•

•

•

The
Anthony Hecht Lectures
in the Humanities

TRUE
FRIENDSHIP

.

.

.

*Geoffrey Hill, Anthony Hecht, and Robert Lowell
Under the Sign of Eliot and Pound*

Christopher Ricks

Yale University Press   ·   New Haven & London

This book was first presented as the Anthony Hecht Lectures
in the Humanities given by Christopher Ricks at Bard College in 2007.
The lectures have been revised for publication.

Designed by Lindsey Joy Voskowsky.
Set in Bembo type by Tseng Information Systems, Inc.
Printed in the United States of America.

Library of Congress Cataloging-in-Publication Data
Ricks, Christopher B.
True friendship : Geoffrey Hill, Anthony Hecht, and Robert Lowell
under the sign of Eliot and Pound / Christopher Ricks.
p. cm. — (The Anthony Hecht lectures in the humanities)
"This book was first presented as the Anthony Hecht Lectures in the
Humanities given by Christopher Ricks at Bard College in 2007.
The lectures have been revised for publication."
Includes bibliographical references and index.
ISBN 978-0-300-13429-2 (alk. paper)
1. Hill, Geoffrey—Friends and associates. 2. Hecht, Anthony, 1923–2004—
Friends and associates. 3. Lowell, Robert, 1917–1977—Friends and associates.
4. Eliot, T. S. (Thomas Stearns), 1888–1965—Influence. 5. Pound, Ezra,
1885–1972—Influence. 6. American poetry—20th century—History and
criticism. 7. English poetry—20th century—History and criticism. I. Title.
PR6015.I4735Z844 2010
821'.9109—dc22
[B]
2009019207

A catalogue record for this book is available from the British Library.

This paper meets the requirements of ANSI/NISO Z39.48–1992
(PERMANENCE OF PAPER).

10 9 8 7 6 5 4 3 2 1

.

.

.

The Anthony Hecht Lectures in the Humanities,
given biennially at Bard College, were established to
honor the memory of this preeminent American poet by
reflecting his lifelong interest in literature, music, the visual arts,
and cultural history. Through his poems, scholarship, and teaching,
Anthony Hecht has become recognized as one of the moral voices
of his generation, and his works have had a profound effect
on contemporary American poetry. The books in this
series will keep alive the spirit of his work and life.

Contents

Prefatory Note

Geoffrey Hill, Anthony Hecht, and Robert Lowell under the sign of Eliot and Pound: the figure of speech comes from T. S. Eliot, who used it in a letter of 18 October 1939 to the scholar Edward J. H. Greene. Of the poems in *Prufrock and Other Observations*, only four (Eliot said) place themselves "sous le signe de Laforgue," under the sign of Laforgue.

Here are five poets who mean a great deal to the world, to me, and—this being the claim of *True Friendship*—to one another. (Though not quite, I grant at once, to every single one of the others.) That Eliot and Pound were as fecundating for each other as had been Wordsworth and Coleridge—this is not news, although in this setting there may be a few new things to notice about it. Eliot and Pound cared diversely about Lowell and his art. Lowell's poems and criticism engage in turn, albeit very differently, with Pound and Eliot. Hill's poems as well as his criticism wrestle angelically with Eliot, with Pound, and with Lowell. Finally, Hecht's criticism and poems undertake their fervent discriminations in apprehending Eliot and Pound, calling Eliot to account and calling Pound's bluff. There is nothing by Pound, so far as I know, that touches upon Hecht or Hill, but there remains only the one two-sided vacancy that is of any moment: that Hill and Hecht, despite the shared respects in which they comprehend their art and its common but far from commonplace concerns, never really met. Which may provide the ground against which the other related figures can be seen.

Something may briefly be said here about my meetings, in person and in pages, with the poets. I never met Pound, and although I shall never forget the exuberated astonishment with which in 1951 I fell upon *The Selected Letters of Ezra Pound, 1907–1941,* I believe that I have never noticed anything about his poems that others have not well noticed already. The most that I have been able to do is express both a precipitated gratitude and some provoked reservations about Donald Davie's two unignorable books on Pound. Eliot, I never met either, and this is scarcely the place to go into the story of his threatening to sue me, but I like to think that in my two books on his art, *T. S. Eliot and Prejudice* (1988) and *Decisions and Revisions in T. S. Eliot* (2003), there was some meeting of minds, mine being the immensely smaller one. Editing Eliot's early unreleased poems, published in 1996 as *Inventions of the March Hare: Poems, 1909–1917,* brought home to me, and not only to me fortunately, the ways in which Eliot's genius had been there from the first and had always grown, in him and then within us. To edit his complete poems in a critical edition now, as I am doing with Jim McCue, is a privilege beyond price and (chasteningly but not as yet cripplingly) beyond any two persons' means.

Personal friendship with Geoffrey Hill, with Anthony Hecht, and with Robert Lowell has been, over the past thirty to fifty years, a more than momentary stay against confusion, and I imagine that it must have gone to the making of the claims in this book, or must at least have gone to the wish to make them. But it doesn't seem to me that my arguments and appreciations, as appreciative argument, derive from or depend upon personal friendship or personal feelings. I have published for more than forty years my gratitude for Hill's art and for Lowell's, and for thirty years my gratitude for Hecht's. It would please me if, after all these years and all that is owed to these poets, the five of them were to form for others as well as for me the mysteriously persuasive shaping that Sir Thomas Browne delighted in: the quincunx. But I should of course settle for something along less far-fetched lines, such as the dear, down-to-earth way of putting it that William Empson came up with: *the right handle to take hold of the bundle.* Or rather, merely *a* right handle to take hold of the bundle.

The invitation to give the Anthony Hecht Lectures in the Humanities in 2007 came as a surprise, a boon, and a blessing; I am very grateful to Helen Hecht, to J. D. McClatchy, and to Bard College and its president, Leon Botstein; this, together with thanks to the good offices of Debra Pemstein.

Jonathan Post is editing the letters of Anthony Hecht, with the support of Helen Hecht; I am grateful that so many pertinent letters have been made available to me. Jim McCue, Lisa Nemrow, Lisa Rodensky, Rosanna Warren, and Jon Westling kindly read various chapters and gave me good advice.

To Yale University Press, I am grateful too. Entirely so, as to Jennifer Banks, Susan Laity, and Christina Tucker. To the Press itself, all but entirely grateful, the withheld 1 percent being a matter of the Press's not permitting footnotes. I have taken up into the body of the text some material which would otherwise have had to be in endnotes and therefore not sufficiently in the immediate vicinity of the passages to which the matter within the notes was ancillary and comparative. The reader is therefore informed that the endnotes consist only of page references and the like, except on the few occasions on which I specifically draw attention to an endnote of a more substantive kind. When quoted poetry is run within the sentence, the final punctuation has sometimes been changed to accord with the syntactical needs. When a block excerpt is given, however, the end punctuation exactly matches the poem, regardless of syntax. Although this may occasionally look awkward, it does not mislead as to cadence and syntax.

1
·
·
·

GEOFFREY
HILL

"Opposition is true Friendship." So William Blake believed, or at any rate hoped. Not but what it would be stretching things to see Blake's opposition to Sir Joshua Reynolds as true friendship. Others of Blake's sayings might better fit the case. "Damn braces: Bless relaxes," perhaps, or "Without Contraries is no progression." Think of how Blake wrote of Reynolds: "This Man was Hired to Depress Art." Or wrote to him, angry urgings from the margin.

REYNOLDS: I found myself in the midst of works executed upon principles with which I was unacquainted: I felt my ignorance, and stood abashed.

BLAKE: A Liar[!] he never was Abashed in his Life & never felt his ignorance.

REYNOLDS: . . . enthusiastick admiration seldom promotes knowledge

BLAKE: Enthusiastic Admiration is the first principle of Knowledge & its last.[1]

No, Blake's proverb would have told more truth (but would not have been as telling) if it had reduced itself to the thought that opposition may on occasion be true friendship.

Then the matter is further complicated by there being no simple opposition to *friendship.* What would friendship's antonym be? An enemy is in opposition to a friend, true, but, despite *Roget's Thesaurus,* which heads its boldly confrontational columns "Friendship" and "Enmity," enmity declines to be simply the opposite of friendship, any more than would be animosity or hostility. Enmity is "the disposition or the feelings characteristic of an enemy; ill-will, hatred" (*Oxford English Dictionary*). Friendship is not limited to—though it is pleased to accommodate—"Friendly feeling or disposition felt or shown by one person for or towards another" (*OED* 2), for friendship is also *OED* 1: "The state or relation of being a friend." So an enmity will never be exactly the counterpart to a friendship. Friendship is mutual by definition; a mutual enmity has to say that it is such. The English language has done without— might even be thought to have wished to do without—an abstract noun from *enemy* that would be to it what *friendship* is to *friend.* Tom Paine had a go at this in 1776: "The nearest and only true way of proving enemyship, if I may so call it." No, you may not, for it is against common sense.

"Opposition is true Friendship." Note by an editor of *The Mar-*

riage of Heaven and Hell: "This line is obliterated in some copies."
Note by a later editor: "This sentence was written in white line
. . . but covered at least partly in all copies except B by washes or,
as here [copy F], by thick opaque colours printed from the plate."[2]
Blake's illuminating thought seems always to have been challenged
as well as challenging.

Of Geoffrey Hill's oppositions, that to Philip Larkin has noth-
ing of friendship about it, though the case made here will be that
it was easier for Hill the critic to repudiate Larkin and all his works
than for Hill the poet. As to Hill and T. S. Eliot (Pound may wait,
though not too long), the grudging respect that Hill has for Eliot
remains respect, even on the occasions when it is palpably outnum-
bered by the grudgings or even the grudges.

Gratitude is a nub. The English language recognizes that there
are such people as ingrates. We are to face the fact that there is not
a corresponding noun for someone who is duly grateful. "What I
dislike about you is that you are an ingrate." But not "What I like
about you is that you are a grate, a great grate."

Going after Eliot has become the sport of bloods no longer
young. William Wootten recently reviewed Frank Kuppner:
"There's nothing like kicking a great writer when he's down. T. S.
Eliot, villain of stage, screen and literary criticism, is now a popular
football for his fellow poets. Tom Paulin let his prose attacks spill
into *The Invasion Handbook,* and even Geoffrey Hill, the most Eli-
otic of contemporary poets, has been using verse and prose to bad-
mouth *Four Quartets.*" (Wootten went on, with Old Possum in play:
"However, when it comes to Eliot-bashing, Frank Kuppner makes
the competition look like pussycats.")[3]

Eliot-bashing? Bad-mouth? Hill's mouth has seldom spoken

with more dignity than on those occasions within his poems when Eliot is a presence, elusive perhaps but a presence not to be put by. Hear the voice of the bard (or rather of the bards) in the closing poem of "The Argument of the Masque," the first section of *Scenes from Comus* (2005).[4] The poem's presentation has been of propositions or postulates: *That* such-and-such is the case (and the world is everything that is the case).

> That weight of the world, weight of the word, is.
> Not wholly irreconcilable. Almost.
> Almost we cannot pull free; almost we escape
>
> the leadenness of things. Almost I have walked
> the first step upon water. Nothing beyond.
> The inconceivable is a basic service.
>
> Hyphens are not-necessary for things I say.
> Nor do I put to strain their erudition —
> I mean, the learned readers of J. Milton.
>
> But weight of the world, weight of the word, is.

The beauty of this poem, most manifest in the sonorous exactitude of its weighting, owes something to the closing words of *Little Gidding* (which were thereby the closing words of Eliot's closing poem, *Four Quartets*): "The fire and the rose are one." For Eliot, the sequence that moves from the plural "The fire and the rose are" to "one" (the most singular word imaginable) manifests the metaphysical union of the one and the many, reconciled at the very last. For Hill, the verb *to be* is likewise to be the mystery and the reconciliation. "Is" simply is. The proposition, "That . . . ," modulates into the turn which is "But."

> But weight of the world, weight of the word, is.

The line, although it comes to open differently, both opens and closes this poem, this sequence of 20 poems, this pause within a longer sequence of 120 poems. Weight of the world and weight of the word are distinguished without being posited as altogether distinct. Had the apothegm ended with *are,* they would have been more differentiated. Are they one and the same, as *is* might insist? Yes and no. Or might it be that they are two and the same? Apposition is true friendship. Feel how immensely different the poem's line is from the prose title of one of the essays collected in *Style and Faith* (2003), an essay which had in 1991 been called "Style and Faith" and which became "The Weight of the Word."

There is in Hill's poem a further and larger debt to Eliot than this, but first there needs to be acknowledged here a smaller debt (like all good debts, going both ways, albeit not equally), an amiable friction that has its connections to opposition and to friendship. Given that I once wrote elaborately on Hill's ways with hyphens,[5] I can be expected to wink or to wince at this poem's asseveration, "Hyphens are not-necessary for things I say." Hill's comedy is often that of a bear; this particular rounding is that of a bull, an Irish Bull, since the very announcement finds it necessary to have recourse to a hyphen, an odd one too, there in "not-necessary." But upon reflection, and upon acknowledgment that Hill is not only precise but a precisian, *not-necessary* is understood as not exactly the same as *not necessary.* (Even as *unnecessary* differs from them both.) To which is added a further glint ("not-necessary for things I say"): can one unmistakably *say* a hyphen? Hugh Kenner pointed out that "the footnote's relation to the passage from which it depends is established wholly by visual and typographic means, and will typically defeat all efforts of the speaking voice to clarify it without visual aid."[6] I am still set to praise Hill's imaginative hyphenation.

GEOFFREY HILL

·

Can't you read English? What
do I meán by praise-songs? I could weep.
This is a praise-song. These are songs of praise.
Shall I hyphenate-fór-you?

(*Speech! Speech!,* 2000, poem 99)

Well, not for me alone. But I do believe that the criticism that I
have devoted to Geoffrey Hill (over the course of forty years) may
play a small part within the complexity that is Hill's relations to
T. S. Eliot. Looking at clippings, I see that I made mention of Eliot
when extolling Hill in 1964, 1968, 1976, 1978, 1984, 1988, and 2001;
this might well have preyed on his nerves, and the present book
may not help. Long ago, I was the recipient of a prize for an essay
that I had written about Hill's poems, an essay that often invoked
Eliot.[7] A friend of mine inquired of Geoffrey Hill how he felt about
this. And he: "Ask the horse how he feels when the jockey wins the
race." As with all the best ruefulnesses, the joke was on both of us.

But the adducing to be italicized is Hill's *Eliot.* "That weight of
the world, weight of the word, is." This particular exactitude would
not have come to be, were it not for Eliot.

If the lost word is lost, if the spent word is spent
If the unheard, unspoken
Word is unspoken, unheard;
Still is the unspoken word, the Word unheard,
The Word without a word, the Word within
The world and for the world;
And the light shone in darkness and
Against the Word the unstilled world still whirled
About the centre of the silent Word.

O my people, what have I done unto thee.

GEOFFREY HILL

·

Where shall the word be found, where will the word
Resound? Not here, there is not enough silence
Not on the sea or on the islands, not
On the mainland, in the desert or the rain land,
For those who walk in darkness

(*Ash-Wednesday* V)

There are other coincidings.

ELIOT: Not on the sea . . . those who walk

HILL: I have walked / the first step upon water

Or the transmutation of Eliot's "those who wait"—which comes a few lines later in Eliot—into the word that is pressed (*peine forte et dure*) by Hill four times: "weight."

Assuredly, Hill's intersection of "world" and "word" would not in itself have needed to resound from or with Eliot's lines. But the syntax that uses the word *is* (in order to hold together two similar but crucially unidentical things) is a corroborative convergence. "That weight of the world, weight of the word, is." "Still is the unspoken word, the Word unheard": the unspoken word is not to be identified with the Word unheard but is not to be distinct from it either, thanks to "is" (not *are*).

In a lecture in 2005 (the year in which he published *Scenes from Comus*), Hill with cogent brilliance chose this line of Eliot's to be a key instance of what was owed to F. H. Bradley. Hill quotes Bradley's *Ethical Studies* (1876), on which Eliot wrote in the *Times Literary Supplement* (29 December 1927), and then most beautifully elicits the interlacing with Eliot's art:

So far religion and morality are the same; though, as we
have seen, they are also different. The main difference
is that what in morality only is to be, in religion some-

how and somewhere really is, and what we are to do is done.

Such passages strain almost hopelessly beyond bearing the conventional understanding of what can be accomplished with verb-tenses within the patterns of ordinary grammar ("somehow and somewhere really is, and what we are to do is done"). It is in this way, in the strangeness of the tense-collocations, that Bradley's prose half-invents the tense-music of *Ash-Wednesday* ("Because I know I shall not know"; "For what is done, not to be done again"; "Still is the unspoken word, the Word unheard").[8]

Furthermore, then, it is in this way, for his part, that Eliot half-invents the tense-music of *Scenes from Comus:* "But weight of the world, weight of the word, is."

Hill writes of Bradley in relation to Eliot: "strain almost hopelessly beyond . . ." And Hill had written in *Scenes from Comus:*

Almost.
Almost we cannot pull free; almost we escape

the leadenness of things. Almost I have walked
the first step upon water. Nothing beyond.

But beyond this parallel with Eliot, there is the accrual by which Hill's "half-invents" is itself half-invented. It may issue from the weight of Wordsworth's world:

of all the mighty world
Of eye, and ear,—both what they half create,
And what perceive;

("Tintern Abbey")

William Empson, sensitive to these mysteries of half-creation, had found it difficult in a way (difficult in a way markedly different from Hill's) to celebrate Eliot. Empson entered his tribute to Eliot's sixtieth birthday in 1948: "I do not propose here to try to judge or define the achievement of Eliot; indeed I feel, like most other verse writers of my generation, that I do not know for certain how much of my own mind he invented, let alone how much of it is a reaction against him or indeed a consequence of misreading him. He has a very penetrating influence, perhaps not unlike an east wind."[9]

Empson's delectable word "invented" ("how much of my own mind he invented") banters the self-importance that would suppose that what great writers do for us is a matter of their helping us discover ourselves. Empson's unrepining warmth can be felt; it is alive, for instance, in the lightness of punctuation that moves on from the word "invented," with the merest of commas, into "let alone . . ." In Hill's prose dealings with Eliot, the prevailing wind is an east wind. Yet in Hill's poems, it is something more—more of a western wind. As in a meeting such as rejoices in this:

> The white sails still fly seaward, seaward flying
> Unbroken wings
>
> And the lost heart stiffens and rejoices
> In the lost lilac and the lost sea voices
>
> (*Ash-Wednesday* VI)

> like a fresh sea-wind
> like the lilac
> at your petrified heart
> as something anciently known . . .
>
> ("Scenes with Harlequins I")[10]

Eliot's art, refreshed, has itself become "something anciently known . . ." and something blessedly *not* "lost." "Someone said: 'The dead writers are remote from us because we *know* so much more than they did.' Precisely, and they are that which we know."[11]

"The lost sea voices" within *Ash-Wednesday* may summon the many voices that are always being conducted within an art as sounding and resounding as that of Eliot and of Hill. In Tennyson, "The deep / Moans round with many voices" ("Ulysses"). Within Eliot, in due course, we hear that "The sea has many voices, / Many gods and many voices" (*The Dry Salvages*). For more many-voices, we might move to Hill, the second poem of *The Orchards of Syon* (2002):

> Something escapes committal; in my name
> recalls itself to being. Mystic
> durables are not the prime good, nor
> lust the sole licenser. Shakespeare
> clearly heard many voices. No secret:
> voicing means hearing, at a price a gift,
> affliction chiefly, whereas despair
> clamps and is speechless. Donne in his time
> also heard voices he preserved on wax
> cylinders. Some of these I possess
> and am possessed by. Persistence tells,
> even when you are past speech, gurneyed
> from *Death's Duel*. As for posterity,
> whose lips are sealed, I do prefer
> Polish to Czech | though, not speaking
> either language, I am unable to say
> why. Starting with these,
> I wish I understood myself

more clearly or less well.
Go back to cast off several lives. Find
all have godlike elements
divided among them: such suffering,
you can imagine, driven, murderous,
albeit under notice of grace.

The incremental confluence in Eliot ("The sea has many voices, / Many gods and many voices") divides its streams here in Hill, flowing via "many voices" into "godlike elements"—elements of which water is one. Much is shared: "such suffering, / you can imagine"—as against "you can't imagine such suffering." For Eliot had imagined such suffering. "Mystic / durables are not the prime good": true, perhaps, but voices can be heard as durables, mysterious even when not mystic, and nowhere more durable than where one poet possesses another.

Donne in his time
also heard voices he preserved on wax
cylinders. Some of these I possess
and am possessed by.

"Donne in his time": "Donne in Our Time" is an essay by Thomas Stearns Eliot. (The full name was preserved in the table of contents and at the head of the essay in *A Garland for John Donne*, edited by Theodore Spencer in 1931.) Preserved by Hill are the voices of Donne, of Webster, and of Eliot.

Webster was much possessed by death
And saw the skull beneath the skin;
And breastless creatures under ground
Leaned backward with a lipless grin.

. . . .

Donne, I suppose, was such another

("Whispers of Immortality")

The "lipless grin" in Eliot is metamorphosed into a differently dark humor in Hill: "As for posterity, / whose lips are sealed." Meanwhile, other poems of Eliot occupy Hill here. Those "godlike elements" have elements of Eliot. Hill: "godlike elements / divided among them." Eliot writes in "Gerontion" of the body and blood of Christ:

To be eaten, to be divided, to be drunk

Among whispers;

Saint Luke 22:17–18: "And he took the cup, and gave thanks, and said 'Take this, and divide it among yourselves: for I say unto you, I will not drink of the fruit of the vine, until the kingdom of God shall come.'" Among the whispers in Eliot are those of immortality and mortality.

It might reasonably be judged that conjunctions of the kind that I am identifying are annotations and belong rather within an edition of Hill's poems than within a critical consideration of writerly gratitude or ingratitude. Certainly I should grant, first, that such noticings would belong equally well within an edition, and, second, that we stand more in need of a thoroughgoing edition of Hill than we do of critical commentary on his art. But the latter does not have to be an obstacle to the former (the obstacles to which are the usual ones: not world enough and time, and not enough learning). Hill's poem from *The Orchards of Syon* is to me diversely beautiful, yet I am not now being directly attentive to all of this but rather to the poem's engagement with Eliot's art, one that is central to Hill's lovely apprehensions though not conterminous with them.

Such engagements are more than matters of likes and dislikes, though in Hill's late work never less than such. It is by fierce courtesy of Dante that Eliot makes an appearance in *The Orchards of Syon* LVII. No main verb in the immediate impatience that opens into self-scathing, of a sort.

> Reading Dante in a mood of angry dislike
> for my fellow sufferers and for myself
> that I dislike them. Dante is exact
> in these conferrals. The words of justice
> move on his abacus or make a sudden
> *psst psst* like farrier's hot iron on horn.

A shriveling and shrinking can be felt in the contraction of "hot iron" to "horn." The words of justice are not easily come by, especially (for Hill) when Eliot declines to be waived. This poem of Hill's ends

> look, ser Brunetto
> whom Dante loved, look, Farinata: the sun
> moves a notch forward on the great wheel.

But Dante's love for ser Brunetto has forever been complemented by Eliot's love for them both, there in *Little Gidding* II where "the brown baked features" of Brunetto precipitate the cry "What! are *you* here?" (a cry that had been, in manuscript, "Are you here, Ser Brunetto?")[12] Within the world of Hill's poem, there is the further cry: Are you here, Mr. Eliot?

He is here, no less than he is there. Robert Lowell witnessed to this: "He can be himself; I feel Eliot's real all through the *Quartets.*

He can be very intelligent or very simple there, and *he's* there, but there are no other people in the *Quartets.*"[13] "No other people" does not quite do justice to the phenomenon, which is rather that, in *Four Quartets,* other people are not altogether other.

(Eliot knew where the positing of *other people* could go wrong: "a Hell for the *other people,* the people we read about in the newspapers, not for oneself and one's friends.")[14]

> So I assumed a double part, and cried
> And heard another's voice cry: "What! are *you* here?"
> Although we were not. I was still the same,
> Knowing myself yet being someone other—
> And he a face still forming; yet the words sufficed
> To compel the recognition they preceded.

"Look, ser Brunetto / whom Dante loved": whom Eliot loved, loved sufficiently to hope against hope, perhaps, that he might partake as much of purgatorial hope as of infernal despair—and this, as Hill's poem goes on touchingly to concede, from within the sequence of poems that may be thought of as Hill's Paradiso. His English publishers at least believe so, supplementing in 2002 the American jacket copy with "*The Orchards of Syon* is Hill's Paradiso."

> From this distance the many barbed divisions
> between Purgatory and Hell appear blurred.
>   (*The Orchards of Syon* LVII)

"The words of justice": my preoccupation here is with the ways in which Hill both does and does not do justice to Eliot. Hill's poems largely (magnanimously) do because they acknowledge that there is a siege of contraries. His critical prose is more narrow, and not only because critical prose always or almost always is.

This, clearly, remains to be shown. For now, the words of justice are the words of Hill's poems. The admission, not only of Eliot into the poems but of the troubled relation with Eliot, is made—with calculable indirectness—in *The Orchards of Syon* XXXVI:

> I did the Lady
> Julian an injustice
> which I will leave for evidence against me,
> configured by the final stroke.

But it is Eliot toward whom Hill is temptable into an injustice: "I have in the past been too ready to accuse the young Eliot of opportunistic toadying; I am more reluctant now. The 1920s were a weird time of slippage and overlap: Saintsbury, Whibley, Riding, and Graves, and of course Eliot."[15] But this does not exactly rescind the accusation of opportunistic toadying. In *Little Gidding* III and then again in V, Eliot did justice to Lady Julian, Dame Julian of Norwich, and to her words of mercy:

> And all shall be well, and
> All manner of thing shall be well

—Eliot, who had anticipated Hill in mustering "the final stroke": "With a dead sound on the final stroke of nine" (*The Waste Land* I). For when Hill speaks of evidence and of the final stroke, he is then moved to speak immediately of Hell and of death.

Certain kinds of life within Hill's late poems constitute a reluctant acknowledgment that Eliot is life-dealing. For this section (XXXVI) of *The Orchards of Syon* may include another nod to Eliot. Hill: "the winged / lion roars his obeisance." True, Eliot does not own the franchise on winged lions, but he is among those who have most notably refused to imp these wings—"Who clipped the lion's

wings?" ("Burbank with a Baedeker: Bleistein with a Cigar") —
with its invocation of Venice. Hill is unwilling to render obeisance
to Eliot; more, he does rather like the thought of clipping Eliot's
wings. Of *The Confidential Clerk* and *The Elder Statesman* (judged to
be "in these senses beyond redemption"), Hill says that "we should
not give credit where it is not due."[16] True. But since it is impossible
to imagine anyone's maintaining that we should, the admonition
feels self-pleasuring.

Again, "The words of justice," or the word *injustice:* "I did the
Lady / Julian an injustice." In 1920, Eliot opened his introduction to
The Sacred Wood: "To anyone who is at all capable of experiencing
the pleasures of justice, it is gratifying to be able to make amends
to a writer whom one has vaguely depreciated for some years. The
faults and foibles of Matthew Arnold are no less evident to me
now than twelve years ago, after my first admiration for him; but I
hope that now, on re-reading some of his prose with more care, I
can better appreciate his position." It was a fine admission to Eliot's
first book of criticism, this thought of what it is to be capable of
experiencing the pleasures of justice. In *Hill's* first book of criti-
cism, which Eric Griffiths declared "the most important first book
of criticism by a major English poet since *The Sacred Wood*,"[17] Hill
calls vividly upon the words of Ezra Pound: "The poet's job is to
define and yet again define till the detail of surface is in accord with
the root in justice."[18] There is (though Hill had no reason to remark
upon this) all the difference in the world between "the root in jus-
tice" and what Pound lapsed into, "the root injustice." The epigraph
to the 2007 edition of *A Treatise of Civil Power* is sixteen lines from
John Skelton beginning "Justyce now is dede." A poem there that
is not found in the 2002 edition but is added in the 2007 edition
opens insistingly:

It is not a matter of justice. Justice is in another world.
Or of injustice even; that is beside the point, or almost.

("On Looking Through *50 Jahre im Bild: Bundesrepublik Deutschland*")

There the dexterous responsible shrug of "or almost" may rival the
word's shifting of its weight in the closing poem of the first section
of *Scenes from Comus* (1, 20):

Almost.
Almost we cannot pull free; almost we escape

the leadenness of things. Almost I have walked
the first step upon water.

Each of these relations is "a matter of justice"—and of injustice.
Does the poem "On Looking Through *50 Jahre im Bild: Bundesrepub-
lik Deutschland*" connect at all with the world of justice and injus-
tice toward or within Eliot? Perhaps, in that it moves at once to a
telling list:

hirelings, the resourceful;
those who are obese—the excellent heads of hair—
the beautiful or plain wives, secretaries and translators.

This, to my eye and ear, is an inspired transporting of Eliot:

The captains, merchant bankers, eminent men of letters.
The generous patrons of art, the statesmen and the rulers,
Distinguished civil servants, chairmen of many committees,
Industrial lords and petty contractors

(*East Coker* III).

When Empson said of Eliot, "I do not know for certain how
much of my own mind he invented," there is no mistaking the gen-
erosity, or rather the reciprocated generosities. With Hill as critic,

somebody—either a reader of Hill or Hill himself—has to be doing some mistaking. Reviewing Hill's *Style and Faith,* P. N. Furbank conceded a perplexity: "If one had the space, and the ability, it would be worth seeking for reasons for the difference between Hill as a prose writer and as a poet. It is a striking one. For his verse, in its response to the world and to history, is both passionate and generous."[19]

There are aspects of this that are not of Hill's making, for poets are characteristically more generous than critics, and poems will often prove more generous than their poets. But then gratitude is itself a form of generosity. There is a revealing (not a betraying) turn in *The Orchards of Syon* XLV:

> The topos
>   of the whole is gratitude.

The tone is that of patiently but firmly setting the reader right as to how such poems of Hill's are to be taken. Sentimentality needs to be fended off, this with the help of "topos," a styptic word that is never on unprofessional lips. The claim is not the warming one that the spirit of these poems is gratitude, and in any case it is not *on the whole,* but "of the whole."

The voice in *Little Gidding* II marvels at its equanimity during the meeting with the familiar compound ghost that is in part Brunetto Latini: "I said: 'The wonder that I feel is easy, / Yet ease is cause of wonder.'" Hill's critical encounters with Eliot, the re-imaginer of that Dantesque encounter, suggest that the wonder that Hill feels is queasy. This last word is from a scrupulous resistance that in 1944 Lionel Trilling put up to Eliot, more particularly to Eliot's too-lavish defense of Kipling: "As anti-Semitism goes these days, I suppose Kipling is not—to use Mr. Eliot's phrase—particularly anti-Semitic. I certainly should not think of isolating for discussion what anti-Semitism he has, but only of mentioning, as one aspect of a complex xenophobia, his queasy, resentful feelings about Jews."[20]

The conviction that it is Eliot's achievement with which Hill's invites comparison is of long standing. Martin Dodsworth was honorably at a loss for instances (and thereby added much with his ellipsis) when he reviewed *Mercian Hymns* (1971): "It is the best English book of poems since . . . But there is no adequate comparison except with Eliot."[21] A corollary of this has been the number of charges uniformly leveled at Eliot and Hill: charges of inaccessibility, obscurity, elitism, inspissation, and foreign paraphernalia; charges of prejudice, nostalgia, and the idealizing of the past; charges of scabrousness and obscenity, and even of mystification and outrage—to take up the terms in which Philip Larkin indicted modernism: "That is my essential criticism of modernism, whether perpetrated by Parker, Pound or Picasso: it helps us neither to enjoy nor endure. It will divert us as long as we are prepared to be mystified or outraged, but maintains its hold only by being more mystifying and more outrageous: it has no lasting power."[22]

The American jacket copy for *Speech! Speech!* conceded that "it may go too far—but then, as T. S. Eliot said, it is only by going too far that you find out how far you can go."[23] Eliot had himself taken his point surprisingly far when praising Harry Crosby's *Transit of Venus* in 1931: "Of course one can 'go too far' and except in directions in which we can go too far there is no interest in going at all; and only those who will risk going too far can possibly find out just how far one can go. Not to go far enough is to remain 'in the vague' as surely and less creditably than to exceed. Indeed, the mentors of pseudo-classicism should consistently content themselves with agnosticism, or at most with the simple faith of Islam; for no extravagance of a genuine poet can go so far over the borderline of ordinary intellect as the Creeds of the Church. And the poet who fears to take the risk that what he writes may turn out not to be poetry at all, is a man who has surely failed, who ought to have adopted some less adventurous vocation."[24] A poem in *King Log* (1968) pictures those who, impelled by zealotry, went too far, those

> Who fell to feasting Nature, the glare
> Of buzzards circling; cried to the grim sun
> "Jehovah punish us!"; who went too far;
>
> ("Locust Songs: Shiloh Church, 1862: Twenty-Three Thousand")

And a poem in *Speech! Speech!* (21) sets itself to "find out how far is HOW FAR."

> Stoics
> have answers, but nót one I go for.

But the ambiguity of "go for" (the pursuit of love, or a harrying?) is among the unsettling energies that lurk within *go*. The word was imperative for Eliot ("Let us go then") when it came to conveying what it was like to be a poet when he was starting out: "I do not think it is too sweeping to say, that there was no poet, in either country, who could have been of use to a beginner in 1908. The only recourse was to poetry of another age and to poetry of another language. The question was still: where do we go from Swinburne? and the answer appeared to be, nowhere."[25] (Swinburne, be it noted, not Tennyson.) "A beginner in 1908": but how about a beginner in 1948, when (five years after *Four Quartets*) the question was still: Where do we go from Eliot?

Where do we go from Eliot? Other poets of (broadly) Hill's time found different answers to the question. For Philip Larkin, where to go from Eliot was back to the poet whom Eliot was unable to read aright: Thomas Hardy. For Ted Hughes, back to Eliot's great antagonist, D. H. Lawrence. For Seamus Heaney, back to a rival tradition (with its own rivalries), the Ireland of Yeats as well as of Patrick Kavanagh.

For Hill, there was no doubt as to which poet constituted the perilous opportunity when it came to influence, influence that would have to be wrestled with, neither spurned nor succumbed to. But then again it is Eliot who knows where to go with all these thoughts about where to go:

People are only influenced in the direction in which they want to go, and influence consists largely in making them conscious of their wishes to proceed in that direction.[26]

A poet cannot help being influenced, therefore he should subject himself to as many influences as possible, in order to escape from any one influence. He may have original talent: but originality has also to be cultivated; it takes time to mature, and maturing consists largely of the taking in and digesting various influences.[27]

Where do we go from Eliot? For him, in the wake of Swinburne, "The only recourse was to poetry of another age and to poetry of another language." For Hill, poetry of other ages has always been a recourse and a resource, in the spirit of Thomas Traherne's noble thought that "Men do mightily wrong themselves when they refuse to be present in all ages and neglect to see the beauty of all kingdoms."[28] As to poetry of another language, for Eliot this had been

French. In 1940 he recalled 1910: "The kind of poetry that I needed, to teach me the use of my own voice, did not exist in English at all; it was only to be found in French."[29]

For Hill, with a sense of the comedy and tragedy of it all, the poetry of another language was written in American English. As a young poet at Oxford, this *Isis* Idol of 18 November 1953 (he was twenty-one) had already been recognized by older poets among whom were two formidable Americans: "Richard Eberhart and Allen Tate (the last offering him an American edition of his poems on the strength of having seen *Genesis,* Geoffrey's best known work)." A few years later, Hill wrote on Tate's poetry in *Geste* (November 1958), and he contributed the entry on Tate to *The Concise Encyclopedia of English and American Poets and Poetry* edited by Stephen Spender and Donald Hall (1963). In Hill's first book, *For the Unfallen* (1959), the sequence "Of Commerce and Society" derives both its title and its six-line epigraph from Tate. In the recent book *Without Title* (2006), "Pindarics" 8, in evoking Cesare Pavese, invokes the Americans:

> redeemed swots,
> you with your Whitman, while I cribbed from much
> maligned beau Allen Tate pindaric odes.

In his fifties, twenty years before retirement, Hill was to move to the land of Whitman and Tate. The move lent itself (not gave itself) to some pat patter, audible in the accents of Daniel Johnson in the *New Criterion* (September 2005): "We must listen to the voices still among us who draw strength from the Judeo-Christian core of British culture. We must listen once more to our poets, chief among them Geoffrey Hill. It is no accident that the greatest living English poet has sought refuge in New England, fleeing the old country and 'her quiet ways of betrayal.'" "It is no accident that . . ." is an idiom better left to the Left, and as so often with these exploitative allegorizings, hardly any time elapsed (a year) before Hill was fleeing the new world for the old country. One of the problems with the *New Criterion*'s account is of course that Hill is not the fleeing type. Max Beerbohm caught forever a glimpse of Byron's petulant left ankle: "Lord Byron, shaking the dust of England from his shoes." Is Hill now shaking the dust of "the old country" back onto his shoes? There is more than one quiet way of betrayal, and the neo-cony-catching or kidnapping of Hill betrays its indifference to art.

But the importance of American poetry to Hill has always been there, with the salience of Eliot's having been both American and English. The narrative within Hill's acceptance speech for the T. S. Eliot Prize in 2000 touchingly tells of the early days: "There is no doubt that High Modernism made me what I am. I grew up in a small Worcestershire village on the extreme fringe of the Midlands' industrial wilderness. Birmingham, some fifteen slow bus-miles away (you had to go three miles south into Bromsgrove, change buses, and ride in the reverse direction, north into the city) was our local metropolis. On one of our rare trips into that alien territory my father purchased for me two books: the *Collected Poems* of A. E. Housman and *A Little Treasury of Modern Poetry*, edited by Oscar Williams. This, I think, was in 1948, the year in which I turned sixteen"—the year in which Eliot turned sixty.

Allen Tate's "Ode to the Confederate Dead" struck me like a bolt from heaven; overnight I became a modernist. The beauty of Tate's "Ode" is that it succeeds in a double economy—the classical economy of the rhymed strophes, the minimal subsistence-economy of the broken unrhymed couplets. I knew nothing, then, of Agrarian political philosophy; I doubt if the phrase "politically incorrect" had yet been coined; I had not read Eliot's *After Strange Gods.* I knew simply and immediately that this was the structural presence, the technical daimon, that would show me how to shape my own work so that its built-in strengths would prove self-sufficient, something quite distinct from an adolescent's yearning for self-expression. At that time I had not read Eliot's "The Function of Criticism" and "Tradition and the Individual Talent" but in being so abruptly and so profoundly affected by Tate's poetry, I was—as I now realize— receiving the Eliotian stresses at second hand.

Gratitude to his father, and to Allen Tate, was complemented by gratitude to Ken Curtis, "an inspired and inspiring teacher" (to whom Hill dedicated *King Log,* 1968): "It was he who insisted that I should not only read, but must also obtain, Eliot's *Selected Essays.* When my parents asked what I wanted for Christmas 1949, I dutifully answered 'T. S. Eliot's *Selected Essays*': the book is still on my shelves, inscribed in my father's hand, the characteristically neat and obedient script acquired by children of his and my mother's generation before they finished with school—or rather, before school finished with them—at the age of thirteen."[30] Such lucid narrative makes me wish that Hill would set down his memoirs.

Hill—the prose Hill, at any rate—was to become estranged from Eliot, but there remain some massive concurrences of principle and of practice. The lucidity that shines throughout Hill's crystalline masterpiece "The Pentecost Castle" is the emanation of two principles of Eliot's.[31] Hill's supreme ways with pointing in the sequence profit immeasurably from Eliot's insight that punctuation "includes the *absence* of punctuation marks, when they are omitted where the reader would expect them" (Eliot on the sleeve of his recorded reading of *Four Quartets*). And similarly with Eliot's conviction that "great simplicity is only won by an intense moment or by years of intelligent effort, or by both. It represents one of the most arduous conquests of the human spirit: the triumph of feeling and thought over the natural sin of language."[32] Simple, but not that simple or easy, as Hill—like Eliot—is aware. "I'm wresting myself into simplicity" (*Scenes from Comus* 1, 18). Or this, from *Canaan:*

> ennobling lowly errors—exacted, from exalted—
>
> tortuous in their simplicity;
>
> ("Mysticism and Democracy [Ill-conceived . . .]")

But then a great many of Eliot's principles are alive for and in Hill. I think of Eliot's characterization of intelligence ("intelligence, of which an important function is the discernment of exactly what, and how much, we feel in any given situation"),[33] and of his refusal to set "literature" against "life," one of his wisest calmings of an age-old fretfulness: "It is the function of a literary review to maintain the autonomy and disinterestedness of literature, and at the same time to exhibit the relations of literature—not to 'life,' as something contrasted to literature, but to all the other activities, which, together with literature, are the components of life."[34]

And then there are all the cruces that Eliot and Hill agree to be inescapable, even if they disagree about just what it would be fully to comprehend them: the recalcitrance of the self in relation to art, the distinguishable but not distinct claims of religion and literature, the centrality of blasphemy, the intertwining of humility with humiliation, and what it might mean to "redeem the time."

GEOFFREY HILL

•

And the force of farce.

Here the trajectory of Hill is the opposite of Eliot's. It was Eliot who established the terms within which much of his early work — and much of Hill's late work — realizes itself.

> If one takes the *Jew of Malta* not as a tragedy, or as a "tragedy of blood," but as a farce, the concluding act becomes intelligible; and if we attend with a careful ear to the versification, we find that Marlowe develops a tone to suit this farce, and even perhaps that this tone is his most powerful and mature tone. I say farce, but with the enfeebled humour of our times the word is a misnomer; it is the farce of the old English humour, the terribly serious, even savage comic humour, the humour which spent its last breath in the decadent genius of Dickens. It has nothing in common with J. M. Barrie, Captain Bairnsfather, or Punch. It is the humour of that very serious (but very different) play, *Volpone*.[35]

Eliot acclaimed "this prodigious caricature." His own art was to move on, or away, or through — elsewhere, anyway. Hill's art, on the contrary, was to move toward an intensity of these energies of farce and caricature. The first stanza of "The Mystery of the Charity of Charles Péguy" (1983) offered a poster for "the new farce," and the sequence's penultimate stanza adduces "Low tragedy, high farce." By the time of *Speech! Speech!* (2000, poem 27), we are in the world of Captain Bairnsfather,[36] the Great War, and Isaac Rosenberg:

> His LOUSE
> HUNTING, nonetheless, remakes, re-masters,
> redeems farce.[37]

There Hill half-acknowledges that he is re-mastering the master who is Eliot as well as the master who is Rosenberg (while perhaps wondering whether to "redeem" Eliot, charged with anti-Semitism and insufficiently appreciative of Rosenberg).[38] "In his essay on Christopher Marlowe, T. S. Eliot observes that a play such as *The Jew of Malta* is not so much a tragedy as it is a tragic farce. I have pondered that definition since my sixth-form days at Bromsgrove High School. To say that *Speech! Speech!* is an attempt to create the equivalent of that genre would be a fairly accurate suggestion."[39] Eliot does not use the phrase "tragic farce," but Hill does (again) in a *Paris Review* interview in spring 2000: "In *The Triumph of Love*, it might be perfectly accurate to describe the rhetorical tone as one of tragic farce—but if it is, then the tragic farce has been written by someone who feels more at home in the world than he felt for the first sixty years of his existence."

The trajectory in Hill has taken him toward tragic farce; the trajectory in Eliot, away from it. In Hill, toward Donne, away from Herbert; in Eliot, toward Herbert, away from Donne. In Hill, toward popular culture; in Eliot, away from it.[40] In Hill, increasingly, toward animosity-as-animation; in Eliot, away from it.[41] You can hear that it is upon Eliot as well as upon Hill himself that the swingeing animus is bent:

> Become vindictive in self-
> vindication? Fall then ∣ victor among
> the secondary infections. Claimed as latest
> pastmaster of the grand infarctions—
> caught in mid-stride—savaged beyond speech—
> (Pray for us sinners)—YOU THÉRE ∣ LÁDY?
>
> (*Speech! Speech!* 107)

Not *just* a smack at Eliot but a smack at him all the same. It is not that Eliot owns the words "Pray for us sinners," for the closing lines of *Ash-Wednesday*'s opening section acknowledge that their source is the close of the Hail Mary, and we are expected to take the force of the movement from *birth* to *death*.

> Pray for us sinners now and at the hour of our death
> Pray for us now and at the hour of our death.

But the sheer (and stylizedly apoplectic) *bad manners* of "YOU THÉRE | LÁDY?" may have a particular pastmaster among the prey. Eliot's immediately ensuing word after the couplet beginning "Pray for us sinners," the word that begins the next section of *Ash-Wednesday,* is the invocation "Lady," which soon becomes "Lady of silences / Calm and distressed." The lines in *Speech! Speech!* have no time for silences; distressed they are, but the opposite of calm.

But it is time to turn to Hill's criticisms of Eliot (from which, in due course, I shall return to the actively constructive elements). In 1984, I remarked that "Hill, who has chosen to write criticism in passionate praise of Yeats, has chosen not to write any criticism at all of the poet even more important to his own poetry: Eliot."[42] Since then, when Hill was in his early fifties, things have changed. Hill, a critic of immense resource, can praise Eliot with eloquent percipience. As here: "It is in the evocation of a not clearly defined boundary between apprehension as fear and apprehension as perception that the early Eliot excels as a poet."[43] Or as in this, where the praise is subsequently qualified but is not rescinded: "It is very much to Eliot's credit that he is found, across a span of more than thirty years, returning upon what is for him a crucial description; knowing each time that something basic has failed to clear its own meaning in, or at, his hands."[44] Yet the strongest impulse remains that of a gravamen. Hill is in some respects the heir of F. R. Leavis,

as is clear in such a shaft as this from Hill on Eliot: "Analytical fi-
nesse and knowing belletrism cohabited in his critical and cultural
writings from the first. It pleased him as a beginner to be approved
by such people as George Saintsbury, Charles Whibley, Desmond
MacCarthy."[45] Leavis would have enjoyed "such people as," assisted
by Hill's granting no *and* before the last name, Desmond MacCar-
thy, so that the chiming satanic trinity (Saintsbury, Whibley, Mac-
Carthy) ends in hostile flatness. Leavis: "Bloomsbury (in a patroniz-
ing way) took up Eliot, who let himself *be* taken up. But that is one
of the less pleasant aspects of his case and career."[46] Hill: "In some
phase of his human progress Eliot ceased to be a Bradleian purist
and became a man-of-letters and a raconteur."[47] And Hill was an-
ticipated in his estimate of *Coriolan* by Leavis, who maintained (of
Eliot's "intense interest in language") that "the nature of that need
as a distinctive portent of our time—that is, as something more
than merely personal—gets direct expression in the two poems of
the unfinished *Coriolan* sequence. I remarked earlier that they seem
to me to be as near to major satiric poetry as anything we are likely
to get in our age."[48]

   If it were the case that Hill's criticisms charged only the failures,
the acquiescences, in Eliot's *late* poems (and in the plays), this might
abolish any contrariety of Hill the poet to Hill the critic. For the
proposition in this book is that Hill's poems make manifest a debt
to Eliot which constitutes one of the highest forms of gratitude,
while Hill's criticism mostly sounds anything but grateful.

   But Hill's wording has long been inspired not only by the
early Eliot and the middle one ("Whispers of Immortality," *The
Waste Land, Ash-Wednesday*) but by late Eliot, too (*Little Gidding*).
It is often late Eliot, the Eliot depreciated by Hill, who gives into
Hill's strong hands something indispensable, not "Into weak hands,

what's thought can be dispensed with," in the words of "Geron-
tion." Since, like Hill, I too find Eliot's plays to be—in varying
degrees—unsuccessful (reminding me of those upon which Tenny-
son embarked in late life, one on the murder in the cathedral), an
honorable but misguided venture, I start off likely to concur with
some at least of Hill's strictures. But I never find myself persuaded
by Hill's insistence that the weaknesses of the plays are endemic in
Four Quartets. Although it is sometimes the failure of the plays that
Hill is primarily addressing, he hands down a wider indictment
when he insists on "the falling away in Eliot's later work" and "the
progressive deterioration of Eliot's creative gifts": "The deepening
failure of Eliot, both as a poet and critic, to focus his powers, I at-
tribute to his increasing inability—and it begins fairly early, in the
late 1920s—to contemplate the heavy cost of being, of becoming,
radically, irretrievably, alienated."[49]

In Hill's earlier formulations of his disappointment with or
at Eliot, the focus had been strictly on the plays. Hill's inaugural
lecture at Leeds more than thirty years ago searchingly narrowed
its eyes at *The Family Reunion* and *The Elder Statesman* and made its
points without scoring them.[50] But Hill's recent judgments widen
to take in *Four Quartets:* "In the distinction here made between the
discursive intelligence and a way, or ways, of apprehension we have
also the distinction in Eliot himself between two major modes of
his poetic comprehension. To the discursive intelligence belong
The Waste Land in the form in which Eliot originally presented
it to Pound's scrutiny, *Four Quartets* and the plays. With the way
of apprehension, the syntax of becoming, we may associate *Ash-
Wednesday, Sweeney Agonistes, Marina,* and—perhaps surprisingly—
the two sections of the unfinished *Coriolan.*"[51] Note the fact that,

despite the air of equipollence, of these "two major modes of his poetic comprehension" only one earns Hill's respect. Admittedly, his concentration upon "the unfinished *Coriolan*" is a rewarding turn, a flash of a feat along the lines of H. A. Mason's thrilling proposal that it was in the translations of the Penitential Psalms that Sir Thomas Wyatt most fully realized his genius.[52] (In *The Orchards of Syon* LXI, Hill moves—within five lines—from "Coriolanus" to "the seven Hebrew-Latin Penitential Psalms.") Hill's passion is itself empassioning: "It is just conceivable that had he found it possible to continue the *Coriolan* sequence beyond 'Difficulties of a Statesman' and the 'Triumphal March' of 1931, he would have possessed an instrument of great range and resonance with which to engage, as well as his progressive confessional motivation, the inner voice of Cyril Edward Parker and the inner voice of his own rage cut into, and cutting across, the public world of the Jarrow hunger marches, the wicked folly of Munich, the limbo of a 'Phoney War' and the many times blundering sacrificial ordeal of 1940–5." So far, so good, or even better. But Hill does not, to my mind, substantiate—partly because he is too eager to harness his speculation—the immediate conclusion that he draws: "*Coriolan* remains one of the major 'lost' sequences in English poetry of the twentieth century and *Four Quartets* is the poorer for Eliot's having 'lost' it."[53] Something of Hill's own discovery is lost once it is enlisted within what itself feels like a Phoney War.

"Eliot's inability or unwillingness to extend—or complete—the *Coriolan* sequence was a tragic failure; and *Murder in the Cathedral*, successful though it is, is none the less a withdrawal from the self-challenge of 'Triumphal March' and 'Difficulties of a Statesman' towards and into a style of less challenging technical problems—the conventions of 1930s choral verse-speaking and the requirement to bring movement and variety to the culturally statuesque." "A successfully completed *Coriolan* sequence, even if as slim a volume as *Ash-Wednesday*, would, I believe, have taken Eliot forward in a direction from which 'Burnt Norton' deflected him: into a synthesis, in twentieth-century terms, of Dryden's two forms of satire—the heroic and the burlesque."[54] But Hill must both wish that Eliot had effected such a synthesis and be thankful that Eliot did not manage it, since the synthesis is one to which Hill has urgently devoted himself, the opportunity having become his to seize. More than one kind of friction is at work and in play here.

"Much in late Eliot that is demonstrably bad stems from two interconnected sources: from elements in his intellectual inheritance and from wrong decisions unconsciously and consciously taken. These too were anticipated in earlier work."[55] Demonstrably, perhaps, but not—for some of us—demonstratedly. Hill's most sustained attempt at this does not earn "Quod erat demonstrandum."

On Hill's reckoning, it is "pitch" that goes wrong in later Eliot. Yet the term, with its concomitant indictment, remains perplexing in the extreme. P. N. Furbank, reviewing Hill's *Style and Faith,* scratched and shook his head: "He behaves rather oddly over Hopkins's special use of the word 'pitch'"; "The puzzle grows more acute in an attack on Eliot's *Four Quartets,* in which the mystifying word 'pitch' is made to do most of the work."[56] Peter Robinson, with the patience that can accompany exasperation, attended closely to the sequence of Hill's reasoning or reasons here, and (for all his admiration of Hill) is unconvinced.[57] Relatedly, Michael O'Neill queries *pitch* vs. *tone:* "Whether the opposition does justice to Eliot is questionable; the very blurring of pronouns in *Four Quartets* of which Hill appears to complain lies behind the success of the encounter with the familiar compound ghost, even though Hill claims that his 'objection . . . has nothing to do with deliberated indeterminacy of pitch.'"[58] "It is not a matter of justice." Truly?

Admittedly, I need to grant that Hill charges me as an accomplice: "I do say, however, that the 'apathy . . . more flagitious than abuse' to which Eliot acutely drew attention in 1920 is a determining factor in the tonality of his own later poetry and in its public reception, and that Ricks is uncharacteristically imperceptive in his response to this factor" (Hill's ellipsis). But grateful though I am for "uncharacteristically," and willing as I am (in principle) to contemplate my imperceptiveness, I am unable to fathom just what Hill means by "pitch" and I am then unable to imagine the grounds for judging "tone" to be not only inferior to "pitch" but inherently contaminated.[59] "I have attempted to show that throughout his argument Eliot aims at pitch but, for the most part, succeeds only in tone. I say 'succeeds' because tone is what people expect and suppose themselves familiar with. It was the pitch of *Prufrock and Other Observations* that disturbed and alienated readers; it was the tone of *Four Quartets* that assuaged and consoled them. That is to say, Eliot's poetry declines over thirty years from pitch into tone, and these late-published papers contribute significant evidence to the history of that decline."[60] But there are things that this averts its mind from. It is conveniently uncertain whether the judgment straightforwardly values pitch above tone ("Eliot's poetry declines over thirty years from pitch into tone"), or whether it judges there to be something wrong, not intrinsically with tone, but with *the tone* of Four Quartets ("it was the tone of *Four Quartets* . . ."). Second, what is wrong with assuaging and consoling? This is left, no less conveniently, in the vague. True, there can be corrupt and sentimental forms of these, but that would not mean that there is no

GEOFFREY HILL

·

33

honorable place for them in literature. Frank Kermode memorably observed that a particular evocation may be too consolatory to console, but this does not constitute a disparagement of consolation in itself. What are the grounds for believing that *disturbing* and *alienating* readers are intrinsically the good or the better things to do? I think we should be told.

"In 'The Love Song of J. Alfred Prufrock' (1910–11) the distinction between I, me, my, we, us, our, you, your, his, her, they, them, one, it, its, is a proper distinction in pitch; in *Little Gidding* (1942) communication is by tone." But even if this were patently so, it would not have to be merely a falling-off, as against being something other, with its own possibilities for revelation.

To be fair, Hill does at once set about quoting and quizzing.

> You are not here to verify,
> Instruct yourself, or inform curiosity
> Or carry report. You are here to kneel
> Where prayer has been valid. And prayer is more
> Than an order of words, the conscious occupation
> Of the praying mind, or the sound of the voice praying.

How is the repeated "you" to be understood? Is it the modern second person singular or the second person plural, or is it the emphatic demotic substitute for what the *OED* terms a "quite toneless, proclitic or enclitic, use of 'one'"? Is Eliot instructing himself, self-confessor to self-penitent, taking upon himself penitentially the burden of common trespass, or is he haranguing the uninitiated, some indeterminate other—or others—caught trespassing on his spiritual property? Do these lines contain, even, a redundant echo from *The Waste Land,* the exclamatory "You" of line 76, the closest Eliot could get, in the grammar of modern English, to the pitch of Baudelaire's "Tu" in line 39 of "Au Lecteur"?[61]

Four consecutive questions, none of them willing to stay for an answer, or even to entertain the possibility of answers which, although in the end they would be likely to be found wanting by Hill, might hope to get a word in. Plus a prompt foreclosing of the possibilities as to tone: "instructing" or "haranguing." Hill's hostility toward tone, or at the very least his low opinion of it as against pitch, has pushed him into indifference to it, or rather into indifference to his responsibility to make good his asseveration as to what the tone may be. For my part, not only do I hear no echo of *The Waste Land,* "redundant" or otherwise, I hear nothing of haranguing in the lines. Although Eliot's own recorded uttering of the lines cannot settle the matter, the entire absence of haranguing in his delivery of them is not to me at odds with how the lines proffer themselves on the page.

In a later essay, Hill returns to the charge:

> Whatever we inherit from the fortunate
> We have taken from the defeated
> What they had to leave us—a symbol;
> A symbol perfected in death.

> One may question the phrase "we have taken." In itself the verb makes us raptors—to take from the defeated is pillage or rape. If the defeated had something to leave us, in what sense can we have taken it—does "take" here simply mean "to receive" as in "take Communion"? What evidence is there elsewhere in *Little Gidding* that "we," ourselves the defeated, have the strength or the nerve necessary for cultural pillage?[62]

GEOFFREY HILL

·

35

Again there is the proliferation of questions that are not actually going to be attended to, and again the unargued insistences. It is asserted, asserted only, that the taking *of a symbol* from the defeated has to be "pillage or rape," and that to "take" is then in itself to become a raptor. But what of these lines from *The Dry Salvages* V?

> But to apprehend
> The point of intersection of the timeless
> With time, is an occupation for the saint—
> No occupation either, but something given
> And taken, in a lifetime's death in love,
> Ardour and selflessness and self-surrender.

This ("given / And taken") steps with grace to the succeeding line, perfectly judged in its give and take.[63]

My objection to Hill's objections is not to any urging that we think about these things; rather the opposite, that there emanates from the impetuosity (there is to be no gainsaying) a strong sense that, about these things, we are not being asked exactly to think.

Granted, Eliot, who used F. H. Bradley as a stick with which to beat Matthew Arnold, would not be in much of a position to complain when Hill puts this through another round and uses Bradley as a stick with which to beat Eliot. But "Bradley is never crass, Eliot is"? "Even at its best, Eliot's critical prose was never more than an epigone of Bradley's philosophical style"?[64] *Never. Never.*

An admirer of Eliot's critical prose feels pressed, then, to give instances. None of the following illuminations strikes me as coming from a less-distinguished Bradley (Eliot himself was always quick to express his enduring gratitude to Bradley). First, Eliot on Henry James and his complex fate: "James's critical genius comes out most tellingly in his mastery over, his baffling escape from, Ideas;

a mastery and an escape which are perhaps the last test of a superior intelligence. He had a mind so fine that no idea could violate it."[65] Second, Eliot on D. H. Lawrence: "Against the living death of modern material civilization he spoke again and again, and even if these dead could speak what he said is unanswerable."[66] Third, Eliot on Shakespeare in comparison with Massinger (scrupulously not slighting Massinger):

MASSINGER:

> *And now, in the evening,*
> *When thou should'st pass with honour to thy rest,*
> *Wilt thou fall like a meteor?*

SHAKESPEARE:

> *I shall fall*
> *Like a bright exhalation in the evening,*
> *And no man see me more.*

Here the lines of Massinger have their own beauty. Still, a "bright exhalation" appears to the eye and makes us catch our breath in the evening; "meteor" is a dim simile; the word is worn.[67]

Every time I read this, it makes me catch my breath.

So my pleasure in Hill's praises of Bradley is diminished by the feeling that the praising gives Hill slightly less pleasure, is less central to him, than the dispraising of Eliot. The same goes for Hill's lauding of Charles Williams, the poet, critic, novelist and theologian. As when Hill raises Bradley in order to lower Eliot, so there is a certain retaliatory humor in using Williams to something of the same end, given Eliot's many public praises of Williams. These praises are acknowledged, to a degree, by Hill: "Williams was greatly admired by Eliot, though perhaps more as an exemplary Christian than as a writer."[68] But Eliot called Williams "a man of unusual genius in several kinds of writing," and Hill's last clause does strike me as a shade grudging if one puts together Eliot's review of *The Descent of the Dove* in 1939, his obituary of Williams in 1945, his broadcast "The Significance of Charles Williams" in 1946, his introduction to Williams's *All Hallows' Eve* in 1948, and the blurb for the *Standard Edition* of Williams's novels (unsigned but written by Eliot), where there comes the tribute to "a man of unusual genius in several kinds of writing": "His work included poetry, drama, literary criticism, and several important volumes in the field of religion and theology; and, in addition, a series of seven remarkable novels. . . . He excels in descriptions of strange experiences such as many people have had once or twice in their lives and have been unable to put into words. . . . These are novels which can be read on a train journey and are likely to carry you past your destination; they are also novels that you will want to keep and read a second and a third time with increased appreciation and deeper understanding."[69]

Those of us who share, in some measure, Eliot's and C. S. Lewis's admiration for Williams are not likely to be flatly resistant to Hill's pitching high claims for Williams: "at his best, a great critic both formally and informally of English poetry."[70] But (to adopt a turn that is dear to Hill) it is one thing to value Williams highly, it is another to deploy these praises of him as a great critic within a summoning of Eliot, a critic from whom such an accolade is here markedly withheld.

The first of the two epigraphs to *Without Title* is from Bradley. Hill has declared that "the heart of Eliot's matter is undoubtedly Bradley." The heart of Hill's matter, the heart of his fertile darkness, is undoubtedly Eliot, Hill's doubts about Eliot. For Hill, "Bradley's memorial in Eliot is in *Ash-Wednesday* and some of the *Ariel Poems* and part, at least, of *Burnt Norton,* and it is an adequate memorial."[71] I learnt much from Hill's demonstration of this. But when he goes on immediately to end his paragraph, "I wish I could give a less qualified testimonial," I have my doubts.

As to Eliot's memorial within Hill, it is to be found not in Hill's prose but in his poems early and late, livingly grateful as they are to Eliot's poems early and late.

Sometimes Hill alludes to Eliot adroitly, deeply. On other occasions, the presence of Eliot does not necessarily imply the calling of Eliot into readerly play, for Eliot's words may have prompted or precipitated or fertilized, without this being in the shaping spirit of allusion. Each case would need to be patiently pondered. The instances that feel like announcements or annunciations of some kind may involve a single word, risky though it can be to emphasize weight of the word. At one end of the range is such a word as *juvescence.* Given that it was not in the dictionary until Eliot gave it to the world, it would probably be imprudent for a poet to use it unless there is to be some intimation of Eliot's immortality. Or there may be the single word that not only has a very plural appearance but is itself about multiplying:

> Polyphiloprogenitive
> The sapient sutlers of the Lord
> Drift across the window-panes.
> In the beginning was the Word.
>
> ("Mr. Eliot's Sunday Morning Service")

In the beginning of this poem was the word "Polyphiloprogenitive." If a poet subsequently wants to use it, he or she had better want to do something with Eliot's drift. Eliot was to turn down a suggestion from John Hayward for *Little Gidding:* "'Easeful' will never be any use until Keats's trade-mark has worn off."[72] What then are we to divine from Hill's adopting a word not often heard on people's lips but memorialized within Eliot's lines, the word *haruspicate.* To divine by inspection of the entrails of animals: the *OED* has the word, though as an adjective, not a verb, despite the inclusion of the noun, *haruspication.*

Speech! Speech! (28) has the word be memorably mentionable:

> LONG TERM counted as thirty days. Hoarding,
> looting, twinned by nature. Haruspicate
> over the unmentionable, the occult signs
> of bladder and bowel. More mental ⏐ hygiene
> urgently called for ⏐ to forget oneself.

Hoarding Eliot, looting Eliot. ("Cultural pillage.") Twinned by nature with Eliot, Eliot as unmentionable, even while inescapable. To forget oneself, or to forget him, or to forget one's relation to him: "mental hygiene."

The next poem (29) capitalizes on the key word:

> The sanctuary hung with entrails. Blood
> on the sackcloth. And still we are not
> word-perfect. HARUSPICATE; what does that
> say to you?

Well (since you ask), what this says to me is that (among much else) the entrails of a poem by Eliot are being inspected.

> To communicate with Mars, converse with spirits,
> To report the behaviour of the sea monster,
> Describe the horoscope, haruspicate or scry,
> Observe disease in signatures,
>
> (*The Dry Salvages* V)

Eliot's auditory imagination is as fine as ever ("horoscope" into "haruspicate," "describe" into "scry"). Hill, whether he altogether wishes to or not, is set to communicate with Eliot as well as with us, to converse with his spirit as well as with ours, to divine all that he can, all round. This not only because *haruspicate* is an altogether outré word but because there is another sign of Hill's being pervious to Eliot. "Haruspicate . . . signs": "haruspicate . . . signatures."

Within Hill's poems, Eliot's poems — the late ones, too — outlast us all, and outlast Hill's prose-wish that things be otherwise.

> Here is a place of disaffection
> Time before and time after
> In a dim light: neither daylight
> Investing form with lucid stillness
> Turning shadow into transient beauty
> With slow rotation suggesting permanence
> Nor darkness to purify the soul
>
> (*Burnt Norton* III)

Nothing transient about Eliot's beauty there, or about the beauty that Hill then duly and amazingly re-creates: "transience . . . shadow," the one turning to the other, with slow rotation suggesting permanence:

> Even now one is amazed
> by transience: how it
> outlasts us all.
> Motley of shadow
>
> dabbles the earth,
>
> ("Scenes with Harlequins" V)

(A sweet swerve, with motley shadow not dappling but dabbling.) Here is no place of disaffection, no room for disaffection. It is in this light, with this light, that we should see Hill's movement from Eliot's "In a dim light: neither daylight" to his own lines near the conclusion to the poem:

> In this light, constrained spirit,
> be a lord of your age.

The spirit of Hill's lines acknowledges the spirit of Eliot's, and this without constraint within a sequence that is "In memoriam Aleksandr Blok." Hill, who is for many of us a lord of his age, does not here repudiate Eliot's right, alongside Blok's, to be esteemed such.

Transitions have always been masterly in Hill, as in Eliot, and therefore punctuation likewise, with a particular resource (or so it still seems to me) to be found in the mark of punctuation that realizes the metaphysical union of the one and the many: the hyphen. First, a return to Eliot.[73]

> Children's voices in the orchard
> Between the blossom- and the fruit-time:
> Golden head, crimson head,
> Between the green tip and the root.
>
> ("New Hampshire")

Here the essence of "between" is incarnate in the two hyphens, both joining and separating, with the first one waiting patiently to be consummated by time: "Between the blossom- and the fruit-time." The tone is unmistakable, and yet the minutiae are ineffable; the voice cannot say a hyphen, and the syntax of the line "Between the blossom- and the fruit-time" is such that "the blossom-" could well be construed or heard as "the blossom." The difference is miniature but substantial, since instead of the quite separated seasons (between season and season?) or manifestations (between blossom and fruit?) there is the seasonal continuity through "between" in the

filament trustingly thrown forward by the hyphen, "the blossom-",
waiting with patient confidence to be fulfilled in and by "time." It is
such a continuity as exists more robustly, though as mysteriously, in
the thought and wording of "Between the green tip and the root."

Hill, with (I believe) some memory of Eliot's achievement here,
has his own pause-worthy hyphenation in *Speech! Speech!* 35:

> love of one's country I bearing with it
> always something under- or over-subscribed,

This bears witness to at least some attachment to *Little Gidding* III:

> love of a country
> Begins as attachment to our own field of action

A hyphenating patience and ripeness can be converted by Hill
to sourness, but not as a sourness toward Eliot, rather toward a city-
scape that instead of being lightened by Eliot's countryside peace
in New Hampshire is shadowed by Eliot's war in London. Here
in Hill the hyphens are eager to compact ("paper-rubble, close-
packed"), almost as compact as the German compacting in the word
Hauptbahnhofsplatz, with the delayed hyphenation awaiting a con-
summation grim not green:

> Even the things that stood,
> stood in unlikeness. The Hauptbahnhofsplatz,
> only, had been bulldozed clear. There were some
> particulars to be recalled; the wind
> bore an unmistakable sour tang
> of paper-rubble, close-packed ream on ream
> scorched into flaking slab, slowly damped down,
> fire- and water-ruin.
>
> (*The Triumph of Love,* 1998, XII)

In the foul fullness of time, ruin was made final by more than one element: "fire- and water-ruin." Hill, with tragic irony, evokes a burning of the books. But not of Eliot's book, within which the German bomber ("the dark dove with the flickering tongue") had rained destruction upon English cities: "This is the death of water and fire" (*Little Gidding* II). What the incendiary air raids did not altogether destroy was then often destroyed by the waters that fought the fires. The enemy elements formed an Axis.

> Water and fire shall rot
> The marred foundations we forgot,
> Of sanctuary and choir.
> This is the death of water and fire.

The wartime memory within Eliot—no Phoney War, this—has become one of the "particulars to be recalled," and (like any allusion or metaphor) it "stood in unlikeness" and in likeness.

In the poem, Hill names Gottfried Benn, which strengthens the association with "the death of water and fire" in *Little Gidding*, since it is in writing explicitly of the Second World War that Hill addressed Eliot's account of Benn. After quoting Simone Weil on the multiple planes of poetry and politics, Hill continued, "Compared to this, Eliot's treatment of Gottfried Benn, in 'The Three Voices of Poetry' (1953), is inane. No discussion of Benn's opinions, eight years after the end of the Second World War, taking as it does Benn's description of lyric 'of the first voice' as being 'addressed to no one' and ignoring as it does Benn's several years of sympathy with, though not membership of, the Nazi Party, should have been received as simply another distinguished contribution to pan-European understanding."[74]

Manifestly, anyone who is unpersuaded that Hill on such a great creative occasion as *The Triumph of Love* XII in any way had Eliot in mind (a wayfinding but wayward thing, the mind) would not feel impelled to wonder appreciatively, more fully, what Hill as a poet makes of Eliot—late Eliot to boot. But it is to Eliot himself that we owe the concept of cumulative plausibility. He wrote of one scholar's adducing "many other parallels, each slight in itself, but having a cumulative plausibility," and of another that "her accumulation of probabilities, powerful and concurrent, leads to conviction."[75]

Here is *The Triumph of Love* CXXI:

> So what is faith if it is not
> inescapable endurance? Unrevisited, the ferns
> are breast-high, head-high, the days
> lustrous, with their hinterlands of thunder.
> Light is this instant, far-seeing
> into itself, its own
> signature on things that recognize
> salvation. I
> am an old man, a child, the horizon
> is Traherne's country.

This tender poem is to me a tissue of truths. The poem is its own man, yes, its own master. Yet one of the truths is that Eliot inescapably means much to it, so that a full appreciation of Eliot within Hill will have to be more positively appreciative than Hill can bring himself to be in prose. Another is that to sense Eliot's compound presence is not a precondition for delighting in Hill's poem (the price of admission) but a felicitous bonus. Hill: "I / am an old man." Gerontion (not T. S. Eliot): "Here I am, an old man," "I an old man," "And an old man." Hill: "Light is this instant, far-seeing / into itself, its own / signature on things that recognize / salvation." Simeon (not T. S. Eliot): "Light upon light," "Having seen thy salvation." Hill in his late sixties imagines in passing these two old men whom Eliot had imagined. True, the horizon is Traherne's country, at once familiar and foreign.

> News from a forein Country came,
> As if my Treasures and my Joys lay there.

And if foreign in some ways, it is by no means "unrevisited." For as well as being Traherne's, it is Eliot's country too, the horizon of his homing. Not, on this occasion, the Enemy's Country.

There are countries of the mind in *Without Title* that, in being Pavese's, turn out to be no less Eliot's. "Pindarics" 21 opens with an epigraph from Pavese, but it then opens into inescapable Eliot.

All these lamentations are far from stoical. So what?

> After the prize-giving the valedictions;
> after the phone call a brief sense
> of what happiness would be like; after
> the forgiveness a struggle to forgive.
> Some discourse is expansive, but some
> composed of opposing blocks. Again
> the award ceremony as paradigm
> for the expected. She gives herself
> to the right man. Their painless composure.

> But, to my purpose, the other, the choice
> that is arbitrary, of the free will,
> moving the unkeyed sections until they lock.

"After . . . after . . . after": this has to be after Eliot.

After the torchlight red on sweaty faces
After the frosty silence in the gardens
After the agony in stony places
The shouting and the crying

(*The Waste Land* V)

But the sequence of "After" moments is not all, for there is too
a particular moment: "after / the forgiveness a struggle to forgive":
"After such knowledge, what forgiveness?" One thing at stake
might be the forgiving of Eliot (and of "Gerontion") by Hill. An-
other might be some acknowledgment that no such forgiveness is
called for. Yet another, any forgiving of Hill in this matter, either by
us or by his most pained prosecutor and judge, himself, the prisoner
of conscience.

But, to my purpose, the other, the choice
that is arbitrary, of the free will,
moving the unkeyed sections until they lock.

The Waste Land V,

I have heard the key
Turn in the door once and turn once only
We think of the key, each in his prison
Thinking of the key,

still, with its note at this point giving half a dozen lines from F. H.
Bradley. One of Hill's epigraphs for the volume that includes "Pin-
darics" is from Bradley.

The epigraph to this particular "Pindarics," it will be remem-
bered, is from Pavese. "*All these lamentations are far from stoical. So
what?*" But it is not from Pavese uncolored, since it takes the um-
brage of this same section of *The Waste Land:*

> What is that sound high in the air
> Murmur of maternal lamentation

Maternal, or paternal, or filial?

"After the prize-giving the valedictions": "He left me, with a kind of valediction" (*Little Gidding* II). No maledictions, at least. "Composed of opposing blocks": such an opposition might constitute true friendship, as might the counterthrust of an arch. "Their painless composure": perhaps, but painless composition?—neither Hill nor Eliot could imagine such a thing.

So one of the things that I hear in the severe beauty of Hill's "Pindarics" 21 is "What the Thunder Said," and rumbling behind that, What T. S. Eliot Said. *The Triumph of Love* CXXI had listened for "their hinterlands of thunder" and for hints of it. *The Triumph of Love* does itself constitute a strange triumph of love, and even—in its hints of earlier and other creation—of friendship.

To move now from Hill's Eliot to Hill's Larkin is not exactly to change the subject since for Hill the two poets are complicit. Unexpected this, in that most of us would have set the two in very different camps or traditions: Eliot as modernist, Larkin as not modernist at all and scarcely even modern. Measure, for instance, the distance between Eliot's "against the sky" in "The Love Song of J. Alfred Prufrock" and Larkin's in "At Grass."

> When the evening is spread out against the sky
> Like a patient etherised upon a table;

> Silks at the start: against the sky
> Numbers and parasols: outside,
> Squadrons of empty cars, and heat,

I should like briefly to draw attention to a similar unexpected-ness as to the modern or modernist when Hill charges John Crowe Ransom with such acquiescences as Eliot is accused of. The con-clusion of Hill's essay on Ransom is this: "Ransom's sorry wit can be distinctly inferior to his grasp of infelicity. He has been led, like Eliot, genuinely to mistake compromise for communication. It is not only the 'bad artists' who are cruelly judged. The good are too. I do not think that Ransom would have wished it otherwise." This stringent ending is in Hill's judgment called for, even while or even because (as is the case with Eliot's presence) Hill's own poems exhibit the most substantial of gratitudes: creativity anew, thanks to the predecessor. Hill's supreme early poem of anguish in love, "The Turtle Dove" of 1954, might never have achieved realization had it not been for Ransom's "Two in August." Hill's formidably at-tentive essay of 1980 lists "Two in August" among Ransom's "poems of 'situation,'" twice quoting the poem and its "stubborn reiterative outcry, disturbing but not halting the ceremonial procedure of his traditional verse-forms."[76] And in 2005 "A Treatise of Civil Power" sets itself courteously to differentiate the two men and their two Muses:

> *Senex iratus* is my present mask,
> not as with John Crowe Ransom and his Muse.[77]

When it comes to Eliot and Larkin, who do not look like sib-lings, Hill diagnoses bad blood brotherhood. "The residual benefi-ciaries of *Four Quartets* have been Larkin and Anglican literary 'spiri-tuality,' two seeming incompatibles fostered by a common species of torpor which Eliot had acutely diagnosed in 1920. If I were to ask Ricks how it is that, against all the evidence his own unrivalled critical intelligence could bring to the process, he is pleased to be numbered among Larkin's advocates, I anticipate that he might answer, 'Because he speaks to the human condition.'"[78]

It is with these words that Hill closes *Style and Faith* (2003). Once again I find myself trundled into the thick of it. Once again, too, I am grateful for a good word ("unrivalled"!) while aware that rivalry is indeed at issue: not Hill's with me, but Hill's with Larkin now as well as with Eliot. With Larkin, perhaps, all the more rivalrous in that Larkin's popularity has been a signal feature of Hill's lifetime as a poet. Yes, I am pleased to be numbered among Larkin's advocates, but no, I would not answer with something about the human condition for I don't find myself uttering those words.

So it is that *Style and Faith* ends. Or does it? For what really ends the book is an endnote, *fifty-three lines long,* beginning with the words "See Christopher Ricks," and then deprecating Eliot and deploring Larkin.[79] From *The Triumph of Love* XXIII we learn about Hill's modes (they are more than moods):

> *Laus*
> *et vituperatio,* the worst
> remembered, least understood, of the modes.

In *Style and Faith,* the endnote that Hill strikes is his *vituperatio* launched explicitly at my *laus* (now not so much my praise of Eliot as of Larkin, but with the one colluding with the other). More in sorrow than in anger, though not *much* more (and as to Larkin, very much the other way round). "The broad integrity of Ricks's critical practice" is soon obliged to give way to something else: "I must conclude that there is a tone that Larkin represents which is stronger even than Ricks's acute sense of pitch." For I am among those who have bought "the Larkin package."[80] A sealed package it is, for at no point in his fifty-three lines does Hill extract words from a Larkin poem. The finishing end of the note is openly aimed at *Four Quartets,* but the damage done earlier to Larkin is not collateral. "During his lifetime Larkin was granted endless credit by the bank of Opinion, and the rage which in some quarters greeted his posthumously published *Letters* was that of people who consider themselves betrayed by one of their own kind. In fact Larkin betrayed no one, least of all himself. What he is seen to be in the letters he was and is in the poems."

Yet what Larkin is in the poems (for Hill and despite Hill) may be better seen not in Hill's prose but in one of Hill's poems and its relation to a Larkin poem. I quote it now in its entirety because Hill has not moved me to shame at my grateful respect for Larkin and I ought to adduce a poem that I have already mentioned and that I believe worthy of such respect.

At Grass
The eye can hardly pick them out
From the cold shade they shelter in,
Till wind distresses tail and mane;
Then one crops grass, and moves about
—The other seeming to look on—
And stands anonymous again.

Yet fifteen years ago, perhaps
Two dozen distances sufficed
To fable them: faint afternoons
Of Cups and Stakes and Handicaps,
Whereby their names were artificed
To inlay faded, classic Junes—

GEOFFREY HILL

•

Silks at the start: against the sky
Numbers and parasols: outside,
Squadrons of empty cars, and heat,
And littered grass: then the long cry
Hanging unhushed till it subside
To stop-press columns on the street.

Do memories plague their ears like flies?
They shake their heads. Dusk brims the shadows.
Summer by summer all stole away,
The starting-gates, the crowds and cries—
All but the unmolesting meadows.
Almanacked, their names live; they

Have slipped their names, and stand at ease,
Or gallop for what must be joy,
And not a fieldglass sees them home,
Or curious stop-watch prophesies:
Only the groom, and the groom's boy,
With bridles in the evening come.

My focus here is not on Larkin's merits but on the appreciation that
"At Grass" might accrue from its having prompted (or more than
prompted) one of Hill's most endearing late poems, *The Triumph of
Love* LII. Hill's immediately preceding poem described the moral
landscape in felicitous geological terms that match Tennyson's ex-
quisite evocations. Here now is LII in its endearing entirety:

Admittedly at times this moral landscape
to my exasperated ear emits
archaic burrings like a small, high-fenced
electricity sub-station of uncertain age

in a field corner where the flies
gather and old horses shake their sides.

"Admittedly": would Hill admit that "At Grass" gained admission there? "At Grass," a poem about the ears, and about old horses, that asks:

Do memories plague their ears like flies?
They shake their heads.

Hill may shake his head at all this.

Plainly it is not a question of his poem sounding like or being like Larkin's; rather, that had it not been for Larkin, it is to be doubted that Hill's poem would have taken the precise form it took. "The moral landscape" is beautifully sketched by Hill, along with its vexations. Sketched, and heard by his "exasperated ear."

Whether Hill faced it or not, his poem owes gratitude to Larkin's. But then both Larkin's and Hill's in turn owe gratitude, deriving as they do from two quatrain poems by Yeats:

On hearing that the students of our new university
have joined the agitation against immoral literature
Where, where but here have Pride and Truth,
That long to give themselves for wage,
To shake their wicked sides at youth
Restraining reckless middle-age?

The Spur
You think it horrible that lust and rage
Should dance attention upon my old age;
They were not such a plague when I was young;
What else have I to spur me into song?

Yeats is at once "plague" and "spur" for Larkin, as is Larkin for Hill.

Larkin, They shake their heads; Hill, shake their sides; Yeats, To shake their wicked sides. Larkin, plague; Yeats, plague. Hill, age; Yeats, middle-age, age. Hill, where; Yeats, Where, where. More loosely, Larkin's horses and Hill's; Yeats, The Spur, to spur.[81]

"My exasperated ear": the very thought of Larkin or (even more) the thought of anyone's thinking that Larkin had a good ear exasperates Hill. In the case of *The Triumph of Love* LII, the exasperation is that of an oyster, and it precipitates a pearl. Larkin's being in the vicinity is confirmed for me by the terms in which Hill spoke in his acceptance speech for the T. S. Eliot Prize, Larkin lurking again within a larger exasperation. Hill's physical hearing (very poor on one side) is not the nub, but it is not irrelevant either: "My ear is haunted by a confused sound of human voices approximating to several conversations occurring at the same time (whether indoors or outdoors I cannot precisely say), a cacophony which in some way I know I have to transform into polyphony. In the broadest sense I can tell you what this cacophony is—it is the clamor of Opinion together with the hissing of my own animus."[82]

The acceptance speech doubles as a rejection speech (the Larkin Booby Prize), "the clamor of Opinion" being debited by Hill as this: "Larkin was granted endless credit by the bank of Opinion." And "the hissing of my own animus" (*psst psst*) is the sound of the branding that is vituperation. "Animus," with Larkin a target. Eliot too, Eliot who had said of English: "The language demands an *animosity* which is singularly lacking in those authors who are most publicly glorified for their style."[83]

Animus
is what I home on, even as to pitch.

(*Speech! Speech!* 90)

—and if even as to "pitch," then even as to Eliot.

Recalling his young self, Hill spoke of how Eliot first came to him: "In being so abruptly and so profoundly affected by Tate's poetry, I was—as I now realize—receiving the Eliotian stresses at second hand." Allen Tate does not seem ever to have exasperated Hill, though there is one matter that Hill feels obliged not to let pass: "If my talk were to degenerate even further into diatribe I would here begin to rant against each and every post-modernist school of Creative Writing. It is, though, somewhat embarrassing to have to acknowledge that creative writing schools were looked on with favor, sixty and more years ago, by practitioners of that self-same New Criticism to which Allen Tate, among others, gave unstinting service. I have known scholars and teachers who, as young men, were in Tate's creative writing classes, or corresponded with him, or met him. Neither of the two friends I have immediately in mind devoted his later life to the writing of poems."[84]

Since Hill brings up this matter of Tate and creative writing schools (on which Hill looks with marked disfavor), I should like to proffer a fine poem written in a manner utterly different from any that one can imagine Hill or Eliot or Larkin adopting. Syllabics! The Higher Anecdotalism!! It is poem 42 in *More Poems From Robert's Book* (2004) by the California poet Fred Smith, and it is about writing poems under the sign of Eliot and Pound.

I asked Allen Tate—this was
after class while we were standing
around before he could return

to his office—if he thought all
poets were fakers. Yes, he said,
but he preferred the word mounte-
bank since that at least implied
entertainment. It takes a good
imagination and a good
ability to read to think of
Tate's poems as entertainment.
But poetry, to use Wallace
Stevens' words, must give pleasure.

Students like me, would-be poets,
knew we didn't need any more
imitations of Eliot
and Pound, or Yeats for that matter,
but our problem was what would come
after them. In some ways that's still
a problem for poets. I asked
Tate if he felt this pressure.
No, because he and Eliot
were near enough in age he
considered himself Eliot's
contemporary. But this wasn't
the whole story. He told how he
and Hart Crane reacted when they
read "The Waste Land" for the first time.
It was, he said, as if all the poems
that needed to be written or
could be written had been written.
Small wonder Pound, after cutting

the manuscript down to size, wrote
Complimenti, you bitch. I am
wracked by the seven jealousies.

Rejoicing in *The Waste Land,* Pound had written to Eliot: "The thing
now runs from April . . . to shantih without break. That is 19 pages,
and let us say the longest poem in the Englisch langwidge. . . .
Complimenti, you bitch. I am wracked by the seven jealousies, and
cogitating an excuse for always exuding my deformative secretions
in my own stuff, and never getting an outline."[85] Unable to re-
joice, Eliot wrote back to Pound, "Complimenti appreciated, as
have been excessively depressed."[86] Eliot was later (with the paren-
thetical power that he directed so well) to bring back the word
compliment as ironically salutary for the pair of them: "The opinion
has been voiced, that Pound's eventual reputation will rest upon
his criticism and not upon his poetry. (I have been paid the same
compliment myself.) I disagree."[87]

Hill often finds it excruciatingly difficult to offer to Eliot un
qualified "complimenti" (less difficult as to Pound). "Complimenti
appreciated." But in the deepest sense Eliot is appreciated by Hill,
for no appreciation could be greater, no compliment more endur-
ing, than to be moved to unique creativity by this earlier creator, as
Hill so often is within his poems. Writing of *Ulysses,* Pound promul-
gated a principle that is of the highest importance: "The best criti-
cism of any work, to my mind the only criticism of any work of art
that is of any permanent or even moderately durable value, comes
from the creative writer or artist who does the next job; and *not,*
not ever from the young gentlemen who make generalities about
the creator. Laforgue's Salomé is the real criticism of Salammbô;
Joyce and perhaps Henry James are critics of Flaubert."[88]

Agreed, and yet how very good the less-than-best criticism that is not "the next job" of creation may sometimes be. Pound himself as critic, for instance, or Hill on Pound. But there is no stimulating discrepancy between what Pound means to Hill the critic and what he means to Hill the poet. There is, in my judgment, no counterpart within the engagement that is Pound/Hill to what Eliot, *pace* Hill (who cannot be at peace with Eliot), can effect for and within Hill's poems.

Hill writes illuminatingly of Pound in a way that is forthright and right, admiring and dismayed. "Ezra Pound, who wrote magisterially on behalf of poets 'All values ultimately come from our judicial sentences,' in the end found himself cruelly and impotently at odds with the US judiciary. Seeking to attribute causes, or even reasons, for this savage contretemps one is presented with several possibilities. It may be that Pound misjudged a critical matter of status or perhaps he misconstrued a fine point of semantics"; "He is vulnerable to accusations that he naively or wilfully regarded his wartime broadcasts as being in some way traditionally privileged and protected by his status as poet, 'boasting of the sanctity of what [he] carried'; an attitude at best archaic and at worst arrogantly idiosyncratic."[89] This comes from "Our Word Is Our Bond" (1983), one of Hill's most searching critical explorations, in essence his Apology for Poetry. But his most sustained engagement with Pound is the twenty-page chapter on "Envoi (1919)" in *The Enemy's Country* (1991). Pound's exquisite, rather too exquisite, poem begins, "*Go, dumb-born book.*"[90] Hill's chapter begins, "'Envoi (1919)' recalls in its title the form of the alba (e.g. 'Alba Innominata,' a version of which Pound had included in his *Exultations* of 1909) and in its opening lines the melody of Waller's 'Goe lovely rose' which had been set by Milton's friend and collaborator, the Royalist musician Henry Lawes. From the time of his first discovery of Lawes's music Pound held it in the highest esteem."[91]

Hill, too, holds Lawes in the highest esteem, while not lacking esteem for Waller, "in that song which acts as Pound's point of departure and remonstrance ('The common fate of all things rare')."[92] I found myself wishing, and still find myself wishing when I return to Hill's persuasively intricate and exactly weighed account of Pound's insinuating verses, that Hill had brought himself at some point to let us hear the whole of Waller's superb song. Hill contents himself, and this only in his notes, with quoting the first of its four stanzas (the one stanza renewed by Pound, it is true, but a stanza that is to be perfectly consummated as the song becomes entire). An anthology piece, supreme as that and not only as that.

Song

  Goe lovely Rose,
Tell her that wasts her time and mee,
  That now shee knowes,
When I resemble her to thee,
  How sweet and fayr shee seems to bee.

  Tell her that's young,
And shuns to have her graces spide,
  That hadst thou sprung
In deserts where no men abide,
  Thou must have uncommended dy'd.

  Small is the worth
Of beauty from the light retir'd:
  Bid her come forth,

Suffer her selfe to bee desir'd,
>   And not blush so to be admir'd.

>   Then dye, that shee
The common fate of all things rare
>   May read in thee,
How small a part of time they share,
>   That are so wondrous sweet and faire.

Pound's poem, which owns its gratitude to Waller and to Lawes (by name, in both cases), has its renewed music.

Envoi (1919)

Go, dumb-born book,
Tell her that sang me once that song of Lawes:
Hadst thou but song
As thou hast subjects known,
Then were there cause in thee that should condone
Even my faults that heavy upon me lie,
And build her glories their longevity.

Tell her that sheds
Such treasure in the air,
Recking naught else but that her graces give
Life to the moment,
I would bid them live
As roses might, in magic amber laid,
Red overwrought with orange and all made
One substance and one colour
Braving time.

Tell her that goes
With song upon her lips

But sings not out the song, nor knows
The maker of it, some other mouth,
May be as fair as hers,
Might, in new ages, gain her worshippers,
When our two dusts with Waller's shall be laid,
Siftings on siftings in oblivion,
Till change hath broken down
All things save beauty alone.

Anthony Hecht, admiring but not awed, was imaginatively open to the tragedy and the comedy of the poem's mannered matter.

Take Waller's stoic, gladiatorial rose,
Saluting you as it prepares to die
On orders, simply to make a vulgar point.
("A Love for Four Voices")

Elsewhere, Hecht wrote, "In praise of both Wallers, Edmund and Fats" ("To L. E. Sissman").

Pound's recording of his poem is at least a tour de force, and Hill draws this out with adjudicatory precision.

One would claim no more for Pound's performance of his own work, as on the 1939 disc which includes a reading of "Envoi (1919)," than that it sounds "full of certitude and implacable, and unswerving" and might "exalt" the listener, making him feel that he is in contact with something arranged more finely than the commonplace. The pace and pitch of the voice do not solve the "whole question of tempo" as it affects one's understanding of this and other poems; but they emphatically confirm an attitude of mind and must, of course, be susceptible to the charge of vocal attitudinizing and moral portentousness. . . . When Pound recites what

GEOFFREY HILL

·

he has written—"One substance and one colour ⏐ Braving time"—his word "braving" is already so placed, so cunningly circumstanced, that it can sustain not only the intermingled, interacting portentousness and irony of the poem itself but also the overweening, gratuitous sonorities of Pound's recital.[93]

Pound's cadences move Hill to a feat of appreciative discrimination that outdoes any of his critical (as against poetic) wrestlings with Eliot. This because of (not despite) the fact that Hill in his poems is exasperated with Eliot, whereas Pound—exemplary for Hill in some ways—is constitutive in none. One might start where honoring often starts, with an epigraph adopted by Hill. Of the three epigraphs to Hill's *Collected Poems* (1985), one is from Pound. It illuminates, but it does not fertilize.

> In the gloom, the gold gathers the light against it.
>
> (Canto XI)

This is Hill the gatherer, not the hunter home from the hill.

Or there may be the single phrase that is not so much the presence of Pound as a present from Pound.

A Song from Armenia
Roughly-silvered leaves that are the snow
On Ararat seen through those leaves.
The sun lays down a foliage of shade.

A drinking-fountain pulses its head
Two or three inches from the troughed stone.
An old woman sucks there, gripping the rim.

Why do I have to relive, even now,
Your mouth, and your hand running over me
Deft as a lizard, like a sinew of water?

Is the culmination of this haunting poem in *The Songbook of Sebastian Arrurruz* from Armenia or from Ezra?

Twisted arms of the sea-god,
Lithe sinews of water, gripping her, cross-hold,

. . . .

Lithe turning of water,
     sinews of Poseidon,
          (Canto II)

Hill's final, far-from-rhetorical question — "Why do I have to relive, even now, / Your mouth, and your hand running over me / Deft as a lizard, like a sinew of water?" — is itself a lithe twisting and turning of Pound, gripping him, cross-hold. The transformation of "sinews" to "a sinew of water" is a singular triumph. Something has been relived.

But such incorporation of Pound is not just different from but less deep, or more momentary, than what it is for Eliot to possess the body of Hill's verse. Something similar might be said of the moments when Pound appears by name. This parallels Pound's quirky pleasure in naming Eliot within his poems, sometimes as Mr. Eliot, sometimes as Old Possum. (Old Possum, Hill calls him too, without affection, in "A Treatise of Civil Power" XII.)[94] In Hill's ways with Pound, the naming is sometimes of the poet, sometimes of the work:

Partial, impartial, unassailable
though many times assailed, like poetry—
The Pisan Cantos, The Confucian Odes

    ("On Reading *Burke on Empire, Liberty, and Reform*")

At these recent moments in his poetry, Hill is *contemplating* Pound, with compassion assuredly, but without the fecund discomposure that works within his fascination with Eliot.

I'm spent, signori, think I would rather
crash out than glide on through. Pound glided
through his own idiocy; in old age
fell upon clarities of incoherence,
muteness's epigrams, things crying off.

    ("Pindarics" 14)

            Pound
was a Ruskinian, so it works out, so it

fits and sits fair to being plausible;

    ("Pindarics" 18)

Cursed be he that removeth his neighbour's mark:
Mosaic statute, to which Ruskin was steadfast.
(If Pound had stood so, he might not have foundered.)

    (*The Triumph of Love* CXLVI)

[The wording of Hill's *Selected Poems* in 2006 is no longer tentative: "(If Pound had stood so, he would not have foundered.)"]

    I should go so far as to say (too far?) that, when Hill the poet comes to Pound, it is only if Pound meets Eliot too that Hill is moved to his most valuably disconcerted achievements. All the more so when a poem by Hill has Pound be overtly and Eliot covertly unmistakable.

GEOFFREY HILL

·

64

Nothing is unforgettable but guilt.
Guilt of the moment to be made eternal.
Reading immortal literature's a curse.

Beatrice in *The Changeling* makes me sweat
even more than Faustus' Helen, let alone
Marlowe's off-stage blasphemous fun with words

or Pound's last words to silence. Well,
let well alone. The gadgetry of nice
determinism mákes, breáks, all comedy.

All the better if you go mad like Pound
(*grillo,* a grasshopper; *grido,* a cry from the fields).
The grief of comedy ǀ you have to laugh.

      (*Scenes from Comus* 3, 19)

It is appropriately hideous, the transition from the first to the sec-
ond line there, the second line being so momentaneously sealed,
hard on the heels of what had been a full sentence but now crying
out for a verb that would allow it to (as abject people say) *move on.*

Nothing is unforgettable but guilt.
Guilt of the moment to be made eternal.

Hill's allusions to Pound are well-lit and open: "Grasshopper is
loud" (Canto LII), and "Be welcome, O cricket my grillo" (Canto
LXXVIII). Those to Eliot are darkly closed though patent. For it
is to Eliot, not mentioned by name, that the modern age owes its
alert understanding not only of "Marlowe's off-stage blasphemous
fun with words" but of *The Changeling,* with the further twist that
it was to *The Changeling* that Eliot himself owed one of the sharpest
moments in one of his most ranging poems, "Gerontion":

I that was near your heart was removed therefrom

To lose beauty in terror, terror in inquisition.[95]

Hill has long been drawn to Eliot's account of Middleton, contrast-
ing it with Eliot elsewhere:

> The poet as I envisage him is quite unlike the Baudelaire of
> Eliot's celebrated panegyric ("Baudelaire was man enough
> for damnation"); whereas the craft of poetry itself, as I de-
> scribe it, comes close to resembling that "frightful discovery
> of morality" to which Eliot alludes in one of his finest pas-
> sages, the account of the nature of Beatrice in Middleton and
> Rowley's play *The Changeling:*
>
> > In every age and in every civilization there are in-
> > stances of the same thing: the unmoral nature, suddenly
> > trapped in the inexorable toils of morality—of morality
> > not made by man but by Nature—and forced to take
> > the consequences of an act which it had planned light-
> > heartedly. Beatrice is not a moral creature; she becomes
> > moral only by becoming damned.[96]

It cannot be doubted, then, that Hill's poem beginning "Nothing is
unforgettable but guilt" wants us never to forget, ever to be aware
of, Eliot. Also perhaps, to beware of suffering either too much or
little guilt when it comes to confronting (to adapt the title of Eliot's
remarkable tribute to Dante in 1950) What Eliot Means to Me.

Eliot dogs Hill. "Beatrice in *The Changeling* makes me sweat / even
more than Faustus' Helen." I don't think that I am alone in scent-
ing the presence of Eliot here, the smell of many men's fear. "Iago
frightens me more than Richard III; I am not sure that Parolles, in
All's Well that Ends Well, does not disturb me more than Iago. (And

I am quite sure that Rosamund Vincy, in *Middlemarch,* frightens me
far more than Goneril or Regan.)"[97]

It was in Canto LXXXI that Pound moved from naming his love
for Lawes and Waller to love and its relation to all that is lasting.

> What thou lovest well remains,
> > the rest is dross
> What thou lov'st well shall not be reft from thee
> What thou lov'st well is thy true heritage
> Whose world, or mine or theirs
> > or is it of none?
> First came the seen, then thus the palpable
> > Elysium, though it were in the halls of hell,
> What thou lovest well is thy true heritage
> What thou lov'st well shall not be reft from thee

Eliot, considerably more than Pound, belongs within Hill's "true
heritage." Hill chastens Eliot, but then the Lord loveth whom he
chasteneth. "What thou lovest well remains": to love *well* might be
to do so not only fervently but with salutary discrimination. Hill's
poems love Eliot's well; Hill's prose, less so.

"What thou lovest well remains." This might be the particular
triumph of love.

> What remains? You may well ask. Construction
> or deconstruction? There is some poor
> mimicry of choice, whether you build or destroy.
> But the Psalms—they remain; and certain exultant
> canzoni of repentance, secular oppugnancy. *Laus
> et vituperatio,* the worst
> remembered, least understood, of the modes.
>
> (*The Triumph of Love* XXIII)

What remains? We may well ask. For one alternative to *construction* may be not *deconstruction* but destruction, and *laus et vituperatio* may be for Hill not two modes but one symbiosis, a living union.

Eliot knew where he needed to turn when contemplating what it is that remains. "Thou, Lord, Who walkest in the midst of the golden candlesticks, remove not, we pray Thee, our candlestick out its place; but set in order the things which are wanting among us, and strengthen those which remain, and are ready to die": in 1928, Eliot set in order this epigraph for his "Essays in Style and Order" (*For Lancelot Andrewes*). Eliot's subtitle was to prompt in 2003 Hill's title, *Style and Faith,* with—on its sleeve—the word *Essays.*

One answer to the question "What remains?" must remain the sane social civility of Alexander Pope, or at any rate of his wise Clarissa in *The Rape of the Lock.*[98]

> What then remains, but well our Pow'r to use,
> And keep good Humour still whate'er we lose?
>
> (V, 29–30)

Good humour or (come to that) ill humour. *Laus et vituperatio.*

But I need to return to Hill's deployment against Eliot of Charles Williams's "critical masterpiece," *The English Poetic Mind* (1932). "It was at this time, from the 1930s to the mid 1940s (Williams died in 1945) that Eliot was falling into a kind of dereliction of the critical imagination. Dereliction: 'the action of leaving or forsaking (with intention not to resume),' 'the condition of being forsaken or abandoned'; 'a morally wrong or reprehensible abandonment or neglect.'"[99]

I cannot reconcile this, except as rhetorical exigency, with Hill's invocation (a dozen lines later) of "the unfinished *Coriolan*": "Had Eliot been able to finish *Coriolan,* as a book about the size of *Ash-Wednesday,* the future pattern and direction of his own poetry would have been different. To say this is not to accuse Eliot of wilful dereliction; these things are out of our control, and his inability to complete that sequence was an unwilled dereliction of the creative faculty." The protestation ("To say this is not to accuse Eliot of wilful dereliction") does not altogether ring true or ring clear. Does it mean that Eliot is not being accused, or that it is not of willful dereliction that he is being accused? Hill has just glossed *dereliction* not solely as "the action of leaving or forsaking (with intention not to resume)," or as "the condition of being forsaken or abandoned," but concludingly as "a morally wrong or reprehensible abandonment or neglect." Hill's syntax ("To say this is not to accuse Eliot of wilful dereliction") palters as to whether the word "dereliction" is accusatory. This from someone who is most exact and exacting with words. It is of Hill that I admiringly think whenever I recall Walter Savage Landor's declaration: "I hate false words, and seek with care, difficulty, and moroseness for those that fit the thing."

It is not difficult to sympathize with Hill's vexed frustration at those disparagers who believe his art to manifest no evidence of dramatization or of what is alive in Henry James's conviction that the artist is concerned to *place* what is presented in the art. Hill is right to protest at the reviewers' protest "that there is something disgusting in seeing a writer describe on the same level the Shoah, the First and Second World Wars and his petty resentments. And all I can say is that no such claim is made by the author. The author is perfectly aware of the grotesque difference between his own resentments and the plight of millions, between the claims that he makes for himself and the several holocausts of his age."[100]

In Hill's art, though not always in his argumentations, resentment at Eliot becomes something altogether other by being exactly placed and by being nourished by so much more than resentment. I greatly admire and relish the conclusion of a remarkable recent poem from *A Treatise of Civil Power,* "On Reading *The Essayes or Counsels, Civill and Morall*":

> The poor are bunglers: my people, whom I
> nonetheless honour, who bought no landmark
> other than their graves. I wish I could keep
> Baconian counsel, wish I could keep resentment
> out of my voice.

Two things act here as a prophylaxis against resentment's infection, even while something like an admission is being made. First, that the cadence breaks what might have been the complacency of a full-blown line. Not, as conclusion,

> wish I could keep resentment out of my voice.

but

>   wish I could keep resentment
> out of my voice.

Second, that the ruefulness knows perfectly well what the imaginary heckler will burst out with. "Shouldn't you wish that you could keep resentment out of your heart and your soul? You and your voice." ("Well, if I could just keep it out of my voice, that might do for a start.")

It will now come as no surprise that I again invoke Eliot, not only because of Hill's phrase "my people" ("My people humble people who expect / Nothing") but because of what had been uttered five lines earlier in *The Waste Land:* "I made no comment. What should I resent?" (A broken-backed line with a broken rhyme.) Lifelong,

Eliot felt for what in *The Dry Salvages* II he called "the failing / Pride or resentment at failing powers."

In 1928, E. M. Forster found the right terms in which to look back at what the Eliot of *Prufrock and Other Observations* had meant to him: "In all the years that have followed, this early fragmentary sympathy has remained, so that still when I read him it is for the witty resentment followed by the pinch of glory."[101] Eliot knew well the power of resentment and could imagine another's feeling it and feeling her or his way around it:

> Stand on the highest pavement of the stair —
> Lean on a garden urn —
> Weave, weave the sunlight in your hair —
> Clasp your flowers to you with a pained surprise —
> Fling them to the ground and turn
> With a fugitive resentment in your eyes:
> But weave, weave the sunlight in your hair.
>
> ("La Figlia Che Piange")

She may wish she could keep resentment out of her eyes, he out of his voice.

2

·

·

·

ANTHONY

HECHT

Within Tennyson, "The deep / Moans round with many voices" ("Ulysses"). Eliot quoted this as "a true specimen of Tennyson-Virgilianism"—and therefore "too *poetical* in comparison with Dante, to be the highest poetry."[1] Within Eliot himself, "The sea has many voices, / Many gods and many voices" (*The Dry Salvages*). Meanwhile, there is Eliot on Pound: "Meanwhile, in *Lustra* are many voices."[2]

Anthony Hecht was interviewed by J. D. McClatchy, who inquired with imaginative pertinence as to the poems in *The Hard Hours* and how Hecht used "formal 'limits' both to define and prompt the different *voices* that sound and overlap in them. The verse units become characters in the poem's drama." Hecht proved himself at once duly grateful and duly modest, the hinge being an honorable "But":

You put the matter flatteringly, and I was certainly trying for the effect you describe. But in this, of course, I am doing no more than what Lowell did in, say, "The Quaker Grave-yard," by incorporating Milton and Thoreau and scripture and Melville into his poem, and what Frost did when sneak-ing a line or so of Herrick or Waller into a poem, or what Milton himself did so strikingly in "Lycidas." It means that as I am writing, certain texts that have meant much to me by their power or beauty are summoned by the theme or thoughts that preoccupy me, and when this happens I some-times try to work a relevant phrase or passage into the fabric of my own poem as seamlessly as possible, so that the know-ing reader will spot it, but another reader will not be intimi-dated by obscure allusions, like some of those in the Cantos, for example. The borrowed voices, I should like to hope, lend a sort of ancestral authority to what I am trying to say, but they also represent a kind of homage on my part. And so, if I have determined to employ a borrowed voice in this way, without quotation marks, without calling undue attention to the borrowing, I may find myself compelled (but pleased) to adopt the formal limitations of the poet from whom I am borrowing, and use them as if they were my own invention. An obvious example from "Rites and Ceremonies" is the ap-propriation of the "form," as well as several lines, of George Herbert's "Denial."[3]

"Are summoned": the poet who introduced himself with *A Summoning of Stones* (1954) was a summoner of voices. This issued in his becoming a realizer of his own voice.

As always with Hecht's critical thinking, there is the richness that William Empson, who was much admired by Hecht, characterized as readiness for argument unpursued.[4] There is the felicity of "preoccupy me" (for it is simply true of the forbear poets that they pre-occupy us). There is the corollary that is tact, concerned to do right both by the knowledgeable readers and by the intimidable ones (this alive to the fact that there is no formula or theory that will not find itself at a loss when it comes to tact). There is the delicate matter of "homage." There is the unflippant comedy of "as if they were my own invention," in the consciousness that here too there is tacit homage: chapter 8 of *Through the Looking Glass* is headed with the White Knight's reiterated claim, "*It's My Own Invention.*" And to fulfill the arc of Hecht's appreciating the art of allusion (his own and others'), there is the entrance of the poet who enjoyed a special place in Hecht's heart and mind: George Herbert. Herbert had in T. S. Eliot's heart and mind, too, a special, albeit a different, place—ever deeper as the years went by, as was likewise the case with Hecht's Herbert.

Hecht speaks to McClatchy of the *ancestral,* itself a concomitant of any true art of allusion, fortified by Hecht with an allusion to the ancestral itself, since his "ancestral authority"—with "voices" ten words earlier in his sentence—is preoccupied by Coleridge: "Ancestral voices prophesying war." The next line of "Kubla Khan" is "The shadow of the dome of pleasure"; Hecht's next sentence to McClatchy has "compelled (but pleased)."

He is a poet who holds in crucial tension with the prospective duty of "prophesying war" the retrospective duty to build a memorial. Of two early poems among others, "A Deep Breath at Dawn" and "Christmas Is Coming," he said, "In writing those poems I felt I was performing duties that pulled me in opposing directions: one was to honour and commemorate the tragedies and horror of war, while the other was to compose elegant and well-crafted poems in the manner of those poets who were still my models."[5]

To turn now to the place of Eliot in Hecht's composing of poems is to discover how much may be achieved by an art that flinches neither from being needled nor from needling. "The Venetian Vespers," a superb poem, is (like all superb poems) a great many things. One of them is an unremitting engagement with Eliot. It is an engagement, necessarily, by the poet first of all—first of all but not first-and-foremost since the crucial engager duly becomes the excruciated consciousness brought into existence by the poem. The presence of Eliot's imaginings—within the imaginings not only of Hecht but of Hecht's brooder—has long been recognized. But then how could it not be, given such an incitement as this?

> Virtues
> Are forced upon us by our impudent crimes.
>
> ("Gerontion")

> Thus virtues, it is said, are forced upon us
> By our own impudent crimes.
>
> ("The Venetian Vespers")[6]

"Thus virtues, it is said, . . ."? What might have been the crime of theft must force upon us many kinds of pertinent impudence. First, there is the spatula that is "Thus," a flat word that is never "said" except with a sense of something dead. Second, there is the flat-tongued affront that takes a level pleasure in not attributing the dark saying either to Mr. Eliot or to the little old man who is

ANTHONY HECHT

•

75

Gerontion. Third, there is the re-lineation (not unlike what Eliot visits upon Oliver Goldsmith in *The Waste Land*), so that Eliot's mid-line "us" is hoisted up to find itself prominent on the promontory of the line. Fourth, there is the addition of the little sly word "own" when manifestly the words are not simply the speaker's own. As much is admitted by "it is said," with exactly that blend of factitious confessing and self-exculpation that is the Dantesque abjection of the consummate monologuist who sways the enterprise.

> "The Venetian Vespers" is about an invented character, largely a man I knew in Ischia, partly my brother, and necessarily something of myself. But for the most part, the character is invented. He is a deeply troubled, neurotic, hampered man, and his misery only exacerbates his self-concern. . . . My speaker in "The Venetian Vespers" is alert enough about himself to recognize the egotism engendered by his unhappiness, and to want to escape from it.[7]

A fluent run of questions by this hampered man may not know what it seeks but does know where to look:

> Where to begin? With the white, wrinkled membrane,
> The disgusting skin that gathers on hot milk?
> Or narrow slabs of jasper light at sundown
> That fit themselves softly around the legs
> Of chairs, and entertain a drift of motes,
> A tide of sadness, a failing, a dying fall?

"That strain again, it had a dying fall." Again and then "again," energized first of all by the interplay of the desirous and the disgusted, the clamorous and the cloyed, at the opening of *Twelfth Night*—and then, still within this tradition of conflicted dismay, in "The Love Song of J. Alfred Prufrock":

I have measured out my life with coffee spoons;
I know the voices dying with a dying fall
Beneath the music from a farther room.

—and then yet again, defying surfeit (as though immediately challenging the reader to object to so prompt a recurrence), in Eliot's next poem, "Portrait of a Lady," which ends:

This music is successful with a "dying fall"
Now that we talk of dying—
And should I have the right to smile?

Hecht:

Where to begin? With the white, wrinkled membrane,
The disgusting skin that gathers on hot milk?

Measure this against "I have measured out my life with coffee spoons." Stir in a memory of the membrane in "Gerontion": "Excite the membrane, when the sense has cooled."[8] But the excitements in "The Venetian Vespers" are not exactly those of the poet; they own the man whom the poet has summoned, the exacerbated history of a self-tormentor. Tormented too, haunted, by T. S. Eliot. Take the light around the legs of chairs, falling and rising: some light is shed on this by the spirit of "Animula":[9]

"Issues from the hand of God, the simple soul"
To a flat world of changing lights and noise,
To light, dark, dry or damp, chilly or warm;
Moving between the legs of tables and of chairs,
Rising or falling,

So it is that four or five moments of Eliot converge upon Hecht's six lines. If we ask to what end, one answer is this: to the mingling of what impels with what repels, this mingling being itself an enactment of the poet Hecht's struggle with the poet Eliot, a struggle that is then one that rightly takes place within Hecht's own feelings and thinkings. "Unable to fare forward or retreat"? Not so for Hecht (though it would be true of many poets who found themselves paralyzed by Eliot), since Hecht's achievement in the face of Eliot is his being able both to fare forward and to retreat. (See note 10 for a sampling of the many alignments of Hecht with Eliot that a fully annotated edition of Hecht would delight to bring home.)[10]

Hecht's mellifluous fluency (like his notable but also notorious *elegance*) has been held against him, as though such an appeal is never that of poetry but of poesy. So it is worth both recalling and contesting the objections that F. R. Leavis made to the mellifluous fluency of a poet whom Hecht praised: Alfred Tennyson. For Leavis, "Tears, idle tears" was characterized by its "simply plangent flow." When Leavis repeated what was for him an accusation, he modified the adverb "simply"—or rather brought it forward a few words and then added another adverb opprobrious for him, "sweetly": "It moves simply forward with a sweetly plangent flow, without check, cross-tension or any qualifying element. To give it the reading it asks for is to flow with it, acquiescing in a complete and simple immersion: there is no attitude towards the experience except one of complaisance; we are to be wholly in it and of it."[11] "Simply plangent," "simply forward," "simple immersion":

"I have said it thrice:
What I tell you three times is true."

From *The Hunting of the Snark,* for which the first of the original illustrations by Henry Holland in 1876 featured Tennyson as the Bellman, "Supporting each man on the top of the tide."

Those of us who think that Leavis's description of the manner

and movement of "Tears, idle tears" is ill-judged will want to draw
attention to many a "cross-tension" within the poem.

> Tears, idle tears, I know not what they mean,
> Tears from the depth of some divine despair
> Rise in the heart, and gather to the eyes,
> In looking on the happy Autumn-fields,
> And thinking of the days that are no more.

There is the disconcerting interplay of the sound of the long *i*, rest-
lessly changing its meaning: "idle tears, I . . ." arriving (via "Rise")
at "the eyes." There is the cross-tension by which the lines feel so
rhymed while being no such thing, and the cross-tension by which
the line that looks set to be the poem's refrain ("And thinking of the
days that are no more") proceeds to allow only the last six words to
remain constant, thereby bringing it about that the opening words
of this, the closing line in each stanza, are there no more. So, *pace*
Leavis, there is within the lines cross-tension and a check and a
qualifying element (exactly that) as the poem and its moods—not
a single mood inviting "complete and simple immersion"—move
from "And thinking of the days that are no more" through "So sad,
so fresh, the days that are no more" and then (qualifying "fresh")
"So sad, so strange, the days that are no more" to what is doubly
a cross-tension, not only of death and life but of the one so en-
sconced within the other: "O Death in Life, the days that are no
more."

Leavis has no misgivings: "No new definitions or directions of
feeling derive from these suggestions of imagery, which seem to
be wholly *of* the current of vague emotion that determines them."
But what exactly is vague about the emotions—again, not just
one emotion—of the poem? Leavis exhibits a physical distaste: the

poem "seems to offer a uniform emotional fluid" (well, does it seem to or does it do so?). "It is plain that habitual indulgence of the kind represented by *Tears, idle tears*—indulgence not accompanied and virtually disowned by a critical placing—would be, on grounds of emotional and spiritual hygiene, something to deplore."

> Where to begin? With the white, wrinkled membrane,
> The disgusting skin that gathers on hot milk?
> Or narrow slabs of jasper light at sundown
> That fit themselves softly around the legs
> Of chairs, and entertain a drift of motes,
> A tide of sadness, a failing, a dying fall?

"Supporting each man on the top of the tide" (*The Hunting of the Snark*): I find in Hecht's loveliness of wording and phrasing many of the same kinds of crosscurrent, of check, of cross-tension, and of qualifying element, that are there in Tennyson for those who have ears to hear. Listen for the relations of the thoughts to the feelings in the opening sentence of "Devotions of a Painter":

> Cool sinuosities, waved banners of light,
> Unfurl, remesh, and round upon themselves
> In a continuing turmoil of benign
> Cross-purposes, effortlessly as fish,
> On the dark underside of the foot-bridge,
> Cast upward against pewter-weathered planks.[12]

No justified suspicions as to aestheticism and its cult of Beauty escaped the attention of either of these two poets who delight in beauty but decline to worship it.

Hecht repudiated half the poems from his first volume, *A Summoning of Stones*. (The others formed the second half of his second book, *The Hard Hours*.) He spoke of the early work as that of an "advanced apprentice," and then glossed this: "I believe that when I made the dismissive remark I meant that the general tone of the book, taken as a whole, was jaunty and distant, cool and artificed, and I still think this is true. I knew perfectly well at the time that I wasn't able to do justice to some of the horrors of existence I had reason to know about." Four of "the more serious poems . . . all put the terror of reality at an artistic distance, and were too full of 'devices.'"[13]

Such crosscurrents are characteristic of Hecht's deepest poems, in which an astonishing fluency of phrasing coexists with an appalled admission of frustration, of being blocked or balked. As in Eliot's art, the condition that is evoked with eerie cogency is one of spiritual, psychological, erotic, and moral contrariety, all aswirl. There is at once a security of movement in Hecht's suasive lines and many a threat both to and from this very security, including the threat of congealed Eliotry. Ease and malaise. That strain again.

"Where to begin": Hecht's art, at one with his characterization of his enterprise in the revelatory conversation with McClatchy, seems to me very different in tone and weight from the terms in which critics, even some of the best, are wont to acknowledge his principles and practice. To one commentator on "The Cost," "The allusive machinery of the poem is considerable."[14] (But "machinery" makes it too mechanical.) To another commentator, on "The Venetian Vespers": "The reader with a well-stocked literary imagination will doubtless find allusions to works by Ben Jonson, Otway, Byron, Shelley, perhaps James, 'Baron Corvo,' Proust, and Mann. Venice has been a favorite setting for corruption, if not death, for centuries. The literary references are only incidental to the subject, but they certainly allow Hecht to create an unusually rich poetic texture when he wants to."[15]

But there is more to Hecht's apprehended allusions than can be contained by the thought of the "well-stocked," or "literary references," or "when he wants to." And "only incidental to the subject"? No, what is deeply and valuably disconcerting (there to be heard in the sounding-composed but the being-discomposed) about the presence of Eliot's flux in Hecht's lines is how much of "The Love Song of J. Alfred Prufrock" and of "Portrait of a Lady," of "Gerontion" and of "Animula" is the opposite of incidental, finding itself compacted into half a dozen lines that seethe all the more sinisterly because they move with style and grace.

"A tide of sadness, a failing, a dying fall": but also a tide that proved to be not a failing but a success, the bringing of new life to a dying fall. Doing so, in part, with the twist that makes the phrase part of a question, ending with a question mark, as had not been the case in Shakespeare or in Eliot. "A tide of sadness, a failing, a dying fall?" This counteracts any dying fall since it lifts, not lets fall.

The grace of self-reflection, by which part of art's attention is well turned upon itself, upon its own proceedings, has rightly been valued of late by much criticism, especially as a power for wit and humor, and as a reminder, in its admission of its own art, that "the truest poetry is the most feigning." The principle of self-reflection has proved to be of deep, wide, and delicate application, from the proper respect in which the art of Saul Steinberg is now held to the profound rotation effected by Walter Jackson Bate's comprehension of the burden of the past and the English poet.[16] But the principle, like all others, has always been tempted to escalate its claims, to make itself the one thing necessary, as if art's own nature were the only thing with which art were ever occupied. Then a proper self-attention becomes solipsism and self-regard, and poems are held to have no other subject than their own poemness.

Few things are more important in literary criticism than to protect the restored insights into the worth of disciplined self-reflection against its foes: those who have never had the imagination to see how much self-reflection could honorably effect, and those who have never had the imagination to see how it cannot honorably effect very much unless it be continually braced—as by the thrust of an opposing arch—against an equal respect for all the ways in which the reflection of something other than self (other than art itself) is indispensable.

So one starting point for the relation of Hecht's art to that of Eliot (upon which it draws so often and so imaginatively) would be the moments when something self-reflecting may perhaps be being proffered for us in turn to reflect upon. As in these lines (956–62) from the translation of Aeschylus's *Seven Against Thebes* (1973) by Hecht and Helen Bacon:

> King Oedipus, who sowed
> his outrageous agony
> in the inviolate field
> of his mother, the same womb
> that bore and cherished him;
> and planted there in blood
> the wrath-bearing root.

"I am, in retrospect, not at all happy about that translation," Hecht later said. "The problem, which I failed to solve, was to find an idiom in English that could be intelligible to a modern theatre audience and still seem as freighted as the Greek. . . . My own English lines are rigid and stilted, and unconvincing."[17] But (valuably) "the wrath-bearing root" both is and is not Hecht's own. For the deeply planted conclusion there would never have flourished (could never have been flourished) had it not been for "Gerontion": "These tears are shaken from the wrath-bearing tree." The Aeschylean lines are born of, planted in, rooted in, Eliot's inviolate field as well as Aeschylus's. The epithet "wrath-bearing" becomes a hyphenated Eliot-Hecht. This is saved from being "outrageous" only by the conviction that Eliot's achievement is itself cherished here, is itself finally left inviolate.

Hecht's lines are manifestly post-Eliot, post hoc, but is it proper to see them as propter hoc? Hecht himself compacts the matter in "A Love for Four Voices," a poem in the tradition of the dendrophile poets such as Andrew Marvell and Alfred Tennyson (and George Herbert: "I read, and sigh, and wish I were a tree"), with their delight in such trees as are not wrath-bearing:

> Between post oak and propter oak
> Falls the inevitable shade.[18]

Any positing of allusion cannot but raise the possibility of the fallacy (after it and so because of it?) post hoc, ergo propter hoc. But there is also the more inspired apprehension of what is post-, caught in Keats's surprised delight in achievements of which the full meaning becomes clear to him only in retrospect: "He has said, that he has often not been aware of the beauty of some thought or expression until after he has composed & written it down—It has then struck him with astonishment—& seemed rather the production of another person than his own—He has often wondered how he came to hit upon it."[19] "Until after": Keats wrote in a letter, "For things which [I] do half at Random are afterwards confirmed by my judgment in a dozen features of Propriety."[20]

One of the voices in "A Love for Four Voices" might be under-
stood to be that of Eliot, or more tellingly that of his Hollow Men.

> Between post oak and propter oak
> Falls the inevitable shade.

Eliot:

> Between the idea
> And the reality
> Between the motion
> And the act
> Falls the Shadow
>> *For Thine is the Kingdom*
>
> Between the conception
> And the creation
> Between the emotion
> And the response
> Falls the Shadow
>> *Life is very long*
>
> Between the desire
> And the spasm
> Between the potency
> And the existence
> Between the essence
> And the descent
> Falls the Shadow

And then to Eliot's voice might be added the voice of the poet-
critic who both impelled and repelled Eliot (rather as Eliot does
Hecht): Matthew Arnold. For Hecht's thoughts within the wood

may recall Arnold's within the bowering wood of "The Scholar-Gipsy." The alluder may be something of a scholar-gipsy. Arnold rhymes "shade" with "branches of the glade," and his next line has "forest." Arnold has "the inviolable shade" and Hecht "the inevitable shade." There is the further knot within the wood, in that "inviolable" is not only Arnold's word but Eliot's: the "inviolable voice" of the violated Philomel in *The Waste Land* II.

For a poet with Hecht's disposition toward old poems in the creation of new poems, literary allusion is at once inevitable, inviolable, and eager not to violate. If Eliot is at times a shade and even a shadow, the shades of the dead are for Hecht — as for many poets — the conceivers of new life. If the preposition *between* can be heard to command not only Eliot's elegiac lines in "The Hollow Men" but Hecht's epigrammatic ones in "A Love for Four Voices" (which has its own serious play with the preposition *for*), well then, *between* may be judged to be just the preposition that an art of allusion needs, since *between* is an axis that comprehends both joining and dividing.[21]

The triangle that is composed of Hecht's art, Eliot's art, and the art of the self-reflecting within allusion can catch many colors and many shades. The Aeschylean moment is blood red; the oak moment, dappled green. Then there may be the violet moment. Eliot saw in his mind's eye, or rather in the mind's eye of Tiresias, the evening homecoming:

> At the violet hour, the evening hour that strives
> Homeward, and brings the sailor home from sea,
> The typist home at teatime,
>
> (*The Waste Land* III)

Eliot's Note chose to tell part of the story: "This may not appear as exact as Sappho's lines, but I had in mind the 'longshore' or 'dory' fisherman, who returns at nightfall." Sappho (in Guy Davenport's translation):

> Dusk and western star,
> You gather
> What glittering sunrise
> Scattered far,
> The ewe to fold,
> Kid and nanny home,
> But the daughter
> You send wandering
> From her mother.
>
> [   ]
> Hesperos, most beautiful
> Of stars.[22]

A further poet will have returned to mind and will have gone to the graving of Eliot's lines:

> This be the verse you grave for me:
> *Here he lies where he longed to be;*
> *Home is the sailor, home from sea,*
> *And the hunter home from the hill.*
>
> (Robert Louis Stevenson, "Requiem")

It was left to Hecht to change Eliot's whole manner and movement so that "Seascape with Figures" might scud along:

> Turn of the screw in time and water speeds
> The French hairdresser home, flutters the gripped
> Hearts of the trim-coifed nuns in bevy shipped

To that poor quarter where their host still bleeds,
To Patrick's Ireland, green and without snake.[23]

Yet this speeds far less far from Eliot than it might seem. Eliot's
typist could have done with a French hairdresser. (She smoothes *her*
hair with "automatic hand.") The poetic turn by Hecht is a turn of
the screw, yes (turning courteously to Henry James in passing), but
it is an evocation not of pain but of the liner's screws, which "speed"
both fast and in success, doubling the elements — and they are both
"in time" and in "water." So the tone of Hecht's turn toward Eliot
is blithe as spray.

It is the extended sequences within Hecht, his syntactical flow-
ings and unfoldings, that make most clear how imperative it is to
him to move with Eliot, sometimes in time with him or in tune
with him, sometimes in supple yet stringent divergence. "Memory"
is a poem whose title modulates its sound to fulfill the first line,
"memory" undulating into "family": "Sepia oval portraits of the
family."[24] The memories proceed from "the hue of ancient news-
paper" through "Tail-feathers sprouting from a small-necked vase"
to "A Bible and a magnifying glass." And then there is an expatiation
into this form of memory that allusion can constitute and that then
constitutes the poem's conclusion. Once again there is an allusion
to Eliot, and once again this reflects something about the nature of
allusion itself. But it is not allusion that in the first place gives such
shape and form and evocative shading to these lines; it is powers
of deep observation, concerned above all to render the truth of an
inward place:

> Green velvet drapes kept the room dark and airless
> Until on sunny days toward midsummer
> The brass andirons caught a shaft of light

ANTHONY HECHT
·
88

For twenty minutes in late afternoon
In a radiance dimly akin to happiness—
The dusty gleam of temporary wealth.

This is pure Hecht in the complicated gratification of its paradoxes (the "dusty gleam," the "radiance dimly akin to happiness"), in its feeling for allusion's essences, allusion being something that radiates and is akin, something that reaches through time for wealth but is more than a merely temporary wealth. Something that is a shaft of light and that catches one. Hecht's lines are happy (more than just akin to happiness) to acknowledge that Eliot's lines of light are in the room.

Sudden in a shaft of sunlight
Even while the dust moves

(*Burnt Norton* V)

The two immediately preceding lines in Eliot are these:

Caught in the form of limitation
Between un-being and being.

Hecht's own allusive illumination appositely escapes being caught in the form of limitation between un-being and being.

Until on sunny days toward midsummer
The brass andirons caught a shaft of light

Allusion at its best does catch something but in the form of the illimitable, bringing into being a new being.

If allusion can be seen under the aspect of a shaft of light, it can be seen too as a slant of light. Hecht gives the salience of a title to Emily Dickinson's supremely lucid opening line ("There's a certain Slant of light"), wording that is alight with paradox, "slant" being askant while "certain" is at once manifest and shrouded. "Determined, fixed, settled" (*OED*), but also "left without further identification in description; thus often used to indicate that the speaker does not choose further to identify or specify them." Eliot availed himself of this in "Preludes" IV: "And evening newspapers, and eyes / Assured of certain certainties."

"A Certain Slant" (from *The Darkness and the Light,* be it noted) — but to follow on this occasion the usual convention of putting the titles of short poems within quotation marks might mislead as to Hecht's practice, which was "to work a relevant phrase or passage into the fabric of my own poem as seamlessly as possible," as he said to McClatchy, and "to employ a borrowed voice in this way, without quotation marks, without calling undue attention to the borrowing."

Hecht gives this particular title without quotation marks although it is a quotation; elsewhere he proceeds differently, to different purposes, for instance giving to the title "More Light! More Light!" actual quotation marks, so that, as with his poem "Gladness of the Best," the quotation marks are Hecht's, not the commentator's convention.

The words "A Certain Slant" will call due attention to Emily Dickinson's certain slant, but the poem promptly and patently does not look or sound anything like a Dickinson poem. Such a scene, such syntax as Hecht displays: Where have we heard and seen and followed something like it? We are present at a serious game of which *homo ludens, homo alludens,* will know the moves: "A Game of Chess."[25]

A Certain Slant
Etched on the window were barbarous thistles of frost,
Edged everywhere in that tame winter sunlight

With pavé diamonds and fine prickles of ice
Through which a shaft of the late afternoon
Entered our room to entertain the sway
And float of motes, like tiny aqueous lives,
Then glanced off the silver teapot, raising stains
Of snailing gold upcast across the ceiling,
And bathed itself at last in the slop bucket
Where other aqueous lives, equally slow,
Turned in their sad, involuntary courses,
Swiveled in eel-green broth. Who could have known
Of any elsewhere? Even of out-of-doors,
Where the stacked firewood gleamed in drapes of glaze
And blinded the sun itself with jubilant theft,
The smooth cool plunder of celestial fire?

This is finely "Etched," at the edge of the first line, with "Edged"
likewise at the second line. In its precise finesse, in its unembar-
rassed self-consciousness, the effect is echt Hecht. (I know, I know,
but our poet did advocate "*mens sana* in men's sauna," and he meta-
morphosed Horace's "Pyrrha" into "piranha," as well as Wallace
Stevens's "Le Monocle de Mon Oncle" into "Le Masseur de Ma
Soeur." And he is the justly proud author of *Civilization and Its Dis-
cothèques.*)

The slant of light finds itself modulated into "a shaft of the late
afternoon" (a shrewd shaft again). The line which enters with the
word "Entered" turns to entertain—somewhat as both guests and
thoughts may be entertained; and then the undulation resumes its
sway, alert to the crosscurrent within "sway" (to govern, or to be
governed and swing from side to side):

Entered our room to entertain the sway
And float of motes, like tiny aqueous lives,

—how light, this "float of motes." Hecht returned to the scene with the exquisitely ghostly poem "Motes," which was posthumously published in the *New Yorker* on 1 November 2004:

They wandered out of gloom
Into some golden shaft
Of late-afternoon light,
Those tiny filaments
That filled me with delight,
Lifted by an updraft
Or viewless influence
There in the living room.

In the cognate poem "A Certain Slant" the decor, with its antique luxuriance, has its affinity to the consummate scene in *The Waste Land,* but it is Eliot's syntax, and particularly the interaction of past participles ("burnished") with past tenses ("Glowed"), that most secures our seeing Hecht's scene against the backdrop of Eliot's, which has as *its* backdrop not only Cleopatra's barge in *Antony and Cleopatra* but Belinda's dressing table in *The Rape of the Lock,* Belinda joining Cleopatra and Philomel among women "so rudely forced."

The Chair she sat in, like a burnished throne,
Glowed on the marble, where the glass
Held up by standards wrought with fruited vines
From which a golden Cupidon peeped out
(Another hid his eyes behind his wing)
Doubled the flames of sevenbranched candelabra

Reflecting light upon the table as
The glitter of her jewels rose to meet it,
From satin cases poured in rich profusion.
In vials of ivory and coloured glass
Unstoppered, lurked her strange synthetic perfumes,
Unguent, powdered, or liquid—troubled, confused
And drowned the sense in odours; stirred by the air
That freshened from the window, these ascended
In fattening the prolonged candle-flames,
Flung their smoke into the laquearia,
Stirring the pattern on the coffered ceiling.
Huge sea-wood fed with copper
Burned green and orange, framed by the coloured stone,
In which sad light a carvèd dolphin swam.
Above the antique mantel was displayed
As though a window gave upon the sylvan scene
The change of Philomel, by the barbarous king
So rudely forced;

    (*The Waste Land* II)

William Empson seized upon a double-edged syntax ("If referring
to *glitter, poured* may, in any case, be a main verb as well as a parti-
ciple") and then poured forth one of his most glitteringly illumi-
nating exegeses:

> The ambiguity of syntax in *poured* is repeated on a grander
> scale by
>
> > Unguent, powdered, or liquid—troubled, confused
> > And drowned the sense in odours; stirred by the air . . .
>
> where, after *powdered* and the two similar words have acted
> as adjectives, it gives a sense of swooning or squinting, or the

ANTHONY HECHT

·

93

stirring of things seen through heat convection currents, to think of *troubled* and *confused* as verbs. They may, indeed, be kept as participles belonging to *perfumes*. . . .

For *stirred,* after all this, we are in a position to imagine three subjects as intended by *these; perfumes, sense,* and *odours* (from which it could follow on without a stop); there is a curious heightening of the sense of texture from all this dalliance; a suspension of all need for active decision; thus *ascended* is held back in the same way as either verb or participle in order that no climax, none of the relief of certainty, may be lacking to the last and indubitable verb *flung*.[26]

But in "A Certain Slant," there is none of the relief of certainty, for there is nothing corresponding to Eliot's "last and indubitable verb *flung*." It is to other ends that Hecht's poem plays Eliot's passionate game, one kind of *-ed* against another, the past participles ("Etched," "Edged," "stacked"—and, with an elegant savoir-faire, "pavé") against the past tenses ("Entered," "glanced," "bathed," "Turned," "gleamed," "blinded"). It is the wit of self-reflection that offers, at the opening or jamb of the line, the word "Swiveled" as the hinge between the two kinds of *-ed,* since it may be either the past tense (they swiveled) or the participle (their being swiveled):

> Where other aqueous lives, equally slow,
> Turned in their sad, involuntary courses,
> Swiveled in eel-green broth.[27]

Hecht's art turns to Eliot, in its happy voluntary course. What jubilant theft, what smooth cool plunder.

Eliot is repeatedly present.

After the torchlight red on sweaty faces
After the frosty silence in the gardens
After the agony in stony places
The shouting and the crying

(*The Waste Land* V, "What the Thunder Said")

Hecht:

After the closing of cathedral doors,
After the last soft footfall fades away,
There still remain artesian, grottoed sounds

("Meditation II")[28]

In conversation with Philip Hoy:

I'm intrigued by "Meditation"'s echoes of "What the Thunder Said." How deliberate was this?

Yes, you're right. Isn't it curious that one has only to begin two consecutive pentameter lines with the words "After the" for an alert reader to say: "Ha! Eliot! *The Waste Land.* 'What the Thunder Said.'" It's an index of the authority and durability and resonance of his words. And yet I think this echo, if that's what it is, was quite unconscious, a faint reminiscence of a familiar music ("That strain again") buried obscurely in the back of my mind. The general tenor of my lines is really unlike Eliot's. Mine are vaguely hopeful, and at least gentle, whereas his are agonized and full of despair.[29]

"That strain again, it had a dying fall." Hecht's words have his characteristic lucidity and scruple. One might, though, separate out some of the thoughts that are entwined there. Probably unconscious, yes. Back of his mind, yes (often the poet's best feature, the back of his or her mind). "Really unlike Eliot's": yes (though

Hecht's "at least gentle, whereas . . ." rightly preserves something tentative)—but it would be a mistake to suppose that the corollary of "really unlike" is that there is no point in bringing Eliot's lines into play as part (only part, but still) of an ample response to Hecht's lines. For the art of allusion makes creative use of both likeness and unlikeness. In this it is like the art of metaphor, and allusion may be seen under the aspect of metaphor, in their both bringing into relation a similitude and a dissimilitude. Hecht's contrastive imagination is at one with Eliot's own practice and principle. Of the allusion to Meredith in his "Cousin Nancy," Eliot said in 1961, "In one of my early poems, I used, without quotation marks, the line 'the army of unalterable law . . .' from a poem by George Meredith, and this critic accused me of having shamelessly plagiarised, pinched, pilfered that line. Whereas, of course, the whole point was that the reader should recognise where it came from and contrast it with the spirit and meaning of my own poem."[30] Eliot's principle and practice here are in line with Hecht's acknowledgment of why for "The Venetian Vespers" he pairs with a harsh epigraph from the Venice of *Othello* this sentence from *The Stones of Venice:* "We cannot all have our gardens now, nor our pleasant fields to meditate in at eventide"—"I wanted the Ruskin sentence because its calm tone of pastoral resignation would contrast with the tone of my own, very urban poem."[31]

And the other of Hecht's own poems?

Meditation II
After the closing of cathedral doors,
After the last soft footfall fades away,
There still remain artesian, grottoed sounds
Below the threshold of the audible,

The infinite, unspent reverberations
Of the prayers, coughs, whispers and *amens* of the day,
Afloat upon the marble surfaces.
They continue forever. Nothing is ever lost.
So the sounds of children, enriched, magnified,
Cross-fertilized by the contours of a tunnel,
Promote their little statures for a moment
Of resonance to authority and notice,
A fleeting, bold celebrity that rounds
In perfect circles to attentive shores,
Returning now in still enlarging arcs
To which there is no end. Whirled without end.

The feat of the allusion is furthered by the dexterity with which
the very nature of allusion is invoked, repeatedly yet not repeti-
tively, by so many of the words that take off from and then in due
course come in for their landing thanks to Eliot's words. The self-
reflecting, with allusion as itself these things, "sounds" that will
sometimes be "Below the threshold of the audible." And com-
pounding this, there is a conjunction: first, of the self-reflecting,
for is not an allusion a "reverberation" even though that word does
not derive from the Latin word for a word?

Reverberations (from the Latin, *verber*,
Meaning a whip or lash)[32]

Hecht evokes "The infinite, unspent reverberations." Eliot:

After the torchlight red on sweaty faces
After the frosty silence in the gardens
After the agony in stony places
The shouting and the crying

> Prison and palace and reverberation
>
> Of thunder of spring over distant mountains

Hecht hears "the sounds of children, enriched, magnified, / Cross-fertilized by the contours." Eliot: "the leaves were full of children, / Hidden excitedly, containing laughter"; "the hidden laughter / Of children" (*Burnt Norton* I and V). Hecht envisages infinity and eternity: "Returning now in still enlarging arcs / To which there is no end. Whirled without end." Eliot whirled "world" into "whirled," and vice versa.[33]

"Meditation II" speaks of "resonance" and "authority." In conversation, Hecht spoke in these terms of "After the . . ." and its calling up Eliot: "It's an index of the authority and durability and resonance of his words." Durability: in the words of the poem, "Nothing is ever lost."

A comedy that is weighty and dark is brought into play when Hecht uses the self-reflecting possibilities of allusion (and especially of allusions to Eliot) contrariously. That is, setting the sense of the lines not parallel but athwart. The first half of "The Hunt" is a broody prose poem that skulks and hides, as is always a good idea if the hunt is on (whether the hider be the hunter or the hunted). "I am hidden."[34] But what is not then hidden at all, what is evident, overt not covert, is what the lines are feeding upon.

> That was a tasty one. Just to go down, there with pale roots
> and hidden waters. O hidden. Is anyone hungry?

Earlier in "The Hunt," "I am hidden" moved then through "hidden waters" to "O hidden." What is the point, the still point?

> O hidden under the dove's wing, hidden in the turtle's
> breast,

Under the palmtree at noon, under the running water
At the still point of the turning world. O hidden.
　("Coriolan I: Triumphal March")

Hecht's darkness is enlightened by Eliot. A hunt is no triumphal
march (but then Eliot's poem is scarcely that), yet there is some-
thing of a triumphal tribute to Eliot, even if a disturbed one. The
most unexpected words that Eliot ever wrote—

　　　　Don't throw away that sausage,
　It'll come in handy.

—are not lost on Hecht. Don't throw away that mess of pottage,
it'll come in handy.

　That was a tasty one. Just to go down, there with pale roots
　and hidden waters. O hidden. Is anyone hungry?

　The Eliot sausage may or may not have been pork. The last qua-
train of a poem by Hecht hungers and thirsts after righteousness.[35]

Pig
In the manger of course were cows and the Child Himself
　　　　Was like unto a lamb
Who should come in the fulness of time on an ass's back
　　　　Into Jerusalem

And all things be redeemed—the suckling babe
　　　　Lie safe in the serpent's home
And the lion eat straw like the ox and roar its love
　　　　To Mark and Jerome

And God's Peaceable Kingdom return among them all
　　　　Save one full of offense

ANTHONY HECHT
·
99

Into which the thousand fiends of a human soul
     Were cast and driven hence
And the one thus cured gone up into the hills
     To worship and to pray:
O Swine that takest away our sins
     That takest away

Flippant, callous, the grim play upon "cured"? Yet it would not vitiate, it would further vitalize, Hecht's wording to allow into one's consciousness the very different cast of mind that prompted Hugh Kingsmill's notorious parody of A. E. Housman's penchant for hangings:

Like enough, you won't be glad,
When they come to hang you, lad:
But bacon's not the only thing
That's cured by hanging from a string.

Hecht's pig is that supreme scapegoat, a scapepig. The pig is the Jewish scapegoat. The poet is well aware of the irony and even the agony by which he, a Jewish poet, finds himself turning to Eliot (*of all poets!* would be shrill but not outré) for his inspired close.

And the one thus cured gone up into the hills
     To worship and to pray:
O Swine that takest away our sins
     That takest away

This is a close that takes away any hope of a full stop, a period. A conclusion in which nothing is concluded. A close that declines to close. A close of which the final sound is the unterminable sound "away." Over the hills and far away.

It was one of Eliot's profoundest principles that punctuation "includes the *absence* of punctuation marks, when they are omitted where the reader would expect them."[36] It was one of his greatest realizations of this principle that brought to an end, an end of a kind, "The Fire Sermon":

> To Carthage then I came

> Burning burning burning burning
> O Lord Thou pluckest me out
> O Lord Thou pluckest

> burning

From the words "O Lord Thou pluckest me out" (which he plucked out from Saint Augustine) Eliot proceeded to pluck out the words "O Lord Thou pluckest." From the fourfold

> Burning burning burning burning

he plucked out a single

> burning

—a brand from the burning.

Then from this evocation of worship and prayer, Hecht takes up "pluckest," turns it to "takest," and takes it away in a direction that is not Eliot's but that does have in common with Eliot a conviction that there is no end of it, the voiceless wailing.

> And the one thus cured gone up into the hills
> To worship and to pray:
> O Swine that takest away our sins
> That takest away

The two words "our sins," which are still all-too-present in the penultimatum, are taken away at the very end, literally. But only in a way, for is there a very end?

To Eliot then he came. And to Eliot's sins.

For the Love of Books (1999) presented "100 Celebrated Writers on the Books They Love Most."[37] Or in Hecht's case, They Mostly Love. For his love of Eliot's poems was instinct with caveats and reservations, being neither a simple love nor that simplifying thing, a love-hate relationship. Hecht's letter to the editor honored Eliot, this side idolatry:

> When I was seventeen or eighteen (who now am seventy-four) I bought for a class in modern poetry a copy (which I still have) of *Collected Poems, 1909-1935* by T.S. Eliot. He was the first modern poet I tried to read, well before becoming acquainted with Pound, Williams, Crane or any of the others. I was immediately mystified, and enchanted by the very perplexities that made the poems so difficult to understand. All by themselves, the "notes" to *The Waste Land* I found mesmerizing. There was, at that time, no great body of commentary on Eliot's poetry, and my professor was little better prepared than his students to interpret the texts, a student advantage that was itself very rare and the more, therefore, to be cherished. I read those poems, if not with much comprehension, at least with enormous assiduity and a kind of devotion, committing a number of them to memory, not on assignment but because of frequent readings. And, as I have found to happen with poems of the highest quality (including, of course, Shakespeare's plays and sonnets) I continued to discover more and more riches the longer I lived with and reconsidered the Eliot poems. There was in a number of them something undeniably provoking and humiliating: the unapologetic note of anti-Semitism, which I found personally wounding. With the passage of time my comprehen-

sion of the poems has become more assured, my admiration for them has become more solidly based, and my sense of affront at their bigotries has remained undiminished. And this troubles me far more than the anti-Semitic outbursts of Pound, which are a sort of thoughtless and purgative rant, and therefore dismissable as a sort of temper tantrum. Eliot's racism is deeper, haunting and more sinister because while Pound simply repeats medieval slanders and libels, invoking "usury" etc., Eliot gives the distinct impression that he finds the physical appearance and the cultural vulgarity of Jews offensive to his own fastidiousness. My experiences in the front lines of the infantry in WWII, including the liberation of the Flossenbürg Concentration Camp, and a good deal of reading about the Holocaust in the ensuing years confirmed my initial discomfort, though by this time I had come to see that anti-Semitism was a widespread feature of the "polite" intellectual life of that time, and could be found, alas, in far too many authors and poets of considerable stature. Whatever it may have been with others, with Eliot it was more than a fashionable sentiment; it was so deeply lodged that he was partly unaware of it, and baffled when accused of it. In any case, its presence in poems I was unable to dismiss was itself a cause of fascination and of much thought. And it has kept my continued reading of Eliot from ever falling into a settled and uncomplicated pleasure.[38]

Not that Hecht took a settled and uncomplicated pleasure in his reading of Pound.

While acknowledging that EP had a major hand in the poetic revolution of his days, that he was generous to many fellow artists, that he helped Yeats get rid of his early cloudiness, and that his own pleasure in hard, clear features was often a healthy and useful influence, that his interest in other cultures and literatures (somewhat neglected in those days) had a broadening and enriching effect — even granting all this, I still find him, for the most part, unrewarding, when not infuriating, to read. In my crotchety latter years I find myself becoming increasingly impatient with anti-semites, and my impatience increases if, at the same time, they regard themselves as infallible prophets.[39]

Hecht's patience increased when he gave sustained attention to *The Merchant of Venice* and to usury within theology and history: "The prohibitory texts have been used by Gentiles to stigmatize both the practice and the Jews (as if they were the solitary practitioners) from the earliest times right down to so late and vehement an anti-Semite as Ezra Pound, whose fulminations upon usury constitute some of the most interesting and musical parts of the *Cantos.*"[40]

From Canto XLV, Hecht quotes "a segment," with ample fairness:

With Usura

With usura hath no man a house of good stone
each block cut smooth and well fitting
that design might cover their face,
with usura
hath no man a painted paradise on his church wall
harpes et luthes
or where virgin receiveth message

. . . .

WITH USURA

wool comes not to market
sheep bringeth no gain with usura
Usura is a murrain, usura
blunteth the needle in the maid's hand
and stoppeth the spinner's cunning. Pietro Lombardo
came not by usura
Duccio came not by usura
nor Pier della Francesca; Zuan Bellin' not by usura
nor was 'La Calunnia' painted.
Came not by usura Angelico; came not Ambrogio Praedis,
Came no church of cut stone signed: *Adamo me fecit.*
Not by usura St Trophime
Not by usura Saint Hilaire,
Usura rusteth the chisel
It rusteth the craft and the craftsman
It gnaweth the thread in the loom
None learneth to weave gold in her pattern;
Azure hath canker by usura; cramoisi is unbroidered
Emerald findeth no Memling
Usura slayeth the child in the womb
It stayeth the young man's courting
It hath brought palsey to bed, lyeth
between the young bride and her bridegroom
                        CONTRA NATURAM
They have brought whores from Eleusis
Corpses are set to banquet
at behest of usura.[41]

Whereupon Hecht pays Pound the compliment not only of prais-
ing the lines but of contesting them.

ANTHONY HECHT
·

There is undoubted power here, and a certain manifest beauty of incantation, along with what we are doubtless supposed to regard as high and moral indignation. But it is not entirely clear just what the poet means. Apart from the traditional, Thomistic condemnation of usury as "contra naturam," against nature in that money is made to beget money without the essential participation of *labor*—an unnaturalness to which Shakespeare is apparently referring when he has Shylock declare that he can make gold and silver "breed as fast" as ewes and lambs, and for which Dante coupled usurers with sodomites in the same circle of *Inferno*—there is in Pound's Canto the puzzle about the specific artists and works of art mentioned. If he is declaring that certain particular artists were not usurers, this is not very wonderful. But some of the works, like the churches, for example, are by unknown artists, and the Canto as a whole suggests strongly that the greatest, the loveliest and the most pious works of art of the Middle Ages and the Renaissance *could not have been produced* "with usura." But this is flatly wrong, and the chances are good that Pound knew it, which a good deal undermines his lofty stance and condemnatory tone.[42]

"I still find him for the most part, unrewarding, when not infuriating, to read." Unrewarding not only to Hecht the reader but to Hecht the writer. Pound, so fertile in himself and for many other poets, was never to be the cause of fertility in Hecht. (For another story, think of Pound's effect upon Louis Zukofsky and upon Basil Bunting.) Hecht writes of Eliot's poems as haunting; he was haunted, too, by *The Merchant of Venice,* as is the man whom he brought to troubled life in Venice.

Something profoundly soiled, pointlessly hurt
And beyond cure in us yearns for this costless
Ablution, this impossible reprieve,
Unpurchased at a scaffold, free, bequeathed
As rain upon the just and the unjust,
As in the fall of mercy, unconstrained,
Upon the poor, infected place beneath.

   ("The Venetian Vespers")

PORTIA: Then must the Jew be merciful.
SHYLOCK: On what compulsion must I? Tell me that.
PORTIA: The quality of mercy is not strained,
      It droppeth as the gentle rain from heaven
      Upon the place beneath. It is twice blest,
      It blesseth him that gives, and him that takes,
      'Tis mightiest in the mightiest.

   (*The Merchant of Venice,* IV.i)

By its nature, allusion may itself be twice blest, it blesseth him that
gives, and him that takes. Hecht's allusion to Portia's immortal lines
is shielded against sentimentality by the awareness that they can all
too easily be sentimentalized. They have their nobility, but they
course with an ignoble energy too, for they are laced with the anti-
Semitism that is the animating animosity of the play. The central
word "gentle" (central to the line and to the speech) combines gen-
erosity of feeling, an appeal for generosity, with something dis-
tinctly ungenerous, which is why the sentiment, divorced from
its context, lends itself to facile employment and deployment. We
are not to forget that the contrast of "Jew" with "gentle" and "un-
gentle" comes more than a dozen times, including "Hie thee, gentle
Jew," along with the Christians' unseemly relish at the thought of

the bond cracked 'twixt daughter and father ("my old Master the Jew . . . my new Master the Christian . . . gentle Jessica"; "his gentle daughter's sake"). "Now by my hood, a gentle, and no Jew."[43]

All of which means that the tender cadence of "It droppeth as the gentle rain from heaven" needs to be heard against the back-sound of an untender murmur.

"The gentle rain from heaven": the thought, with its ancient positive sense of what "condescension" should be, has biblical authority behind and above it. "He maketh his sun to rise on the evil and the good, and sendeth rain on the just and on the unjust" (Saint Matthew 5:45). Shylock is being asked by Portia to do himself the mercy of being among the just. This with the conviction that justice may be something other than the opposite of mercy; rather, mercy may itself minister to justice. "Then must the Jew be merciful."

The thought of the rain from heaven duly invited a bringing down to earth. There is poetic justice in its being a judge (a Victorian one, Lord Bowen) who notoriously drew attention to the realities:

> The rain, it raineth on the just
> And also on the unjust fella:
> But chiefly on the just, because
> The unjust steals the just's umbrella.

This is not without its own "jubilant theft."

There is nothing jubilant about Hecht's treatment of the biblical-Shakespearean befalling. But his monologuist does take his liberties, half-hoping and half-fearing that we shall register what he commits, rather as he half-reveals and half-conceals his distortion of Eliot within "Thus virtues, it is said, are forced upon us / By our own impudent crimes."

ANTHONY HECHT

·

108

                    bequeathed
As rain upon the just and the unjust,
As in the fall of mercy, unconstrained,
Upon the poor, infected place beneath.

Hecht's monologuist is by way of being a teacher (many a teacher masquerades as a dialoguist), and he is happy to gloss the Shakespearean phrase "is not strain'd" as "unconstrained." There is a characteristic blend of the helpful and the condescending in this thinker's turn; we (his readers? his listeners? his overhearers?) are no longer constrained by our unfamiliarity with Shakespearean English. So the way is prepared for those changes and additions that will wrest the Shakespearean moment to the service of the self-serving. No longer does the rain fall "from heaven," and no longer is it "gentle": "gentle" and "from heaven" have been dropped. Those assurances (which did have their crosscurrents but were assurances still) are no longer available. (The words "from heaven" did not gain admission to Samuel Beckett's "A Piece of Monologue" either, for all its loveliness of cadence: "Room once full of sounds. Faint sounds. Whence unknown. Fewer and fainter as time wore on. Nights wore on. None now. No. No such thing as none. Rain some nights still slant against the panes. Or dropping gentle on the place beneath.") In "The Venetian Vespers" there arrive—not to take the place of "gentle" and "from heaven" but to occupy a different place—two words that were not to be found in Portia's speech of mercy: "Upon the poor, infected place beneath." This has the steely insistence that goes beyond an emendation to an erratum: for "the place," read "the poor, infected place." It is likely to be a coinciding rather than a coincidence that it should have been Ezra Pound who

ANTHONY HECHT
•
109

urged, with harsh realism, "pity, yes, for the infected, but maintain antisepsis, let the light pour."[44]

Pound's poems, some of them, were worse than affected by his anti-Semitism; they were infected by it. But then so were Eliot's, some of them. I differ from Hecht as to the scale and the nature, and as to the endorsement (is it always that?) of the anti-Semitic animosities within Eliot's poems of 1920–22, but there is no ignoring any of this, and I have long been grateful to Hecht for making me not only think but re-think about it.[45] Eliot is haunted, and Hecht acknowledges that he finds this haunting.

Ghosts haunt Hecht's poems. (In note 46 many representations or representatives of them are raised.)[46] Some of them appear to be ghosts pure and simple. (Yet what would that be, exactly?) But most of them are ghosts who breathe the air of allusion, who are there in allusion's immediate vicinity with an apprehension of how allusion may itself function as a spirit summoned, at once dead and alive. There is the ghost of Hamlet's words in Hecht's "Despair," which opens:

> Sadness. The moist gray shawls of drifting sea-fog,
> Salting scrub pine, drenching the cranberry bogs,
> Erasing all but foreground, making a ghost
> Of anyone who walks softly away;[47]

Hamlet, I.iv:

> By heaven, I'll make a ghost of him that lets me!
> I say away!

And behind Hecht's line "There comes no manager hither to explain," there is the ghost of a line from the greatest of ghost plays.[48]

There needs no ghost, my lord, come from the grave
To tell us this.

(*Hamlet,* I.v)

Multiple allusion permits of provocatively divergent im-
pulses. For instance, "The Witch of Endor" will immediately call
up 1 Samuel 27, the woman of Endor who calls up the ghost of
Samuel.[49] But to this dark summoning, with the unsupernatural aid
of Shakespeare, Hecht adds the salutary skepticism of Shakespeare's
Hotspur. "The Witch of Endor" opens:

I had the gift, and arrived at the technique
That called up spirits from the vasty deep
To traffic with our tumid flesh,

recalling Shakespeare's Glendower. (The superstitious will register
that the name Glendower has within it, in sequence, *endo r.*)

GLENDOWER: I can call spirits from the vasty deep.
HOTSPUR: Why so can I, or so can any man:
But will they come, when you do call for them?

(*Henry IV, Part I,* III.i)

This is the question that every allusive poet who calls spirits—or
who calls up or who calls upon spirits—had better ask himself or
herself. Will they come, when you do call for them?

Two of Hecht's titles may alert us to this spirit in his work. Both
poems explicitly invoke ghosts; both titles let their imagination
play over the concept of life and of what contrasts with life.

The one title, "Still Life," pictures what the French language
stiffens into *nature morte.* In Hecht's hands, this title is alive to life
and death, and far-from-incidentally it constitutes a memento
(*vivere* and *mori*) of how painterly this poet is.[50] A ghost is still life.
"Still Life," as the poem opens, is about to dawn:

ANTHONY HECHT

•

111

Sleep-walking vapor, like a visitant ghost,
    Hovers above a lake
Of Tennysonian calm just before dawn.
Inverted trees and boulders waver and coast
In polished darkness. Glints of silver break
Among the liquid leafage, and then are gone.[51]

Again there is the concurrence and divergence—similitude and dissimilitude, as in a successful metaphor—of more than one current of allusion. For the calm may be and is Tennysonian, without our being meant to forget how uncalm the poet of *In Memoriam* and *Maud* recurrently is—but then Tennyson at his best is not Tennysonian, and in any case Tennyson does not have a monopoly of calm—but the calm and the coast and the concluding syntax are an Arnoldian opening.

    The sea is calm to-night.
    The tide is full, the moon lies fair
    Upon the straits;—on the French coast the light
    Gleams and is gone.
        ("Dover Beach"; for Hecht's poem "The Dover Bitch" see note 52)[52]

How precarious the moment is, in Arnold, as in much of Tennyson, here within one of Hecht's most tingling poems of the war. "Still Life" (*still* as "making no movement" and as "for now, at least") moves to its last two stanzas:

    Why does this so much stir me, like a code
        Or muffled intimation
    Of purposes and preordained events?
    It knows me, and I recognize its mode
    Of cautionary, spring-tight hesitation,
    This silence so impacted and intense.

ANTHONY HECHT

·

As in a water-surface I behold
> The first, soft, peach decree
Of light, its pale, inaudible commands.
I stand beneath a pine-tree in the cold,
Just before dawn, somewhere in Germany,
A cold, wet, Garand rifle in my hands.

What is perfect is the placing: "somewhere in Germany" is the G.I.'s
not being quite sure where, in this foreign country and in a war, he
finds himself, and is at the same time the necessary keeping of his
location quiet if he did know, even in (say) a letter to a loved one,
back home (headed "Somewhere in Germany," like the journalists'
reports from the battle zone). It is then the timing that makes pos-
sible the fit of such different things: of all that is calmly outside time
or at least proffers the hope of being so (in the worlds of nature, of
art, and of the forms of peace that they differently make real to us)
set in tension ("impacted and intense") with the realities—let us
hold to the hope that we really mean the *other* realities—of war, of
weaponry, of imminent death for at least someone.

This ghostly poem, with "Tennysonian" in its opening sentence,
calls upon intimations of allusion. An allusion is like a ghost in
being an "intimation," within a "mode" that has been and is to be
"recognized," something "preordained" and "impacted." The lines
circle round, with the return of "just before dawn" (from the first
stanza) as "Just before dawn" in this the last stanza, where the capi-
tal in "Just" brings out, tacitly and tactfully, that the phrase is dif-
ferently deployed now; and then there is the return of "cold," like-
wise not altogether the same as at its earlier appearance, numbed
down:

ANTHONY HECHT
•
113

I stand beneath a pine-tree in the cold,
Just before dawn, somewhere in Germany,
A cold, wet, Garand rifle in my hands.

All contemplation of the horrors of war must face the peril of two opposite half-truths: that of being sure that peace will win and that of being sure that war will. This siege of contraries is there for me in the poem's contrast of two names: Tennyson and Garand. The epithet from a proper noun that is "Garand" (the standard U.S. Army rifle then) in the closing stanza cannot destroy the epithet from a proper noun, "Tennysonian," in the opening stanza. Or vice versa, be it remembered. *Wenn ich Kultur höre . . . entsichere ich meinen Browning.* "Whenever I hear the word culture I release the safety catch of my Browning."[53] But it will not do simply to retort, Whenever I hear the word *safety catch,* I release my *culture.* A Browning cannot destroy a Browning. Either way.

Art, like everything else including the soldier at dawn, must take its chances. The allusions are ancestral voices prophesying war, recalling war, recording war. Recording it all the more unforgettably because never forgetting how much there is that is neither war nor warfare. The life of a wit is a warfare upon earth; the end of art is peace. The respective convictions of Alexander Pope and Seamus Heaney.

The title of another ghost poem, "Curriculum Vitae," is couched in a dead tongue, and yet the phrase formulates the run of a life, with some touch of the dead hand of the pedagogical curriculum, given that the poem is about schoolchildren and schoolbooks. The businesslike phrase presses toward earning a living rather than exercising a life. Hecht sets the fact that *curriculum vitae* (like *rigor mortis*) is a phrase from the ancient world against the phrase's pointing inescapably to the professionalized modern world, and he succeeds in doing this by *not* italicizing the title. The opening poem in *The Transparent Man,* "Curriculum Vitae," like "Still Life," begins at dawn, being again an aubade of a sort. In "Still Life" the love—unlike in the traditional aubade—was not for a loved one but for nature, for art, and, yes, for life. In "Curriculum Vitae" the love is for sight, for sights literal and imagined, but above all the love (a pained love) is for young loved ones, for young lives, for the life that is schoolchildren boarding a bus. "Curriculum Vitae" (but these lives are still to be run) sets its scene at once, nothing splendid or splendiferous but lovely withal. Schoolchildren have their wars, and there are even child soldiers to make the heart sink and ache. But here the sound of war is distant, being muted to metaphors.

Curriculum Vitae

As though it were reluctant to be day,
    Morning deploys a scale
    Of rarities in gray,
And winter settles down in its chain-mail,

Victorious over legions of gold and red.
    The smokey souls of stones,
    Blunt pencillings of lead,
Pare down the world to glintless monotones

Of graveyard weather, vapors of a fen
    We reckon through our pores.
    Save for the garbage men,
Our children are the first ones out of doors.

Book-bagged and padded out, at mouth and nose
    They manufacture ghosts,

George Washington's and Poe's,
Banquo's, the Union and Confederate hosts',

And are themselves the ghosts, file cabinet gray,
Of some departed us,
Signing our lives away
On ferned and parslied windows of a bus.

The ghosts of "some departed us" include an earlier departure, the ghost of a ghost: "It is, or seems to be, a choice of whether to consider ourselves the ghosts of ghosts, or the immensely favored beneficiaries of priceless heirlooms."[54] To Banquo's ghost, within Macbeth's world of civil war, are joined ghosts from within the American Civil War, "the Union and Confederate hosts'." (The plural hosts' ghosts.) A tiny, telling syntax this, with the apostrophe that tacitly hyphenates "the Union and Confederate" to make the warring parties one.

These men, and those who opposed them
And those whom they opposed
Accept the constitution of silence
And are folded in a single party.
(*Little Gidding* III, on the English Civil War)

Hecht's is a telling rhyme, the sequence "ghosts" into "hosts," the former word entirely folding the latter up into itself. The quatrain compounds the pressure by returning to the sound effect of the opening quatrain, with the practice of entire assonance—"day," "scale," "gray," "chain-mail" (doubled there)—putting in a second appearance or apparition as "nose," "ghosts," "Poe's" (with the immediately ensuing word being "Banquo's"), "hosts'."

Among the things that generations generate are ghosts. Among the things that ghosts generate is commonalty. In *Hamlet,* Gertrude can urge her son,

> Do not for ever with thy veilèd lids
> Seek for thy noble father in the dust;
> Thou know'st 'tis common, all that lives must die,
> Passing through nature, to eternity.
>
> (I.ii)

Hamlet turns this commonplace (Latin and everywhere) to his sardonic purposes by setting *common* as shared by all mankind against *common* as, oh, frequent. "Ay Madam, it is common." But then it is not in the dust that Hamlet has sought for his noble father but on the battlements, where the ghost has opened his eyes.

New life is there in "Curriculum Vitae," to be seen in the young ones' visible breath, a sight at once bizarre and everyday or every-cold-day. The breath, in the cold open air, beats any séance's ectoplasm when it comes to issuing ghosts: "at mouth and nose / They manufacture ghosts." (For ectoplasm and ghosts in Hecht, see note 55.)[55] Then the warm young breath, soon to be on the windows of the bus, is to be set against the frosty-paned beauty that is crisply caught in the unexpected terms of "ferned" and "parslied." The verb *to fern* is not entirely a novelty (the *OED* has two instances, 1420 and 1862), and it incites the verb *to parsley,* unknown to the *OED,* and effects a combination of the hitherto unseen and the crystal clear.

Asking myself why "Signing" feels so right ("Signing our lives away"), I find myself wondering about the convergence not only of the directions of the verb (one toward signature, the other toward signal) but also of an exquisite moment in Tennyson.

As when a soul laments, which hath been blest,
    Desiring what is mingled with past years,
In yearnings that can never be exprest
    By signs or groans or tears;

("A Dream of Fair Women")

The muted force of "signs" there is a matter of its looking for a mo-
ment as though it might be a typo. "By signs or groans or tears": it
is as if the line cries out for *sighs* but then does not go in for crying
out after all. The pressure upon "signs" that in Tennyson's line is
exerted by "or groans or tears" is exerted in Hecht's line ("Signing
our lives away") by all the breath in the air of the poem, the warmth
against the frost.

And are themselves the ghosts, file cabinet gray,
    Of some departed us,
    Signing our lives away
On ferned and parslied windows of a bus.

It is the small word "bus" that consummates this haunting poem. A
strange word in that it is entirely everyday and even demotic while
being at the same time an imaginative appropriation of Latin. In
full, it had been *omnibus.* Omnibus, because *for all.* The *OED*'s first
quotation for the vehicular "omnibus" is 1829. The popular abbre-
viation arrives a mere three years later in 1832, without even an
apostrophe to its name. Eliot knew what he was doing when he
used the full form in a poem of 1914 that combines the calculatedly
proper and the uncalculating erotic:

The girl who mounted in the omnibus
The rainy day, and paid a penny fare
Who answered my appreciative stare
With that averted look without surprise

ANTHONY HECHT

•

118

Which only the experienced can wear

A girl with reddish hair and faint blue eyes

An almost denizen of Leicester Square.

("Paysage Triste")[56]

Was *she* for all, one wonders?

At its most ordinary, public transport; at its most ordinary and extraordinary, what is in store for all: "all that lives must die." Signing our lives away and trying not to lapse into sighing them away. The school bus is suddenly glimpsed, with calm drama and with no melodrama, as something for all to be schooled by.

The breath of the schoolchildren on the cold day can manufacture ghosts at dawn. More than thirty years earlier, Hecht had recalled "A Deep Breath at Dawn."[57] Of the early morning light:

I have watched its refinements since the dawn,

When, at the birdcall, all the ghosts were gone.

The ghost of Hamlet's father is gone at the birdcall. (Rather later in Hecht's poem, "The cocks cried brazenly against all ghosts.") But it is not ghosts in the plural who haunt Hecht's poem, it is a singular ghost.

What if he came and stood beside my tree,

A poor, transparent thing with nothing to do,

His chest showing a jagged vacancy

Through which I might admire the distant view?

Hecht came to judge that the poem was itself something of a vacancy; he not only left it unreprinted, he leveled a charge: "The lines in 'A Deep Breath at Dawn' about admiring a distant view through the shell-penetrated body of a dead soldier who returns as a ghost is too fanciful and unreal, and almost embarrassing. Though not because it involves ghosts. Hardy and Yeats and Eliot all wrote about them well enough."[58]

"Eliot was a poet who appears in his poetry in a very remote and ghostly way."[59] The self-tormentor in "Gerontion" may say, "I have no ghosts," but the poet who invented him had his ghosts. They aptly move gently when it is within a poem "To Walter de la Mare" that they appear:

> Or when the lawn
> Is pressed by unseen feet, and ghosts return
> Gently at twilight, gently go at dawn,
> The sad intangible who grieve and yearn;

Elsewhere his ghosts—as Eliot admitted—were sometimes sadly tangible. Of the Furies in *The Family Reunion,* he wrote, "We put them on the stage, and they looked like uninvited guests who had strayed in from a fancy dress ball" (uninvited ghosts); in whatever way the play is directed, "They never succeed in being either Greek goddesses or modern spooks." And so, when it came to *The Cocktail Party,* "no chorus, and no ghosts." Two figures from *Hamlet* met when Eliot wrote in 1917 that "the ghost of some simple metre should lurk behind the arras in even the 'freest' verse; to advance menacingly as we doze, and withdraw as we rouse."[60]

Hardy and Yeats and Eliot—and Shakespeare. The conjunction of Eliot and Shakespeare (particularly by courtesy of *Hamlet*) often opens for Hecht into an invaluable triangle. The spirit that informs his art is then one that on the appropriate occasions delights in the *discordia concors* of comedy with tragedy, as in much of Eliot and of Shakespeare. "The comedy of the grotesque" that G. Wilson Knight identified and demonstrated within *King Lear* (in *The Wheel of Fire,* 1930, with an introduction by T. S. Eliot) is a feat that Hecht

emulated in a poem with a title à la Laforgue that therefore has
more than a smack of Eliot.[61]

Humoresque

> *Passengers will please refrain*
> *from flushing toilets while the train*
> *is standing in the station. I love you.*

From sewage lines, man-holes, from fitted brass
Sphincters and piston chambers, from the dark
Gastro-intestinal corridors of hell,
Deep among wheels and oily underbellies
Of *Wagon Lits* emerge these screeching ghosts,
Doomed for a certain time to walk the night,
Erupting there and there in baggy forms
That cloud, occlude and spirit away the luggage,
Facteurs and passengers from this vast barn
Of skeletal iron and grimed membranes of glass.
This pestilent congregation of vapors sings
In Pentecostal tongues, now shrill, now soft,
Mixed choral dolorosos by Satie
To the god Terminus, the living end
Of every journey, whom the Romans charmed
With gifts of blood and ashes, and who today
Comes up from under as pale S. Lazare,
Come back to tell us all, and tell us off,
And tell and tell, as the bells toll and trains
Roll slowly to their sidings, issuing ghosts.
These rise and fade into the winter air
Already gray with souls of the departed
Through which indifferent pigeons lift and bank

ANTHONY HECHT

•

And flutter in the vague and failing warmth,
Which, like the curling lamias of *Gauloises,*
The shiny rigor mortis of the rails,
Blends with the exhalations of my love.

Twice we hear of ghosts: "screeching ghosts" and "issuing ghosts," where disconcertingly the -*ings* have different grammatical functions in the body of the lines. The poem is haunted by a great many ghosts, allusive and elusive, and is as crowded as a railway station or the railway station S. Lazare. Two or three allusive appearances or apparitions stand out: Hamlet (Young Hamlet and old Hamlet) and young/old J. Alfred Prufrock. Old Hamlet returns:

I am thy father's spirit;
Doomed for a certain term to walk the night.

The latter line is given by Hecht the certainty and the doom-mood of italics:

these screeching ghosts,
Doomed for a certain time to walk the night,
Erupting there and there

But here too there is something to tease us into thought, for there are no italics bent upon the line that comes five lines later, Hecht's line that is all but entirely Hamlet's, "This pestilent congregation of vapors sings / In Pentecostal tongues." In Pentecostal tongues, and in the tongue that Shakespeare spake, the very words.

The comedy of the grotesque is there in the way in which the three "fitted" letters immediately preceding "Sphincters" are "-ass" (this is an American, not a British, poem), even while a certain decorum is preserved thanks not only to "[Br]ass" but to the cordon sanitaire of the line ending that keeps "Sphincters" at a decent distance from "ass." Or there is the tacit twist whereby three successive lines contain words beginning with *w*, but these don't alliterate since "*Wagon*" is sounded with a *V*: "wheels," "*Wagon*," "*walk*." (A notorious Answer-&-Question joke: Answer, *9 W*. Question, Do you spell your name with a V, Herr Wagner? Hecht incites the further happy vexation by which "*Wagon Lits*" and *walk* are both italicized but for very different reasons, the one as from another language, the other as quoted from another ghost world.) Again, the grotesque rumbling and grumbling of "Gastro-intestinal corridors of hell" has its own intestinal corridor (and not just because of putting the "gas" back into "gastro-," to say nothing of the relation of "piston" to "flushing toilets"), conducting this ghostly poem back to another ghostly such: "The Witch of Endor," which concluded with the ghost

> Who spoke a terrible otherworldly curse
> In a hollow, deep, engastrimythic voice.

Hecht's poems often find themselves haunted by his own earlier apparitions. Haunted, too, by Eliot. Today the god Terminus

> Comes up from under as pale S. Lazare,
> Come back to tell us all, and tell us off,
> And tell and tell, as the bells toll and trains
> Roll slowly to their sidings, issuing ghosts.

"The Love Song of J. Alfred Prufrock":

> To have squeezed the universe into a ball
> To roll it towards some overwhelming question,
> To say: "I am Lazarus, come from the dead,
> Come back to tell you all, I shall tell you all"—

ANTHONY HECHT

•

123

The ghosts that issue in Hecht's poems are, like Eliot's greatest ghost, a familiar compound ghost. There is the compound of Hamlet's father's ghost with Eliot. There is the compound of Baudelaire and Eliot.

It may be that I am indebted to Baudelaire chiefly for half a dozen lines out of the whole of *Fleurs du Mal;* and that his significance for me is summed up in the lines:

> *Fourmillante Cité, cité pleine de rêves,*
> *Où le spectre en plein jour raccroche le passant . . .*

I knew what *that* meant, because I had lived it before I knew that I wanted to turn it into verse on my own account.[62]

And in turning Baudelaire's lines into verse on his own account, Eliot was moved at once to turn to other lines of Baudelaire. The last line of the first section of *The Waste Land* is famously an entente that is scarcely cordiale: "You! hypocrite lecteur!—mon semblable,—mon frère!" No italics in Eliot. When Hecht summons both Baudelaire and Eliot, the French line is unviolated by a word from perfidious Albion ("You!"), and so can enjoy its italic autonomy. Hecht has moved his "You" to the head of an earlier line:

> You know me, friend, as Faustus, Baudelaire,
> Boredom, Self-Hatred, and, still more, Self-Love.
> *Hypocrite lecteur, mon semblable, mon frère,*
> Acknowledge me. I fit you like a glove.
>
> ("Death the Hypocrite")[63]

Brotherly love? Sibling rivalry? But Hecht is never a hypocritical reader of Eliot, any more than Eliot is of Baudelaire. It is fitting too that this allusive poem, like "Humoresque," needs to speak of what fits or is fitted. The word "Love" in due course fits perfectly within "glove." There's Self-Love for you.

Can simply the word *brother* call up Baudelaire? Probably yes, if Eliot too is of the company, as he undoubtedly is in "The Ghost in the Martini."[64]

> And now, ingenuous and gay,
> She is asking me about what I was like
> At twenty. (Twenty, eh?)
>
> You wouldn't have liked me then,
> I answer, looking carefully into her eyes.
> I was shy, withdrawn, awkward, one of those men
> That girls seemed to despise,
>
> Moody and self-obsessed,
> Unhappy, defiant, with guilty dreams galore,
> Full of ill-natured pride, an unconfessed
> Snob and a thorough bore.
>
> Her smile is meant to convey
> How changed or modest I am, I can't tell which,
> When I suddenly hear someone close to me say,
> "You lousy son-of-a-bitch!"
>
> A young man's voice, by the sound,
> Coming, it seems, from the twist in the martini.
> "You arrogant, elderly letch, you broken-down
> Brother of Apeneck Sweeney!["]

This is a cocktail of a poem, most skillfully mixed and shaken. "Brother" seems to grope drunkenly for Baudelaire (*mon frère*), with "letch" being a slurred semblable of *lecteur*. Apeneck Sweeney never participates in a rhyme on all the occasions that Eliot calls him up. Of Hecht's serving "martini" with "Sweeney," Eliot might have been chafedly envious. ("The waiter brings in oranges / Bananas figs and hothouse grapes.")

> Apeneck Sweeney spreads his knees
> Letting his arms hang down to laugh,
>
> ("Sweeney Among the Nightingales")

Hecht's smooth propositioner who is suddenly accosted by his rough young self is in no mood to laugh. Even the switch by which "the ghost in the machine" becomes the ghost in the martini is hardly philosophical about the contretemps. But then the deliberate allusiveness is to a philosophical term that was itself brought into being in a spirit of deliberate abusiveness.

> OED 3 b. Philos. *the ghost in the machine:* Gilbert Ryle's name for the mind viewed as separate from the body (see quots). 1949 G. RYLE *Concept of Mind* i. 15 Such in outline is the official theory. I shall often speak of it, with deliberate abusiveness, as "the dogma of the Ghost in the machine."

The young self announces, in reprimanding the old one, "I come unwillingly, like Samuel's ghost." All hail, Witch of Endor.

The voice from the twist of the martini is scabrous, a specter at the feast. Elsewhere a voice is at a far remove from any such world.

> A Voice at a Séance
> It is rather strange to be speaking, but I know you are there
> Wanting to know, as if it were worth knowing.
> Nor is it important that I died in combat

In a good cause or an indifferent one.
Such things, it may surprise you, are not regarded.
Something too much of this.

You are bound to be disappointed,
Wanting to know, are there any trees?
It is all different from what you suppose,
And the darkness is not darkness exactly,
But patience, silence, withdrawal, the sad knowledge
That it was almost impossible not to hurt anyone
Whether by action or inaction.
At the beginning of course there was a sense of loss,
Not of one's own life, but of what seemed
The easy, desirable lives one might have led.
Fame or wealth are hard to achieve,
And goodness even harder;
But the cost of all of them is a familiar deformity
Such as everyone suffers from:
An allergy to certain foods, nausea at the sight of blood,
A slight impediment of speech, shame at one's own body,
A fear of heights or claustrophobia.
What you learn has nothing whatever to do with joy,
Nor with sadness, either. You are mostly silent.
You come to a gentle indifference about being thought
Either a fool or someone with valuable secrets.
It may be that the ultimate wisdom
Lies in saying nothing.
I think I may already have said too much.[65]

ANTHONY HECHT

•

Alicia Ostriker hears Eliot and a turning of the tables. "In 'A Voice at a Séance,' Hecht ventriloquizes what sounds unmistakably like the familiar drone of Old Possum at his most disembodied—a sort of *Beyond the Four Quartets*—telling us that there is little to expect on the other side of the grave either."[66] But the voice is more than a feat of ventriloquism, even though the ventriloquial skills of Browning, creator of "Mr Sludge the Medium," are certainly to the point. (Richard Holt Hutton called Browning "a great intellectual and spiritual ventriloquist," with "spiritual" in touch with spiritualism.)[67] Ostriker writes of the relation of "A Voice at a Séance" to parody: "This is so good that it almost seems parody, but I suspect that it is something subtler and more crucial than parody for the poet, perhaps a way of discovering the degree to which he too endorses the silence of a final apathy. If the echoes behind echoes fade back from the composite ghost of *Little Gidding* to the dusty voices that spoke in Hades to Ulysses, so much more grave the experiment." Yes, "A Voice at a Séance" is something more crucial than parody, even though parody can seize a crux. Hecht's voicing of the poem (recorded at Harvard on 17 May 1971) eschews all parody. It is far more touching to hear his recorded voice, now that he has gone but his poems have assuredly not, than it would be to hear a voice at a séance.

The poem compounds Eliot's compound ghost with an attachment to lines that follow very soon after in *Little Gidding,* lines that take up a preceding mention of "indifference":

> Thus, love of a country
> Begins as attachment to our own field of action
> And comes to find that action of little importance
> Though never indifferent.

(*Little Gidding* III)

ANTHONY HECHT

•

"A Voice at a Séance":

> Nor is it important that I died in combat
> In a good cause or an indifferent one.
>
> . . . .
>
>   the sad knowledge
> That it was almost impossible not to hurt anyone
> Whether by action or inaction.
>
> . . . .
>
> You come to a gentle indifference

But there are two further allusions that steady the poem into a new configuration. "It is all different from what you suppose": you are to hear at this séance the voice of the dead, the voice of Whitman, rueful with a difference:

> All goes onward and outward, nothing collapses,
> And to die is different from what any one supposed, and
>   luckier.[68]

A further allusion carries onward the sad knowledge that Hecht always had to bear as to Eliot's flawed greatness. (For one glimpse of Hecht's struggle with these contrarieties, see note 69.)[69] It is an allusion not to Eliot but to the play that haunted Eliot. Hecht:

> Nor is it important that I died in combat
> In a good cause or an indifferent one.
> Such things, it may surprise you, are not regarded.
> Something too much of this.

Hamlet, who died in a good cause (a better cause than Fortinbras's combat), to Horatio:

>   Give me that man,
> That is not passion's slave, and I will wear him

ANTHONY HECHT

·

129

In my heart's core; aye, in my heart of heart,
As I do thee. Something too much of this.
  (III.ii)

It makes a haunting finale when the voice at the séance fades with
a rueful acknowledgment of Hamlet's line, Hecht's line, at once
expanding and contracting the thought:

It may be that the ultimate wisdom
Lies in saying nothing.
I think I may already have said too much.

One of the combat zones where Hecht came to believe that
there could all too easily be "something too much of this" was the
propensity of poets to gather the Holocaust to themselves. "Others
have suffered so much more than I that it would be impudent for
me to speak self-righteously in their behalf."[70]

In these matters, Hecht's best interlocutor is Daniel Hoffman,
who wrote with imaginative discernment on how "The Fire Ser-
mon" (within "Rites and Ceremonies")[71] repeatedly evokes Eliot.
Across a stanza division, Hecht gave the world this:

O hear my prayer,

And let my cry come unto thee.

Eliot had given the world, and had thereby given Hecht, this, which
ends section VI of *Ash-Wednesday* and thereby ends the poem:

Suffer me not to be separated

And let my cry come unto Thee.

Not a *stanza* division but a concluding leap of faith all the same.
Nearer my God to "Thee," not, as in Hecht, to "thee."

Hoffman said with precision that "this homage to the preeminent religious poet of our time is intentionally double-edged."[72] Hecht sent a grateful letter: "Especially I want to thank you for your detailed concern with 'Rites and Ceremonies.' You are the only reader I have ever come across who has not stopped at noticing the debt to Eliot—Lowell remarked as much—but could see the 'double-edged' nature of that allusion to him in a poem about the Holocaust. You were right in detecting the consequent complication of tone, involving homage but bitterness, and both overlaying the horror of historical fact."[73]

The horror is the greater when a poem by Hecht begins in peace, a loving evocation of a landscape of art and more, at once Victorian and Chinese. Immediately following "Still Life" in *The Venetian Vespers,* there is a poem that persists with poems of ghosts.

Persistences

The leafless trees are feathery,
   A foxed, Victorian lace,
Against a sky of milk-glass blue,
   Blank, washed-out, commonplace.

Between them and my window
   Huge helices of snow
Perform their savage, churning rites
   At seventeen below.

The obscurity resembles
   A silken Chinese mist
Wherein through calligraphic daubs
   Of artistry persist

Pocked and volcanic gorges,
　　Clenched and arthritic pines,
Faint, coral-tinted herons' legs
　　Splashing among the tines

Of waving, tasselled marshgrass,
　　Deep pools aflash with sharp,
Shingled and burnished armor-plate
　　Of sacred, child-eyed carp.

This dimness is dynastic,
　　An ashen T'ang of age
Or blur that grudgingly reveals
　　A ghostly equipage,

Ancestral deputations
　　Wound in the whited air,
To whom some sentry flings a slight,
　　Prescriptive, "Who goes there?"

Are these the apparitions
　　Of enemies or friends?
Loved ones from whom I once withheld
　　Kindnesses or amends

On preterite occasions
　　Now lost beyond repeal?
Or the old childhood torturers
　　Of undiminished zeal,

Adults who ridiculed me,
　　Schoolboys who broke my nose,
Risen from black, unconscious depths
　　Of REM repose?

ANTHONY HECHT

•

Who comes here seeking justice,
    Or in its high despite,
Bent on some hopeless interview
    On wrongs nothing can right?

Those throngs disdain to answer,
    Though numberless as flakes;
Mine is the task to find out words
    For their memorial sakes

Who press in dense approaches,
    Blue numeral tattoos
Writ crosswise on their arteries,
    The burning, voiceless Jews.

We are again to contemplate, alike yet eternally different, "ancestral deputations," "the apparitions," "a ghostly equipage," within a world that both is and is not Shakespearean. *Hamlet* opens with "Who's there?" In Hecht, "some sentry flings a slight, / Prescriptive, 'Who goes there?'" Who goes there, and who comes here?

Who comes here seeking justice,
    Or in its high despite,
Bent on some hopeless interview
    On wrongs nothing can right?

It is true that nothing (except God Almighty, for those who believe) can right the wrongs of the Holocaust or of any such murderous injustices. Is it likewise true that nothing can write such wrongs? Hecht, like any honorable writer, is of two minds. He remembers who it was who most memorably wrote of "high despite," the author of *Henry VI:*

By many hands your father was subdued,
But only slaughtered by the ireful arm
Of unrelenting Clifford and the Queen:
Who crowned the gracious Duke in high despite,
Laughed in his face: and when with grief he wept,
The ruthless Queen gave him, to dry his cheeks,
A napkin steepèd in the harmless blood
Of sweet young Rutland, by rough Clifford slain.

(*3 Henry VI*, II.i)

The old-world ruthlessness, slaughter and laughter, both is and is not continuous with the Nazi world. Hecht does not assimilate the one to the other, but he does set the modern horror within a longer history of nightmares than some would wish:

Who comes here seeking justice,
    Or in its high despite,
Bent on some hopeless interview
    On wrongs nothing can right?

Those throngs disdain to answer,
    Though numberless as flakes;
Mine is the task to find out words
    For their memorial sakes

Who press in dense approaches,
    Blue numeral tattoos
Writ crosswise on their arteries,
    The burning, voiceless Jews.

The archaism of "Writ" calls up injustice as of very long standing, and "crosswise" cannot but wonder how it was that the Cross cooperated in the destruction of "The burning, voiceless Jews." It is not only the Jews who bear the tattoo of the Holocaust.

It is not maintained that the Jews are in themselves voiceless; only (*only*) that these are the deputations of the voiceless. Darkling in Hecht's mind will have been the knowledge (After such knowledge, what forgiveness?) of who it was that had most memorably given voice to the epithet "voiceless" in a poem of 1941. "There is no end of it, the voiceless wailing" (*The Dry Salvages* II). "As to whether I regard my work in general as an attempt to memorialize 'the burning, voiceless Jews,' I'm not sure I have a clear, uncomplicated answer. For one thing, I am not a concentration-camp survivor, I feel that undue indignation on my part would be a vulgar appropriation of the suffering of others for cheap rhetorical purposes and a contemptible kind of self-promotion. At the same time, I cannot help identifying with all Jews who have experienced persecution, for I have felt the effects of anti-Semitism throughout the whole of my life, though not *in extremis,* and I invariably wince at finding it widespread in Western literature."[74]

Of the poems by Hecht at which we are invariably to wince, the greatest is "'More Light! More Light!',", whose title is the English for Goethe's dying cry.

"More Light! More Light!"
for Heinrich Blücher and Hannah Arendt

Composed in the Tower before his execution
These moving verses, and being brought at that time
Painfully to the stake, submitted, declaring thus:
"I implore my God to witness that I have made no crime."

ANTHONY HECHT

•

135

Nor was he forsaken of courage, but the death was horrible,
The sack of gunpowder failing to ignite.
His legs were blistered sticks on which the black sap
Bubbled and burst as he howled for the Kindly Light.

And that was but one, and by no means one of the worst;
Permitted at least his pitiful dignity;
And such as were by made prayers in the name of Christ,
That shall judge all men, for his soul's tranquillity.

We move now to outside a German wood.
Three men are there commanded to dig a hole
In which the two Jews are ordered to lie down
And be buried alive by the third, who is a Pole.

Not light from the shrine at Weimar beyond the hill
Nor light from heaven appeared. But he did refuse.
A Lüger settled back deeply in its glove.
He was ordered to change places with the Jews.

Much casual death had drained away their souls.
The thick dirt mounted toward the quivering chin.
When only the head was exposed the order came
To dig him out again and to get back in.

No light, no light in the blue Polish eye.
When he finished a riding boot packed down the earth.
The Lüger hovered lightly in its glove.
He was shot in the belly and in three hours bled to death.

No prayers or incense rose up in those hours
Which grew to be years, and every day came mute
Ghosts from the ovens, sifting through crisp air,
And settled upon his eyes in a black soot.

ANTHONY HECHT

•

The Tudor world of persecution by fellow Christians is horrible enough, and the more so because of the crystalline calm with which the double-edged "Composed" (as composition and as composure) ushers in the poem:

> Composed in the Tower before his execution
> These moving verses,

"And that was but one, and by no means one of the worst": the turn to the worst, the Nazi world, is effected through the wresting of the warmth of "moving" ("These moving verses") to the chill of "We move": "We move now to outside a German wood."

This level, hideous equanimity was achieved by Hecht's accommodating two rifled lines from an early ghost poem (one that reads, "You could not doubt it was an honest ghost") in which he no longer believed, "To a Soldier Killed in Germany."[75]

> Man-eating danger moved to where you stood
> Probing the features of the German wood
> With a slim rifle.

"We move now to outside a German wood."

"To a Soldier Killed in Germany" summons Hitler by name, and—not by name—a "ghost"; there are "Ghosts from the ovens" in "'More Light! More Light!'" Both poems call upon God. "To a Soldier Killed in Germany" fears "the devouring light"; "'More Light! More Light!'" has its devouring "light" a further five times, and then hideously twists this to the light word "lightly":

> No light, no light in the blue Polish eye.
> When he finished a riding boot packed down the earth.
> The Lüger hovered lightly in its glove.
> He was shot in the belly and in three hours bled to death.

Early, "the squinting eye"; later, "the blue Polish eye" and "his eyes." Early, "raised"; later, "rose up." Early, the "dirty grave"; later, "The thick dirt mounted toward the quivering chin." In the soldier's grave, "Deep in your heavy bed"; at the gloating graveside, "A Lüger settled back deeply in its glove." "To a Soldier Killed in Germany" imagines the "death" (rhyming on the word) that "cut away your breath," and the "air"; "'More Light! More Light!'" passes from "be buried alive" to "crisp air."

The entire poem has a terrifyingly crisp air. The quatrains give no quarter. The rhymes, which are for the even lines only, tell the full story and are full rhymes until the end nears: "time"/"crime"; "ignite"/"Light"; "dignity"/"tranquillity"; "hole"/"Pole"; "refuse"/"Jews"; "chin"/"in"—and only then are there the off-rhymes that move in conclusion from clenched teeth to teeth on edge: "earth"/"death"; "mute"/"soot." The poem attends to several death sentences; its own stanzaic sentences feel obdurately alike while seeing to it that no two are the same. The first stanza is one sentence. The second, two sentences (two lines apiece). The third, one sentence but deployed differently, for now each line is end-punctuated. The fourth, two sentences but deployed differently from the second stanza, for now the shape is one line plus three lines. The fifth stanza, where we might have expected the alternation that has taken shape by now (stanzas of one sentence, then of two sentences; of one sentence, then of two sentences), metastasizes into four sentences (one-and-a-half lines, half a line, one line, one line). The sixth stanza, something new again, three sentences (one line, one line, two lines). The seventh, four sentences but deployed differently from the fifth (one to each line now, with the utmost obduracy). Finally, the eighth stanza, which is one sentence,

•

138

like the opening stanza and the third stanza but with determinedly different terminal punctuation from either of its predecessors. Iron quatrains but flexibly disciplined withal. There is one, and only one, commanding enjambment in the thirty-two lines, commanding in that the sense-unit permits of no substantiated pause, the adjective "mute" demanding its fulfilling noun, "Ghosts":

> No prayers or incense rose up in those hours
> Which grew to be years, and every day came mute
> Ghosts from the ovens, sifting through crisp air,
> And settled upon his eyes in a black soot.

The end.

"To a Soldier Killed in Germany" went newly to the making of "'More Light! More Light!'" Not that this earlier poem is in any way *alluded to* by the later one, for there is no reason to suppose that it is being called into play. Its interest is that of a source, not the further interest of an allusion. The same is true of Eliot's going to the making of "'More Light! More Light!'" The poet of *Burnt Norton* II had written of "long forgotten wars" while aware in 1935 that a never-to-be-forgotten war might be looming.[76] Eliot had written there that "We move above the moving tree / In light," something that might have come to Hecht's mind when he wrote, "We move now to outside a German wood." The three stanzas about the four elements that open *Little Gidding* II, proceeding then to the "familiar compound ghost," have their debris of the Second World War. To be buried alive, as people often were in the air raids that throb in *Little Gidding* II: "Dust inbreathed was a house" —

> There are flood and drouth
> Over the eyes and in the mouth,

—"This is the death of air," "This is the death of earth." Hecht rhymes "earth" with "death."

With perhaps some such memory of Eliot, Hecht created a flawless poem from one that he decided was flawed and that he did not reprint, "To a Soldier Killed in Germany." But some of the appreciation that "'More Light! More Light!'" has received fails to do justice to the poem (no criticism does full justice to any outstanding poem) because it shows less vigilance than the poem shows. I am thinking particularly of the way in which the poem, far from endorsing the antithesis of the Jewish and the Polish, prompts us to ponder the antithesis, to repudiate it, or at the least to have misgivings about it—misgivings that are not registered when the poem is paraphrased and its terms acquiesced in but its wariness neglected.

> We move now to outside a German wood.
> Three men are there commanded to dig a hole
> In which the two Jews are ordered to lie down
> And be buried alive by the third, who is a Pole.

But just as, in Germany, German Jews were Germans, however much it assisted Nazism's hatreds to deny it, so in Poland a Polish Jew was no less a Pole. Zinovy Zinik reported recently:

> Last week someone asked the routine question, "Where are you from?", to which I gave my usual reply, "From Moscow." "Are you Polish or Jewish?" he asked and, noticing my surprise, explained his logic: "My experience says that only Jews or Poles from Russia say that they are from Moscow instead of saying simply they're Russians."
> I didn't like this.[77]

Bin gar keine Russin, stamm' aus Litauen, echt deutsch.

"I am not Russian at all; I come from Lithuania; I am a real German."
This is the world of *The Waste Land* I, "The Burial of the Dead." The
world of "'More Light! More Light!'" is that of the burial of the
living.

The world still has not arrived at an undistorting way to speak
of these entanglements of nationality; even the best-intentioned
writers on the Holocaust will lapse into distinguishing Germans
from Jews, which is not a distinction that it is wise to make, al-
though there are honorable and necessary distinctions to be made.

It is characteristic of Hecht's determined justice that his history
tells of how the two all-too-humanly yielded ("Much casual death
had drained away their souls"), even though the one had initially
stood firm:

> Not light from the shrine at Weimar beyond the hill
> Nor light from heaven appeared. But he did refuse.

At the second hideous round, there will be "No light, no light in
the blue Polish eye." The blue eye suggests, even while aware that
it does not prove, that this man is not a Jewish Pole. But then we
know this from the earlier distinction, perilously misguided though
it is, that contrasts "the two Jews" with "the third, who is a Pole."

Finally, there is a distinction that substantiates Hecht's art.
William Empson established the principle when he explained a
slippage within an American poet of an earlier generation, Robin-
son Jeffers, who "often seems to write from his conscience rather
than his sensibility. He chooses painful subjects, one may suspect,
less because he feels strongly about them than because he feels it
shameful not to feel strongly about them; because one cannot be
comfortable and unimaginative, with the world as it is. You may
honour this feeling very much and yet say it does not produce good

writing; it gives an air of poking at the reader, or trying to catch him on the raw, and it tends to falsify a dramatic issue."[78] It is not so much that Anthony Hecht chose painful subjects because he felt strongly about them as that painful subjects chose him. He himself would probably now have urged, after Hamlet, "Something too much of this."

3

.

.

.

ROBERT
LOWELL

Anthony Hecht did not think of himself as being—or yet more liberatingly, did not feel himself to be—the heir to anyone in particular. Great though his respect was for W. H. Auden, he was expansively free from all that can make heirdom a frictive matter. In this fretlessness as to whether he is an heir, Hecht resembles both Eliot and Pound and differs from both Hill and Lowell.

Given that Eliot was American and then English, it is apt to the nature of things that he should have been granted, if that is the word, both an American and an English heir, Hill for England and

Lowell for America, with the pleasing plaiting that Hill lived for years in America, and Lowell for years in England.

Stanley Kunitz opened his praise of Lowell, "Telling the Time," like this: "Robert Lowell is the American poet of his decade—that is, in his forties—who has most conspicuously made his mark. T.S. Eliot must have had this thought in mind when at his last reading at the Poetry Center in New York he requested that Mr. Lowell, who was introducing him, should remain seated on stage during the entire program. The request, coming from Mr. Eliot, had the authority of a dynastic gesture."[1]

"What thou lovest well remains" (Pound). "What remains? You may well ask" (Hill). To remain seated onstage during the entire program.

The simultaneous publication in 1973 of three volumes by Lowell (*The Dolphin, For Lizzie and Harriet,* and *History*) moved Faber and Faber to garland each of them with a tribute by Kathleen Raine that called up not only Eliot but Eliot's very words:

> For last year's words belong to last year's language
> And next year's words await another voice.
> (*Little Gidding* II)

> Robert Lowell is, in more ways than one, heir to T.S. Eliot; his voice the older poet would have recognised as one that "next year's words await."[2]

Not just would have recognized, did recognize, as the decider about poetry at Faber and Faber recognized, for a start.

The stage direction by Eliot to Lowell at the Poetry Center was one kind of tribute. A different kind was paid some years later when Lowell was being introduced at Cambridge University by a senior figure who prided himself on his diplomacy, suavity even.

"I am privileged to introduce to you a man widely regarded as the greatest living American poet." (Pause) "Or perhaps I should take the word *living* out of that sentence." One knows what the praiser meant, and yet. Lowell stood there looking like death; Lowell, who settled for "All's well that ends"; Lowell, whose name ends "well."

Expatriation is at the heart of Lowell's history, as with Eliot— and with Pound (the author of *Patria Mia*). Eliot in 1931 had confronted a further waste land in acknowledging the resistance to the modern world that was being mounted by Dixieland. *I'll Take My Stand* was the anthem of the Southern Agrarians, and Eliot wrote of the book as a New Englander (which, though originally from St. Louis, he had been for a time), one who was now newly an Englander. "A New Englander cannot read the book without admitting that his own country was ruined as the South is ruined, and that New England was ruined first." Last comes a wider dismay: "The American intellectual of today has almost no chance of continuous development upon his own soil and in the environment which his ancestors, however humble, helped to form. He must be an expatriate: either to languish in a provincial university, or abroad, or, the most complete expatriation of all, in New York. And he is merely a more manifest example of what *tends* to happen in all countries."[3]

Three years earlier, the year after he had become a British citizen and had entered the Church of England, Eliot had dated a letter "St. George's Day, 1928." The letter is poignant, baffled, and lucid: "Some day I want to write an essay about the point of view of an American who wasn't an American, because he was born in the South and went to school in New England as a small boy with a nigger drawl, but who wasn't a southerner in the South because his people were northerners in a border state and looked down on all southerners and Virginians, and who so was never anything any-where and who therefore felt himself to be more a Frenchman than an American and more an Englishman than a Frenchman and yet felt that the U.S.A. up to a hundred years ago was a family exten-sion. It is almost too difficult even for H.J. who for that matter wasn't an American at all, in that sense."⁴ Henry James was to put in a similar cameo appearance in the fierce piece that Pound penned in 1938, "National Culture: A Manifesto": "In our own day and voca-tion it can't be said that either Mr. Eliot nor the undersigned have exactly looked up to British contemporaries. It can't be said that an alteration on Mr. Eliot's passport has altered the essential Ameri-canness of his work. H. James' death-bed change of citizenship was the one last and possible defiance that he could hurl at the scum in the White House."⁵ To Pound, prudence and temperance were the cardinal vices.

For more than one generation of expatriate writers, James was unignorable, having himself always been unignoring. Of another expatriate, the ambassadorial James Russell Lowell, James had writ-ten from London in 1891: "Strange was his double existence—the American and the English sides of his medal, which had yet so much in common. That is, I don't know how English he was at home, but he was conspicuously American here."⁶

Consciousness of James as predecessor could induce both kinds of self-consciousness, the good kind that is self-awareness, the bad that is self-paralysis. Robert Lowell: "I'm always very conscious of being an American, in Europe, far more so than at home, but that's as it should be. I haven't got the real expatriate temperament, as I see all the time; only England, in my view, is possible for an Ameri-can forever—look at Eliot . . . You see the risk and reward wonderfully in Pound. He didn't think of himself as an Italian, but as a sort of Idaho, patrician exile, a Landor . . ."[7]

He, Pound, did not think of himself as an Italian (nor did Walter Savage Landor, though he spent twenty years in Italy). The Italian who is my final destination in this book thought of himself not as an Italian but as a Florentine, banished into expatriation. It is Dante upon whom Hill, Hecht, and Lowell converge, the meeting taking place under the sign of Eliot and Pound.

Of the three later poets, Lowell is the one who celebrates explicitly in his art the friendship of Eliot and Pound, a friendship that had often proved to be true opposition. Lowell, unlike both Hill and Hecht, was a personal friend of both Eliot and Pound. It is Lowell who does more than—or rather, does something other than—create poems that are the friends of the predecessors' poems. He brings to life not only his friendship with Eliot and Pound but more crucially their friendship with each other, the strains musical and emotional.

Eliot and Pound, friends, were almost always able to argue without quarreling. Intellectuals, who are people who believe that such a thing is possible, become credulous when they move from believing that it is possible to believing that it is easy. But then Eliot and Pound were unusual intellectuals. For one thing, they were often aware of the temptations and prejudices that beset intellectuals. For another—but let us hear Eliot on John Maynard Keynes. Keynes was, "in any sense of the word, an 'intellectual'. That is to say, he was born into, and always lived in, an intellectual environment; he had intellectual tastes; and he had—what is not always denoted by 'intellectual'—an intellect."[8]

The quality of the friendship between Eliot and Pound is clearest on those occasions when one of them is moved to substantiated dissent and stylized dismay at the other. A few instances. There is Pound's unmisgiving gait in the *New English Weekly* (29 March 1934): "I have for years respected Mr. Eliot because of my belief that he did not and does not read his own Quarterly publication . . ." Or the pounce that launches Pound's "Credo" (1930): "Mr Eliot who is at times an excellent poet and who has arrived at the supreme Eminence among english critics largely through disguising himself as a corpse once asked in the course of an amiable article what 'I believed.'"[9] "At times"! This merely in passing. How equably "excellent" proceeds to "Eminence," with the capital letter affecting subservience (Your Excellency, Your Eminence — no capital E on "English," be it noted). There is punctuational punctilio again — how calmly (not the slightest pause, no comma, between "corpse" and "once") the sequence moves on as though it could not possibly give offence: "the supreme Eminence among English critics largely through disguising himself as a corpse once asked." Amiable indeed, and trusting to amity. For does not an Old Possum stay alive by disguising himself as a corpse? Lowell said of Eliot, "His fierceness was restrained, his dullness was never more than the possum's feigned death."[10]

Again, still in this world of cut-and-thrust that is not out to wound but is something other than shadow fencing, there is Eliot's letter to the editor of the *New English Weekly* (15 March 1934), responding to Pound's comments on *After Strange Gods*. Here are the beginning, the middle, and the end.

> Sir, — I have read with keen interest Mr. Pound's kindly note upon my Virginian lectures, in your columns; and I find myself in cordial agreement with the major part of what I am

able to understand of it. What I do not understand includes statements which, to me, have no meaning.

. . .

I find that paragraph 4 has no meaning for me. That has sometimes been one's experience with statements beginning with the words *the fact is that.*

. . .

I do not understand paragraph 15, but I believe that it contains something which might be put in a form in which it would have some meaning for me.

T. S. ELIOT

Punctuation-power again: "for me. / T. S. ELIOT", as against "for me, T. S. ELIOT." To be heard as "*some meaning* for me," eschewing "some meaning for *me.*"

Eliot let himself go (ah, but where exactly?) in another letter to the same editor about Pound's comments on *The Use of Poetry and the Use of Criticism* in comparison with those on *After Strange Gods:*

Mr. Pound has done your readers a disservice in suggesting that a book of mine, which is an unsatisfactory attempt to say something worth saying, is more negligible than another book of mine which is an unsatisfactory attempt to say a variety of things most of which were not worth saying.

. . .

What Mr. Pound really has to say is this: that my lecture on the Countess of Pembroke (pawky humour) was good enough to include in a new edition of Selected Essays, and that the rest might well be scrapped. I wholeheartedly agree. But I cannot help being exacerbated by a critic who takes a great space to condemn an inferior book for the wrong reasons, and who cannot stick to the point, because he refuses to see it.

Mr. Pound might have been usefully occupied in saying that I overrated the criticism of Dryden; and that through ignorance, inattention, and haste, I both underrated and misunderstood the criticism of Coleridge. He might have told you, in so many words, that my lecture on Arnold was prejudiced, ill thought out, and wholly superfluous. He might have said that my lecture on "The Modern Mind" was undigested. He might have said that I had spent eight hours in coming to no conclusion. But he has done none of these things. Instead, he wastes time flinging tomatoes at Mr. Richards and Mr. Maritain, whose works I do not suppose he has read; for as he says himself, one cannot read everything. Still, one need not call them "racketeer-aesthetes and theorists."

Mr. Pound suggests that "Faber, Fraser, Frobenius, Fenellosa" mean nothing to me. I at least know how to spell Frazer,

and on it goes, to end in Fatigue:

I am, dear Sir, Your outraged,

Possum[11]

The word for *bless*, in some tongues, is the same as the word for *curse*. Eliot on Pound in 1928: "A man who devises new rhythms is a man who extends and refines our sensibility; and that is not merely a matter of 'technique.' I have, in recent years, cursed Mr Pound often enough; for I am never sure that I can call my verse my own; just when I am most pleased with myself, I find that I have only caught up some echo from a verse of Pound's."[12] Or there are the accomplishments that are simultaneously Eliot's and Pound's.

Supremely and most enduringly, the transformation of *The Waste Land* drafts into *The Waste Land*. No less honorably, the imaginative editorial decisions by Eliot that brought into being the *Literary Essays of Ezra Pound* (1954). Eliot's introduction treads warily: "I must add a word about footnotes. I have tried to avoid notes (with the exception of one modest correction bearing my initials) except to supply dates." No page reference is given, but in due course the reader comes upon it. It is a footnote (p. 391) to Pound on William Carlos Williams:[13]

> At any rate he has not in his ancestral endocrines the arid curse of our nation. None of his immediate forebears burnt witches in Salem,* or attended assemblies for producing prohibitions.
>
> *Note: We didn't burn them, we hanged them. T.S.E.

In Pound, not "None of his," rather "None of *his.*" And in Eliot, not "We did not," rather "We didn't." The tone slangy, not slanging. No apologies. Interrupting Pound in mid-sentence. Eliot's "modest correction" is in its way A Modest Proposal.

In any such friendship, there is competition, yes; ruthless competition, no. Pound rightly felt the obligation to admit the thought of *envy* into the world of poets and poems. "Near Perigord" (1915) has Arnaut Daniel in the literary lions' den:

> And the "best craftsman" sings out his friend's song,
> Envies its vigour . . . and deplores the technique,
> Dispraises his own skill?—That's as you will.
> [Pound's ellipsis]

Deploring the technique is itself "not merely a matter of 'technique,'" as Eliot was to say in praise of Pound. In the Library of America edition, the note to "best craftsman" reminds us well, doubly: "In *Purgatorio*, XXVI, 117, Dante calls Arnaut Daniel the 'better craftsman' ('miglior fabbro')—a compliment T.S. Eliot would later pay to Pound in the dedication of *The Waste Land*."[14] Later it was: the famous dedication of *The Waste Land* was not published in any of the 1922 printings of the poem, but Eliot inscribed a copy "for E.P. / miglior fabbro / from T.S.E. / Jan. 1923," and the tribute then appeared in *Poems, 1909-1925* (1925).[15]

Envy can have its own vigor. Each of us has to decide whether to concur with Andrew Marvell's reflection in "An Horatian Ode upon Cromwel's Return from Ireland":

> For 'tis all one to Courage high
> The Emulous or Enemy;
>   And with such to inclose
>   Is more than to oppose.

Estimating more than esteeming Pound's *Quia Pauper Amavi* in 1919, Eliot wrote: "The poems 'contemporaneous' are the most doubtful in the book. I am not at all sure that 'Mr. Styrax' and 'Nodier raconte . . .' are good poems, or that, even with Martial behind it, the modern satirical vein is of permanent importance. The two poems mentioned irritate in a way in which poems should not irritate; they make you conscious of having been written by somebody; they have not written themselves. There are lines in them which are too much the voice of the accidental human being with a smile in conversation."[16]

As for Pound's opposition to Eliot, it is nowhere clearer than on those occasions when, within the Cantos, Pound cites—for some violation or other—Eliot. There is some sympathy for Mussolini and his mistress, and much for the peasant, but little for the Possum (only pretending to be dead):

The enormous tragedy of the dream in the peasant's
    bent shoulders
Manes! Manes was tanned and stuffed,
Thus Ben and la Clara *a Milano*
            by the heels at Milana
That maggots shd / eat the dead bullock
DIGONOS, Δίγονος, but the twice crucified
                where in history will you find it?
        yet say this to the Possum: a bang, not a whimper,
    with a bang not with a whimper,
        (Canto LXXIV)

(Help is to hand in *A Student's Guide to the Selected Poems of Ezra
Pound* [1979], by Peter Brooker: "*Manes:* (?216–?276), a Persian
sage, founder of the sect of Manicheans and crucified for his teach-
ing. *Ben and la Clara:* Benito Mussolini [1883–1945], dictator of Italy
1922–45, and his mistress Claretta Petacci were executed and strung
up by the heels in the Piazzale Loreto, Milan, 29 April 1945. DIGO-
NOS: (Gk.) 'twice born,' the epithet of Dionysus.")

Eliot's unforgettable phrasing from "The Hollow Men" is al-
lowed into Pound's Canto but not so that it be newly active; the
retorted line is simply held to have been passive, itself something of
a whimper, emanating from a hollow man. (Lowell saw something
quite other in Eliot: "In America almost all our gods coarsen into
giants or shrivel into hollow men. Eliot did neither.")[17]

But the lot of 'em, Yeats, Possum and Wyndham
    had no ground beneath 'em.
        (Canto XCVII)

But the lot of 'em, Yeats, Possum, Old Wyndham

had no ground to stand on

(Canto CII)

These are reprimands, and the more so in throwing in Wyndham
Lewis with the lot of 'em. Even when Pound's incorporation of
Mr. Eliot by name may rise to poetry (as against sinking to posi-
tioning), the poetry in question may turn out not to be exactly
Pound's, although the air of puzzlement is his:

but the Saducees hardly give credence
to Mr Eliot's version
Partial resurrection in Cairo.
Beddoes, I think, omits it.
            The bone *luz,* I think was his take off
Curious, is it not, that Mr Eliot
has not given more time to Mr Beddoes
            (T.L.) prince of morticians
        where none can speak his language
centuries hoarded
to pull up a mass of algae
            (and pearls)
or the odour of eucalyptus or sea wrack

(Canto LXXX)

Poetic creativity there is most manifest in the couple of phrases
from Beddoes that Pound had quoted in an essay of 1913 on "Bed-
does and Chronology": "centuries hoarded" and "where none can
speak his language."[18] But Pound brings no new life to or from
Eliot's words.

but the Saducees hardly give credence
to Mr Eliot's version
Partial resurrection in Cairo.
Beddoes, I think, omits it.

    The bone *luz,* I think was his take off[19]

        And God said
Shall these bones live? shall these
Bones live?

    (*Ash-Wednesday* II)

Pound was quite right not to put a question mark after "is it not," since he was not really asking a question but ruminating lordlily. "Curious, is it not," that Pound apparently has so little curiosity in this matter. Anyway Mr. Eliot did give time to Mr. Beddoes (though it is true that he might have given more). There is, for instance, the imaginative pertinence of the adducing in "The Three Voices of Poetry":

What you start from is nothing so definite as an emotion, in any ordinary sense; it is still more certainly not an idea; it is—to adapt two lines of Beddoes to a different meaning—a

    bodiless childful of life in the gloom
  Crying with frog voice, "what shall I be?"[20]

Moreover, there is the ensconcing within "Whispers of Immortality" of Beddoes's sardonic turn, "a lipless grin."[21]

Pound makes nothing of Eliot's words, though he makes free with Eliot's name. This is perfectly compatible with friendship, but it does mean that one form (one, only) that friendship's gratitude may take is not to be found in Pound. Eliot pays Pound the compliment of creating anew, complementarily, thanks to Pound. Complimenti. But not from Pound the returning of such a compliment.

Allusion is always a return, and the word *return* within an allusion will align the use of poetry with the use of memory.[22] Nothing in *Four Quartets* is more of an accomplishment than the return of *Little Gidding* III in section V. From this:

> This is the use of memory:
> For liberation—not less of love but expanding
> Of love beyond desire, and so liberation
> From the future as well as the past. Thus, love of a country
> Begins as attachment to our own field of action
> And comes to find that action of little importance
> Though never indifferent. History may be servitude,
> History may be freedom. See, now they vanish,
> The faces and places, with the self which, as it could, loved
>   them,
> To become renewed, transfigured, in another pattern.

To this:

> We die with the dying:
> See, they depart, and we go with them.
> We are born with the dead:
> See, they return, and bring us with them.

This graced return is not only within Eliot's poem but to Ezra Pound, whose poem "The Return" (1912) Eliot had quoted in his short book on Pound in 1917 and was to include in his *Selected Poems* of Pound in 1928:

See, they return; ah, see the tentative
    Movements, and the slow feet,
    The trouble in the pace and the uncertain
    Wavering!

See, they return, one, and by one,
With fear, as half-awakened;
As if the snow should hesitate
And murmur in the wind,
        and half turn back;

"See, they return": itself returning near the poem's end as "These were the souls of blood." Pound too had become for Eliot one such soul, "of blood" both as close kin to Eliot and as set against him during the Second World War. In 1942 Pound was not a man of tentative movements, not a man to be moved by uncertain wavering. There is poignancy in Eliot's return to Pound, Eliot during the Second World War musing back to the poem he had celebrated during the Great War; the unsentimentality of the poignancy is in the sense of alienation from what Pound had turned to and now seemed likely never to return from.

Lowell honors the memory and celebrates the friendship of Eliot and Pound in two consecutive sonnets: originally published in *Notebook* (where they had been the first two in "Writers," a sequence of seven) and then, in succession although not within a subordinate sequence, in *History*.[23] "T. S. Eliot" tells of a conversation with Eliot about Pound; "Ezra Pound," of a conversation with Pound about Eliot.

T. S. Eliot

Caught between two streams of traffic, in the gloom
of Memorial Hall and Harvard's war-dead. . . . And he:
"Don't you loathe to be compared with your relatives?
I do. I've just found two of mine reviewed by Poe.
He wiped the floor with them . . . and I was *delighted.*"
Then on with warden's pace across the Yard,
talking of Pound, "It's balls to say he only
pretends to be Ezra. . . . He's better though. This year,
he no longer wants to rebuild the Temple at Jerusalem.
Yes, he's better. '*You* speak,' he said, when he'd talked two
    hours.
By then I had absolutely nothing to *say.*"
Ah Tom, one muse, one music, had one your luck—
lost in the dark night of the brilliant talkers,
humor and honor from the everlasting dross!

(T. S. Eliot, born 1888, died 1965. The text above is the one in *History*, revising *Notebook.*) "'It's balls to say he only / pretends to be Ezra'" had been in *Notebook, 1967-68* as "'to say he isn't / the way he is,'" and then in *Notebook* as "'to say he only / pretends to be like Ezra.'" For "your luck," *Notebook, 1967-68* and *Notebook* (1969, 1970) had "the luck." For "humor and honor," *Notebook, 1967-68* had "humor and boredom"; this earlier reading, characteristically surprising, may owe something to Eliot's phrase "the boredom, and the horror, and the glory," itself a variation upon "the kingdom, and the power, and the glory" (Saint Matthew 6:13).[24]

As often with the best of Lowell, the simple directness of anecdote (linear) is unexpectedly at one with multiplicity of suggestion (radiating). The setting at Harvard is able to occasion the meeting not only of Eliot in person but of Eliot in persona: the familiar compound ghost who haunts and is haunted within *Little Gidding* II.

> And he: "I am not eager to rehearse
> My thoughts and theories which you have forgotten.["]

The thoughts and theories may be forgotten, but the turn of phrase — from Dante via Eliot — is not.

> Caught between two streams of traffic, in the gloom
> of Memorial Hall and Harvard's war-dead. . . . And he:
> "Don't you loathe to be compared with your relatives?["]

The London of the Dantesque section of *Little Gidding* is the ground against which the Harvard conversation sets its place, space, pace. Or, to change the figure of speech, wartime London is one of the two streams of traffic within which the graphic photographic moment is caught. The poem is itself a Memorial Hall. "Harvard's war-dead" are allied with Britain's war dead. "Then on with warden's pace across the Yard": this intersection time summons the memory of the raids and of the air-raid warden, realized as poetry within the air raid that had opened *Little Gidding*'s Dantesque section.

> In concord at this intersection time
> Of meeting nowhere, no before and after,
> We trod the pavement in a dead patrol.

Lowell's alighting upon "warden's pace" is inspired, the intersection space of the air-raid warden and then of the world of the incarcerated Pound "in the ward" at St. Elizabeths with its warders and wardens, with perhaps a further touch from the word in a university setting, Oxford not Harvard: Lowell in 1970 was at All Souls College, Oxford, the head of which is the Warden.

ROBERT LOWELL
•

"The dark night" is at once, and at first, that of the wartime memory as well as that of the soul (Pound's, Eliot's, Lowell's— ours?), and then takes on a flickering: "lost in the dark night of the brilliant talkers." Loss and gain.

Lowell is a great reminder. An excursus, or incursus, on the un-rhymed sonnet beckons here. Readers may recall that for all three books published that year (*History, For Lizzie and Harriet,* and *The Dolphin*), the unrhymed sonnet became his instrument—or rather his orchestration. (Of Lowell's predecessors, the most notable are Blake, "To the Evening Star"; Keats, "Oh thou whose face hath felt the Winter's wind"; and Beddoes, "A Crocodile," though there will always be the teasing possibility that what is before us is not an unrhymed sonnet but fourteen lines of blank verse.) But in Lowell's hands the unrhymed sonnet is not entirely so, since he deploys rhymes with truth and cunning—and he crucially deploys, too, the absence of rhyme. The effect of Lowell's unrhymed heroic line in these sonnets is often that which Coleridge stigmatized in "those who, like Mallet & too often my honored Thomson, give us rhyme-less or rather rhyme-craving Pentameter Iambics for Blank Verse."[25] But then rhyme-craving, like any other craving, is not devoid of valuable functions. Lowell's unrhymed sonnet "Milton in Separation" arrives at some such paradox, though unable to rest there, able only to pause:

> His wife was no loss to the cool and Christian Homer,
> blind, paraphrasing Latin and pronouncing
> *divorce* and *marriage* with hard, sardonic R's.
> Through the blank strain of separation, he learned
> he only cared for life in the straits. Her flight

put a live elbow in his marble Eve;
she filled a thirst for emptiness—

(*History*)

(John Aubrey, of Milton: "Extremely pleasant in his conversation, and at dinner, supper, etc, but Satyricall. He pronounced the letter 'R' very hard: a certain Signe of a Satyricall Witt. From John Dryden.")[26]

It fills a thirst for emptiness that the blank strain of separation is achieved through blank verse—blank verse that, like Milton's own, is darkly happy to accommodate rhymes and off-rhymes and para-rhymes when need be. In Lowell, "paraphrasing" into "pronouncing," and "strain" into "straits." In Milton, "wretched matter" into "lame Meeter," in his note on "The Verse" of *Paradise Lost* that was added in 1668: "The Measure is *English* Heroic Verse without Rime, as that of *Homer* in *Greek,* and of *Virgil* in *Latin;* Rime being no necessary Adjunct or true Ornament of Poem or good Verse, in longer Works especially, but the Invention of a barbarous Age, to set off wretched matter and lame Meeter."

Lowell, the author of a magnificent (and dual) imitation that he called with ineffable effrontery *The Vanity of Human Wishes* (1967), is likely to have remembered something that was said about the author of *The Vanity of Human Wishes* (1749). T. S. Eliot wrote of Samuel Johnson's play *Irene* that "we find the blank verse to be that of a writer who thought and felt in terms of the rhymed couplet"; "the phrasing is admirable, the style elevated and correct, but each line cries out for a companion to rhyme with it."[27] Crying out for a companion, or craving one, is among the things that an unrhymed line, or the lines of an unrhymed sonnet, may well do and may do well.

"T. S. Eliot" talks to us about having talked with Eliot about the exhaustive talker Pound. "The dark night of the brilliant talkers" was not where Eliot was either lost or at home. Lowell said in a reminiscential piece when Eliot died: "I have never met anyone more brilliant, or anyone who tried so hard to use his brilliance modestly and honestly." Strange, this, but not more so than Eliot as a leader, "a strange leader, one who gave thousands of speechless hours listening to brilliant monologuists."²⁸ Eliot, speechless? Only in courtesy. Lowell's poem, like the poet whom it honors, is a figure of speech.

Lowell ended his memorial tribute to Eliot in 1965 with an anecdote, one that was to become the poem of two or three years later. Excellent prose, Lowell's, the difference between his prose and his poetry being—as in all the best cases—nothing to do with the prosaic or the poetical, and everything to do with punctuation. "Pause." "Pause again." "Pause."

> When I was about twenty-five, I met him for the second time. Behind us, Harvard's Memorial Hall with its wasteful, irreplaceable Victorian architecture and scrolls of the Civil War dead. Before us, the rush-hour traffic. As we got stuck on the sidewalk, looking for an opening, Eliot out of a blue sky said, "Don't you loathe being compared with your relatives?" Pause, as I put the question to myself, groping for what I really felt, for what I should decently feel and what I should indecently feel. Eliot: "I do." Pause again, then the changed lifting voice of delight. "I was reading Poe's reviews the other day. He took up two of my family and wiped the floor with them." Pause. "I was delighted."

Altogether alive in the telling. There is the agreeable coinciding in "looking for an opening" (in the traffic and in the traffic that is conversation), the opening being followed immediately by "out of a blue sky." There is "took up," descending to "wiped the floor with them." "Behind us" is not only the physical architecture but the poetic architectonics. For when Lowell was "about twenty-five" (that is, 1942), in time of war, Eliot was publishing the very poem, the last of his poems really, that in so many ways furnishes Lowell's sonnet: *Little Gidding*.

At twenty-one, R. T. S. Lowell had given Eliot a fiftieth-birthday present: two paragraphs in the *Harvard Advocate,* "For T. S. Eliot." This was, like many a birthday present, a present for himself, too. Having one eye on himself, he risked squinting or connivance, especially in praising Eliot for being snooty.

> The New Englander is a useful symbol, to which one is per-mitted to attribute a perennial and almost sensual enjoy-ment of starch and morality. Mr. Eliot has been refined and colored by an environment in which experience is neces-sarily circumlocution. As a tireless Calvinist, he has formu-lated Catholic plays and harried his pagan English public with godliness. Otherwise, he has devoured aesthetic crite-ria and actuality from the Symbolists and compatible areas of the arduous European tradition. Turbulence of experience, adroitness of sensibility, and artistry of presentation are fused in the terrifying solution.

> A bias so complicated, snooty and immaterial—hap-pily, psychologically tortured—is desperately precious. Its current worms against our flooding modernity. Form and finesse are its hallowed proprieties. These had to be pro-tracted even among the empty shells, form for form's sake, before they flowered as something better than sensitivity,

something heavily selfish—creation and faith. Mr. Eliot and another unautochthonous New Englander, Miss Marianne Moore, are the last creatures of the savage sophistication. Obviously, they are unparalleled in world literature; but Mr. Eliot, religiously oppressed from the beginning, has gone much farther. They are the last creatures, probably, because antithetical to this massive and mannerless democracy which has dedicated its institutions of learning to a populous pragmatism.

R. T. S. Lowell[29]

To which one feels like saying, You don't say. Luckily, Lowell came to have his say in terms that one could bring oneself to listen to. He himself, a man with astonishing powers of growth, grew to extirpate the snooty; more crucially, he grew to write a great deal that was desperately precious, its preciousness often its understanding of desperation. He came to a very different sense of his likeness to—and unlikeness to—Eliot. "I almost think I'm more varied than Eliot but much more repetitious" (*The Listener*, 4 September 1969).

And he:

"Don't you loathe to be compared with your relatives?
I do. I've just found two of mine reviewed by Poe.["]

Eliot may have loathed to be compared with his relatives, but fortunately London's Russell Square (there you feel free) was far enough from Harvard Square. But however much Lowell may have loathed being compared with *his* relatives, he knew that it was inescapable. As this poem suggests (since it calls up the Lowells and Eliots of their alma mater), Lowell freed himself into poems, often poems directly about his relatives—something that Eliot did not. (With perhaps the sly exception of "Mr. Eliot's Sunday Morning Service," for who is the Mr. Eliot there? TSE, or could there be a glance, too, at his cousin the Reverend Frederick May Eliot? See note 30.)[30]

For Lowell, Harvard was impressively and oppressively the ground of the Lowells. It stamped him for life. Haunted by Harvard, he haunted it; he became the eternal revenant. His exquisite poem about his relatives ("Cousin So, Ancestral Mother-in-Law So") is called "Revenants"; probably it was inspired (as, in small part, was the poem for Eliot) by the final page, the last leaf, of Ferris Greenslet's dynasts, *The Lowells and Their Seven Worlds,* with its evocation of the aged President Lowell as he "plunged across the stream of traffic" in Boston during "the Second World War": "To those not unacquainted with New England history and the part his family had played in it, he came to seem something of a *revenant.* As a last leaf he was an utter misfit, and would have been even if there had not still been green and fruit-bearing branches on the family tree."[31] Such as young Lowell. Off the young man went to Kenyon College, under the illusion that such dust could be shaken off his feet.

Lowell's poem talks of talking of Pound (among "the brilliant talkers" in his way and in his day), Pound who stops not his own mouth but that of the interlocutor Eliot:

> "'*You* speak,' he said, when he'd talked two hours.
> By then I had absolutely nothing to *say.*"[32]

Talking is a human conditioning, and no sect has a monopoly on it, and yet when it comes to talking, a particular privilege is said to attach to a particular class of Bostonian.

> And this is good old Boston,
> The home of the bean and the cod,

ROBERT LOWELL

•

Where the Lowells talk to the Cabots,

And the Cabots talk only to God.

("On the Aristocracy of Harvard," John Collins Bossidy)

Presumably, then, the Cabots trump the Lowells, but in the aristoc-
racy of Harvard the Lowells and the Eliots are equipollent. There
had been a President Lowell and a President Eliot, there is a Lowell
House and an Eliot House. The Lowells had talked quite as much
to the Eliots as to the Cabots. Now in 1942, "Caught between two
streams of traffic, in the gloom / of Memorial Hall and Harvard's
war-dead," *the* Eliot is talking with *the* Lowell.

"Don't you loathe to be compared with your relatives?" The
first letter in *The Letters of Robert Lowell* is one from Harvard dated
2 May 1936.[33] It is not to Eliot but to Ezra Pound, and it opens,

> Dear Mr. Pound:
>
> I have been wanting to write you for several months, but
> haven't quite had the courage to until now. You will prob-
> ably think that I am very impudent and presumptuous, but I
> want to come to Italy and work under you and forge my way
> into reality. I have no right [to] ask this of you, yet let me try
> to describe myself and explain my desire.
>
> I am 19, a freshman at Harvard, and some relation, I don't
> know what, to Amy Lowell.

The second letter in the volume (later that month?) is again to
Pound. It starts by pondering damnation, perhaps lightly: "You
may have meant: 'You're not wholly damned before you start but I
don't see much hope.'" Soon, it touches upon Eliot — with a touch
of condescension: "Eliot's 'Ariel' poems are closely and skillfully
expressed but lack vitality." But the direction is to and at Pound, via
the thought of pounding:

I would like to bring back momentum and movement in poetry on a grand scale, to master your tremendous machinery and to carry your standard further into the century; and I think I have life enough to withstand the years of pounding and grinding before accomplishment. More specifically to work in Italy under your personal direction: plenty of work and plenty of leeway for initiative.

Please don't feel insulted, I have no delusions as to your bulk and my smallness, I am only trying to show you more clearly why I wish to become your disciple.

Subscribed,

> Sincerely yours,
> R. T. S. Lowell

P.S. Relatives have nothing to do with the question.

Don't you loathe having to compare yourself with your relatives? Yes and no. Nearly twenty years later, Lowell's thinking about lineage was still along the same contrarious lines. He wrote to Pound (25 March 1954) about Ford Madox Ford: "I loved Ford, though he would hardly speak to me half the time, because (God Damn it!) he thought I would write undignified gossip about him in his old age, and (on the strength of that I suppose) become president of Harvard."[34] Harvard, waved not waived. On, then, with talking and saying and speaking as the lines along which Lowell's poem lives:

> Then on with warden's pace across the Yard,
> talking of Pound, "It's balls to say he only
> pretends to be Ezra. . . . He's better though. This year,
> he no longer wants to rebuild the Temple at Jerusalem.

Yes, he's better. '*You* speak,' he said, when he'd talked two
   hours.
By then I had absolutely nothing to *say.*"

Nothing to *say.* This, for all the humane comedy in Eliot's affection-
ate exasperation, has its pity and terror, to be heard in the pregnant
silence that is among the tragedies of Pound's final years. His being
unable to speak, or his declining to speak: such is the fatigued re-
frain of all who visited him in his late despair. Lowell wrote of it to
Elizabeth Bishop in November 1969 (the year in which he published
the sonnets on Eliot and Pound): "I saw Pound here last spring, very
silent and gone."[35] This was written two days after Anthony Hecht
had written to Stanley Sultan: "You will be amused to know that I
read with Pound at the Spoleto Festival this past summer. The old
gentleman is very frail and feeble; and rather touching. He observes
a rigorous and self-imposed silence, which I seriously think is a
kind of pennance. Olga Rudge does all his talking for him."[36]

Hear how often over Pound's last few years it is spoken of, this
phase and worse than phase.

1961
   "On 2 February 1961 they endured 'a sad hard 3 hours of
more than his usual silences.'" [Leonard Doob and his wife
Eveline]
   "And when I went to see him, he was in bed and wouldn't
eat. Ezra was very silent." [Olga Rudge]
1962
   "We sat down. Total silence. He seemed to have reached
the end of his resources . . . I started babbling of the most in-
consequential matters . . . He remained sunken; far, far away.
But he never took his eyes off me . . . Then words seemed

unnecessary, even intrusive." [Perdita Schaffner; ellipses in
the original]

"Thin, considerably aged, he lay on a bed in almost com-
plete silence." [Dr. Bacigalupo]

1963

"He simply couldn't talk. . . . he would look at the maid
and be unable to ask for what he wanted. And in company he
really enjoyed—such as Stephen Spender and Isaiah Berlin,
at dinner here once—he still couldn't speak at all for much
of the time. There was nothing self-willed about it, nothing
affected. It was a real psychological or possibly neurological
block." [Dr. Bacigalupo]

1966

"The patient was at this time almost completely silent."
[medical report]

Pound himself tried to summon some hope. "After a long time
he said 'There—can be such—communication—in silence'" (to
Donald Hall in 1960). His family did their unconvincing best to sec-
ond this. His daughter Mary de Rachewiltz called the silence "the
most wonderful thing that happened to him. Silence is an easy eti-
quette." And Olga Rudge was "not inclined to regard the silence as
remarkable: 'Old people become increasingly silent.'"[37] *Silent:* the
number of times this was said. In due course, with a complicated
respect for Pound, Geoffrey Hill was to devote words to "Pound's
last words to silence" (*Scenes from Comus* 3, 19).

> Pound glided
> through his own idiocy; in old age
> fell upon clarities of incoherence,
> muteness's epigrams, things crying off.
>
> ("Pindarics" 14)

ROBERT LOWELL

•

But blessedly, Pound's voice can be heard not only within his own poems but in this of Lowell's.

Ezra Pound

Horizontal on a deckchair in the ward
of the criminal mad. . . . A man without shoestrings clawing
the Social Credit broadside from your table, you saying,
". . . here with a black suit and black briefcase; in the brief,
an abomination, Possum's *hommage* to Milton."
Then sprung; Rapallo, and the decade gone;
and three years later, Eliot dead, you saying,
"Who's left alive to understand my jokes?
My old Brother in the arts . . . besides, he was a smash of a
    poet."
You showed me your blotched, bent hands, saying "Worms.
When I talked that nonsense about Jews on the Rome
wireless, Olga knew it was shit, and still loved me."
And I, "Who else has been in Purgatory?"
You, "I began with a swelled head and end with swelled
    feet."

(Ezra Pound, born 1885, died 1972.) The text above is the one in *History*, revising the versions in *Notebook, 1967–68* and *Notebook*, which had the following version:

Ezra Pound

Horizontal in a deckchair on the bleak ward,
some feeble-minded felon in pajamas, clawing
a Social Credit broadside from your table, you saying,
". . . here with a black suit and black briefcase; in the
    briefcase,

an abomination, Possum's *hommage* to Milton."
Then sprung; Rapallo, and then the decade gone;
then three years, then Eliot dead, you saying,
"And who is left to understand my jokes?
My old Brother in the arts . . . and besides, he was a smash of
    a poet."
He showed us his blotched, bent hands, saying, "Worms.
When I talked that nonsense about Jews on the Rome
wireless, she knew it was shit, and still loved me."
And I, "Who else has been in Purgatory?"
And he, "To begin with a swelled head and end with swelled
    feet."

What had been implicit, or (better) tacit, in the sonnet to Eliot is open in the Pound sonnet: admission to St. Elizabeths, to Pound's life there, if life is the word. Liveliness he clearly still has, and he is heard mustering it in protest against Eliot's playing possum yet once more. Eliot, for his part, had been heard expressing skepticism as to whether Pound only "pretends to be Ezra" (in *Notebook*, "pretends to be like Ezra"), so we may recall the tragedy that is evoked in chapter 7 of the book of Ezra: "let judgment be executed speedily upon him, whether it be unto death, or to banishment, or to confiscation of goods, or to imprisonment." But then, two chapters later, the prophet was to offer hope: "that our God may lighten our eyes, and give us a little reviving in our bondage."

Lowell in life had tried to give more than a little reviving to Pound in his bondage. This by reviving the memory of his, Lowell's, own time as a felon in what was offered to Pound as more than a show of solidarity. *Notebook*'s "some feeble-minded felon in pajamas" (with "felon" swerving away from "some feeble-minded fellow") may bring to mind what Lowell said about his imprisonment, the consequence of his political act: "I slept among eighty men, a foot apart, and grew congenial with other idealist felons."[38] A fragment survives of a letter that Lowell wrote, probably to Pound, probably in September 1947: "During the war I spent a few months in jail as an objector, so I suppose we have a little of that in common as well as verse, which is what matters."[39] Lowell assuredly to Pound, fall 1948:

> Dear Ezra:
>
> I've been meaning to write you for weeks but I've been working like hell on my poem, and somehow that doesn't go well with letters.
>
> Yaddo is a sort of St. Elizabeths without bars—regular hours, communal meals, grounds, big old buildings etc. Details: a bust of Dante with a hole in the top and cigarette ashes inside, framed poems by Henry van Dyke, a man writing a history of Harvard.[40]

Pound might have received with some wryness the thought that the writers' retreat Yaddo, with its privileges and perquisites, was "a sort of St. Elizabeths without bars." But Lowell's letter is saved from crassness not only by its being so manifestly meant with all kindness but also by its being visited by the usual shared hauntings, with "like hell" very much more than an expletive, given the bust of Dante—and, a few lines later, a mention of *Faust*. Plus "a man writing a history of Harvard," of all places (as it likes to think of itself), with Lowell reverting to what had from the beginning been for him a crucial obsession. Lowell's 1948 letter to Pound about Yaddo turned toward William Carlos Williams's "bristling at the thought of meeting Eliot. *'I'm indifferent to him and what he does.'*"

God, damnation, Harvard, and Italy, together with the expletive "hell" ("a hell of a lot better") and an evocation of "the other world," form a knot again in Lowell to Pound (25 March 1954), including this expostulation: "because (God Damn it!) he [Ford] thought I would write undignified gossip about him in his old age, and (on the strength of that I suppose) become president of Harvard."[41]

The sonnet on Eliot moves to the sonnet on Pound. From Harvard to St. Elizabeths:

> ["] an abomination, Possum's *hommage* to Milton."
> Then sprung; Rapallo, and the decade gone;
> and three years later, Eliot dead, you saying,
> "Who's left alive to understand my jokes?

"Harvard's war-dead" are joined with Eliot's report of Pound ("'*You* speak,' he said, when he'd talked two hours. / By then I had absolutely nothing to *say*") to become here, "Eliot dead, you saying." Possum dead, and no longer—in the interests of survival—pretending to be so.

"Then sprung": how this springs, is sprung on us. The sudden leap, abrupt of syntax, is to *OED* 23: "To release (a person) from custody or imprisonment. *slang* (orig. *U.S.*)." "Possum" into "sprung" into "years": behind this, with Lowell's characteristic ability to call upon so much that does not have exactly to be vouched for, is the thinking from "Gerontion": "The tiger springs in the new year." Or to expand and to contract:

> The tiger springs in the new year. Us he devours. Think at
>   last
> We have not reached conclusion, when I
> Stiffen in a rented house.

At St. Elizabeths, Pound had become an old man, stiffening there in what had been worse than a rented house. Pound, who had devoted such attention to the wording of "Gerontion," attention that Eliot almost entirely resisted.[42] Pound, of whom there could be no more telling inquiry than "After such knowledge, what forgiveness?" We have not reached conclusion.

"Yaddo is a sort of St. Elizabeths without bars." For Pound, St. Elizabeths succeeded Italy and the harsher bars, the cage, north of Pisa. It is something of a relief to think back to happier times, the annus mirabilis that was 1922, and to an aspect of the Pound-Eliot friendship that comes to mind when responding to Lowell's sonnets (without necessarily supposing that it had come to Lowell's mind, at least consciously). In his well-intentioned, misguided proposal to help the young Eliot, Pound had turned naturally to a figure of speech that would—in due hideous course—become something other than a figure of speech. "In order that T.S. Eliot may leave his work in Lloyd's Bank and devote his whole time to literature, we are raising a fund . . ."

"Bel Esprit" started in Paris. To release as many captives as possible.

Darkness and confusion as in Middle Ages; no chance of general order or justice; we can only release an individual here or there.

T.S. Eliot first name chosen. Must have thirty guarantors at £10 per year "for life or for as long as Eliot needs it" (anyone who don't like my choice is at liberty to choose some other imprisoned artist or writer, and start another "Bel Esprit" group). . . .

I mean the struggle is to get the first man released. "Release of energy for invention and design" acc best economic theories. AFTER Eliot is freed it will be much easier to get out the second, third and tenth prisoners.[43]

"At liberty to choose some other imprisoned artist": Pound's thought was vivid and kindly, but Eliot was to wish that nothing would come of it as far as he was concerned. He did not forget Pound's generosity of impulse but was careful never to surrender his own precise ways of expressing this. As he said of Pound in 1946:

> He liked to be the impresario for younger men, as well as the animator of artistic activity in any milieu in which he found himself. In this role he would go to any lengths of generosity and kindness; from inviting constantly to dinner a struggling author whom he suspected of being under-fed, or giving away clothing (though his shoes and underwear were almost the only garments which resembled those of other men sufficiently to be worn by them), to trying to find jobs, collect subsidies, get work published and then get it criticised and praised. Indeed, he was ready to lay out the whole of life for anyone in whose work he was interested—a degree of direction which not all the beneficiaries deserved, and which was sometimes embarrassing. Yet, though the object of his beneficence might come to chafe against it, only a man of the meanest spirit could have come to resent it.[44]

"Only a man of the meanest spirit" could have resented, as against resisted, Bel Esprit.

Eliot remembered Pound's shoes. Lowell would have thought of them when he revised "some feeble-minded felon in pajamas"

ROBERT LOWELL
•
175

(*Notebook*) into "A man without shoestrings" (*History*). The man is not Pound (despite there being a passing strange effect in the syntax of Lowell's sequence, which has the apposition "Horizontal on a deckchair in the ward / of the criminal mad. . . . A man without shoestrings"), for the man is a felon fellow inmate, and yet the phrase "without shoestrings" is tied to Pound, Pound in past trouble and Pound in present trouble. His daughter Mary brought together, as life had brought together, the cage near Pisa and the hospital in Washington, three times remarking that they had taken away his shoelaces: "It was only years later when I visited him in St. Elizabeths Hospital in Washington that he described the gorilla cage in detail and how he had felt threatened by the sharp iron spikes. He had been deprived of belt and shoelaces to ensure that he could do himself no harm." "He also apologized to her for his untidy appearance, pointing at the unlaced shoes." He was "in a U.S. Army blouse and trousers, in unlaced shoes without socks."[45]

Lacing together many of these suggestivenesses is the thought of treason, for Pound had been accused of treason, been found mentally unfit to stand trial, and was incarcerated in St. Elizabeths so that he might suffer a less extreme penalty than would have been his had he been convicted. What has all this to do with Eliot, the visitor not altogether welcome for all the friendship?

> you saying,
> ". . . here with a black suit and black briefcase; in the brief,
> an abomination, Possum's *hommage* to Milton."[46]

A link might be prompted by the word "recanted" in the note on the Lowell line by Frank Bidart and David Gewanter: "In 'Milton II' (1947), Eliot recanted many of his earlier strictures against Milton."

Not really true of Eliot's recanvassing of the matter, but it is likely to have seemed so to Pound, who never forgave Milton "his asinine bigotry, his beastly hebraism, the coarseness of his mentality," and who would not have taken kindly to Eliot's taking more kindly to the perpetrator of *Paradise Lost*.[47] Eliot himself was a touch gingerly here: "Pound's disparagement of Milton, for instance, was, I am convinced, most salutary twenty and thirty years ago; I still agree with him against the academic admirers of Milton; though to me it seems that the situation has changed."[48]

The thing is that one man's recantation may be another man's treason. One may think this even while wishing that Pound had undertaken much more of a recantation instead of giving a fascist salute when, released from St. Elizabeths, he hit Rapallo.

Two of Pound's words, which then become Lowell's words, seethe for attention: "an abomination, Possum's *hommage* to Milton." For the word "abomination" pays a certain kind of homage to the book of Ezra, occurring three times in chapter 9: "doing according to their abominations," "with their abominations," "Should we join . . . in affinity with the people of these abominations?" Lowell, who attended to wives and whose sonnet has Pound speak of his wife, Olga, may have noticed that chapter 10 of the book of Ezra makes much of "strange wives": "taken strange wives" (six times), "separate yourselves . . . from the strange wives." Added to which, there is the fact that for Pound himself the word *"hommage,"* or even "homage," had come to seem something of an abomination. Lowell is likely to have been aware of Pound's letter to Thomas Hardy (31 March 1921), a letter in which Pound berates himself for the misdirection in what (over the years) has come to seem an exceptional and unexceptionable title, *Homage to Sextus Propertius*:

ROBERT LOWELL

•

177

Dear Thomas Hardy,

It is very good of you to answer—and though you seem to think you have said little or nothing, you have really said a great deal and diagnosed the trouble with nearly all art and literature of the past thirty years.

I ought—precisely—to have written "Propertius soliloquizes"—turning the reader's attention to the reality of Propertius—but no—what I do is to borrow a term—aesthetic—a term of aesthetic attitude from a French musician, Debussy—who uses "Homage à Rameau" for a title to a piece of music recalling Rameau's manner. My "Homage" is not an English word at all.

There are plenty of excuses—and no justification. . . . I imitate Browning. At a tender age London critics scare me out [of] frank and transparent imitation—even "Propertius Soliloquizes" would sound too much like one of R.B.'s titles.[49]

True, for Browning had given the world "Artemis Prologizes."

In any case, Lowell lets Pound put it right at last; if the word *homage* is going to be used à la française, let the word and the phrase have their full complement of *mm*s: "Possum's *hommage* to Milton." For which treason of Eliot's, Pound might have wished to say "There are plenty of excuses—and no justification." But the thing about an excuse is that it fails to excuse.

Purgatory, on the other hand, can purge. Here is the exchange between Lowell and Pound that the poem brings itself to "end with."

> And I, "Who else has been in Purgatory?"
> You, "I began with a swelled head and end with swelled
> feet."

In the Pound sonnet as originally published (in *Notebook, 1967-68*),
"And I" had been followed immediately by "And he":

> And he, "To begin with a swelled head and end with swelled
> feet."

In this final line of the Pound sonnet, the change to "You" comes
in the course of all such changes of "he" to "you." Pound is now
spoken *to*, within the poem, no longer spoken *of*, although the time
has now come for the poem to speak of him, here and now, as well
as to him, back then and there.

> And three years later, Eliot dead, you saying,
> "Who's left alive to understand my jokes?["]

Eliot dead, and by the time that Lowell publishes this poem, Pound
dead too. Both of them were destined to live anew, as does Lowell
(1917-77), who within a decade of publishing these sonnets had
passed in his turn.

> So may som gentle Muse
> With lucky words favour my destin'd Urn,
> And as he passes turn,
> And bid fair peace be to my sable shrowd.
>   ("Lycidas")

"And he": perhaps Lowell discarded this from the Pound sonnet
because it constituted too palpable a nudge at the sonnet on Eliot
immediately preceding:

And he:

"Don't you loathe to be compared with your relatives?["]

And he: Don't you loathe to be nudged into *relations*? Into *Only connect*? But what thou lovest well remains, and a connection to Dante remains in the Pound sonnet ("And I"), and, with it, a sufficient but less insistent connection with the sonnet on Eliot. Eliot and Pound: the Two Musketeers, One for Both and Both for One. Whereupon the threesome, the triangle, finds itself completed by Lowell, and then completed again into a foursome, a quadrangle, by Dante, who is invoked in both of the Lowell sonnets and in so much of both Eliot and Pound.

Dante in English (2005), edited by Eric Griffiths and Matthew Reynolds, prefaced its selection from Eliot with a headnote succinctly suggestive about the intersection of Eliot, Dante, and Pound:

> After Shakespeare, Dante was the sharpest and most lasting influence on Eliot's writing, and, unlike Shakespeare, served Eliot as a deliberately adopted model of style, though Eliot tended to exaggerate into world-historical antithesis the contrasts he saw between the detailed practice of the two writers. Eliot's first book of poems, *Prufrock and Other Observations,* has an epigraph from Dante (*Purgatorio* 21.133–6), as does the first poem in that book, "The Love Song of J. Alfred Prufrock" (*Inferno* 27.61–6); allusions to Dante persist throughout his poetic life and culminate in *Little Gidding* II (1942). He read Dante at first in the bilingual Temple Classics edition, and may be said to have learned Italian from and for Dante. There are more references to Dante in his *Selected*

Essays than to any writer apart from Shakespeare; lines from Shakespeare and Dante appear side by side in three sections of *The Waste Land,* as if dividing the poem between them. In his obituary notice for Eliot, Pound wrote (implying a humbled comparison between himself and Eliot) "His was the true Dantescan voice"; there seems no good reason to dissent from that judgement.[50]

The comparison, humbling to the point of accepting the possibility of humiliation, was not easy for Pound or easy on him. Writing for Eliot in *The Criterion* (April 1934), he had reviewed Laurence Binyon's translation of the *Inferno:* the heading, HELL. But Inferno and Hell are not synonymous, not conterminous. The triple alliance presented its shifting challenges, as Pound noted in 1960: "It is difficult to write a paradiso when all the superficial indications are that you ought to write an apocalypse. It is obviously much easier for an inferno or even a purgatorio."[51] Pound's friend and commentator Noel Stock "noticed that he was reading *Four Quartets,* which was surprising, since he had earlier seemed to dislike them. 'He was anxious to assure me, though,' says Stock, 'that he had simply been criticizing *other* aspects of TSE's work.' He added that Eliot 'had already been through his 'Purgatory.'"[52]

In *The Criterion* in 1934, Pound's first page had referred to "the nature of Dantescan verse." In the fullness of time, once more for Eliot (but now for Eliot the poet, not for Eliot the editor), Pound was touchingly to voice Dantescan verse as Dantescan voice.[53] In Memoriam T.S.E.

FOR T. S. E.

His was the true Dantescan voice—not honoured enough, and deserving more than I ever gave him.

ROBERT LOWELL

•

I had hoped to see him in Venice this year for the Dante commemoration at the Giorgio Cini Foundation—instead: Westminster Abbey. But, later, on his own hearth, a flame tended, a presence felt.

Recollections? let some thesis-writer have the satisfaction of "discovering" whether it was in 1920 or '21 that I went from Excideuil to meet a rucksacked Eliot. Days of walking—conversation? literary? le papier Fayard was then the burning topic.[54] Who is there now for me to share a joke with?

Am I to write "about" the poet Thomas Stearns Eliot? or my friend "the Possum"? Let him rest in peace. I can only repeat, but with the urgency of 50 years ago: READ HIM.

E. P.

Pound, honoring Eliot in 1965: "Who is there now for me to share a joke with?" Lowell, honoring Pound and Eliot, the thought and its rhythm, in 1969: "And who is left to understand my jokes?" In 1973 yet another report from Lowell, a related thought with a different rhythm, movingly *alive:* "Who's left alive to understand my jokes?"

In lapidary inscriptions a man is not upon oath. (These poems by Lowell are lapidary inscriptions of a sort.) The truest poetry is the most feigning.

Eliot told us of "What Dante Means to Me" (1950). But then there is what "Dantescan" means to us. Dante has formed many an adjective for our tongue. *Danteish* is one that the language willingly let die (as daintyish). But *Dantean* is from 1785, *Dantesque* from 1813 (this being Eliot's choice in "What Dante Means to Me"), and *Dantescan*—Pound's majestic preference—is from 1834, when an ear heard "the Dantescan harmony."

ROBERT LOWELL
·

Eliot had met Dante in the company of Pound near Périgord in early days, earlier even than 1920 or 1921. He had praised Pound's 1915 poem in *To-Day* (September 1918) and was to include it in his *Selected Poems* of Pound in 1928:

> "Near Perigord" expresses a situation of a man and a woman; it is also an appreciation of a particular time with much historical and geographical knowledge, and incidentally contains a beautiful translation of half a dozen lines of Dante:

> *Surely I saw, and still before my eyes*
> *Goes on that headless trunk, that bears for light*
> *Its own head swinging, gripped by the dead hair . . .*

"Incidentally"? More than that, as not only the poem but time would tell. For it is the poem "Near Perigord" that sang out the turn which was to mean so much to Eliot by courtesy of and in courtesy to Pound: "And the 'best craftsman' sings out his friend's song." Il miglior fabbro.

Yet a moment later in Pound's poem a question will insist on being asked: "Do we know our friends?" For there is more than one kind of severance in life, and the vision that Pound brings from Dante, and that Eliot praised in 1918, is "half a dozen lines," of which Eliot gave only the first three:

> *Surely I saw, and still before my eyes*
> *Goes on that headless trunk, that bears for light*
> *Its own head swinging, gripped by the dead hair,*
> *And like a swinging lamp that says, "Ah me!*
> *I severed men, my head and heart*
> *Ye see here severed, my life's counterpart."*[55]

Pound himself was to sever and be severed from so much. His life's counterpart did not bring him to a cry as simple as "Ah me!" Remorse it seems that he did come to feel, but it would take strange turns. "He was quite strong and active for a while, though plagued by all kinds of remorse. Mr. Eliot was one: 'I should have listened to the Possum.'" There is something concertedly right about the syntax of this, with Mr. Eliot's being a remorse. But then there is something disconcertingly wrong about what directly follows the words "I should have listened to the Possum." For the next sentence is this: "And we all had to read *After Strange Gods.*" Does *After Strange Gods,* which is the book about which Eliot himself felt some remorse, offer a worldview that Pound, in his remorse, did well to urge upon his loved ones? At which point it is a mercy that an inadvertent comedy immediately intervenes in Mary de Rachewiltz's account. "I wrote to Mr. Eliot begging him to come and see Babbo [her nickname for Pound]. He sent a birthday telegram saying: 'You are the greatest poet alive and I owe everything to you'—or words to that effect."[56] There is something delicious about a poet's daughter who can straightfacedly set down the sequence (Eliot to Pound) "'You are the greatest poet alive and I owe everything to you'—or words to that effect."

But *After Strange Gods* remains a dark presence. In Pound's eyes, this book (which for most of us and for Eliot himself had gone too far) had not gone far enough. "Eliot, in this book, has not come through uncontaminated by the Jewish poison. Until a man purges himself of this poison he will never achieve understanding. It is a poison that lost no time in seeping into European thought." "Poison": tolled three times. "Until he succeeds in detaching the Jewish from the European elements of his peculiar variety of Christianity he will never find the right formula. Not a jot or tittle of the hebraic alphabet can pass into the text without danger of contaminating it."[57]

Pound did come to detach himself from something hereabouts, but it was not a dissociation from *After Strange Gods* and the book's injustices; rather it was from what had been Pound's own injustice (so he felt) to the book. He added and dated "1959" a footnote to a 1937 essay: "Mr. Eliot's *Primer of Heresy* (*After Strange Gods*) was not examined with sufficient care, nor did the present author chew on it sufficiently, especially in regard to the distinction between A Church, an orthodoxy, and a collection of intelligent observations by individual theologians, however brilliant."[58]

But a cry was often wrung from him. Noel Stock recorded in 1962: "Olga put on tape in living room . . . [Ezra] reading Cantos, including 'Pull down.' EP broke down—depressed— 'harm I have done.' I tried to reassure him. As Olga left with me EP called out— asking her back: 'I have done enough evil.'"[59]

> The shame
> Of motives late revealed, and the awareness
> Of things ill done and done to others' harm
> Which once you took for exercise of virtue.
>
> (*Little Gidding* II)

It is this section of *Little Gidding,* with its awareness of Dante's Brunetto Latini, to which the mind turns. Hecht's essay on Eliot in *Literary Imagination* 5 (2003) moves to an end with the acknowledgment that "the mere attainment of calm after so much violence, including contempt and self-contempt, is somehow stirring in a way that rises at last to a condition of dignity, and exhibits its own austere and genuine beauty." The final words of Hecht's essay, which was published the year before he died, are these words of Eliot's:

ROBERT LOWELL

•

185

And last the rending pain of re-enactment
Of all that you have done, and been; the shame
Of motives late revealed, and the awareness
Of things ill done and done to others' harm
Which once you took for exercise of virtue.

For Eliot, the Brunetto Latini encounter in Dante constituted more than an Arnoldian touchstone. Identifying the parts of the *Inferno* which certainly remained (he says) in his memory and first "convinced" him, Eliot chose "especially the Brunetto and the Ulysses episodes, for which I was unprepared by quotation or allusion," and he then gave further force to what might have been the single thought of his having been "unprepared," by proceeding to

the quality of *surprise* which Poe declared to be essential to poetry. This *surprise,* at its highest, could by nothing be better illustrated than by the final lines with which Dante dismisses the damned master whom he loves and respects:

Poi si rivolse, e parve di coloro
che coronno a Verona il drappo verde
per la campagna; e parve di costoro
quegli che vince e non colu che perde.

Then he turned back, and seemed like one of those who run for the green cloth at Verona through the open field; and of them he seemed like him who wins, and not like him who loses.

One does not need to know anything about the race for the roll of green cloth, to be *hit* by these lines; and in making Brunetto, so fallen, *run like the winner,* a quality is given to the punishment which belongs only to the greatest poetry.[60]

Eliot's evocation of Dante's evocation is haunting and radiant, for instance in the apposite contrariety within the word "dismisses" ("the final lines with which Dante dismisses the damned master whom he loves and respects"), since "dismisses" is at once what happens as narrative and what emotionally can never happen, Brunetto being forever the master whom Dante loves and respects. Or there is Eliot's sequence sighing out its interjection of "so fallen," pausing before it runs on ("in making Brunetto, so fallen, *run like the winner*"), with a double memory of elegiac allusion, or so it seems to me. There is the memory of the poem by Dryden that Eliot loved, which he quotes in its entirety at the end of his Dryden essay, following it with the words "From the perfection of such an elegy we cannot detract." "To the Memory of Mr. Oldham" brings home what it is to be fallen as well as to run like the winner, in the Virgilian story of the race that is competition and friendship:

> Thus Nisus fell upon the slippery place,
> Whilst his young friend performed and won the race.[61]

And there is the other memory, of another damnable change: "If thou beest he; But O how fall'n! how chang'd." The fallen angel, so fallen. If I am right in hearing Milton, too, behind Eliot's "so fallen," this may be in part because *quantum mutatus* has its further mutation, of a different order, within Dante's double feelings at parting from Brunetto, not only because of the change from what and who he had once been but in the mutation within the simile itself, so unexpectedly and yet so familiarly mingling the damned, the loved, and the respected: "in making Brunetto, so fallen, *run like the winner.*" At which point one might realize, with that same "quality of *surprise,*" how much Eliot had effected, earlier in the paragraph, by means of an unobtrusive preposition, for the Brunetto episode "is Dante's testimony of a loved master of arts," not simply his testimony *to* a loved master of arts.

There is Eliot's earlier testimony, a decade before, in "Tradition and the Individual Talent" (1919): "Canto XV of the *Inferno* (Brunetto Latini) is a working up of the emotion evident in the situation; but the effect, though single as that of any work of art, is obtained by considerable complexity of detail. The last quatrain gives an image, a feeling attaching to an image, which 'came,' which did not develop simply out of what precedes, but which was probably in suspension in the poet's mind until the proper combination arrived for it to add itself to. The poet's mind is in fact a receptacle for seizing and storing up numberless feelings, phrases, images, which remain there until all the particles which can unite to form a new compound are present together."[62] This prose waited until the proper combination arrived for the poet. For in suspension in this poet's mind, stored up, were these feelings, phrases, images, which would remain there to form a new compound, the Brunetto Latini passage in *Little Gidding:*

> The eyes of a familiar compound ghost
>
> . . . .
>
> And he a face still forming; yet the words sufficed
> To compel the recognition they preceded.

"To form a new compound . . . an image, which 'came,' which did not develop simply out of what precedes."

"The last quatrain gives an image, a feeling attaching to an image, which 'came.'" What the last quatrain of Dante's Canto XV gave to Robert Lowell was an opportunity to vie with Eliot (a loved master of arts), to compete with him in a vivid race. Lowell emulates not only Dante but Eliot's Dante. What "came" to Lowell was

something at which he had three goes. In this proliferation, he ex-
ercised the right (one that flourished for Whitman) to conceive of
poetry as though it had the freedom associated with a performing
art such as song, the freedom to do the same thing again differently
and thereby have it not be the same. Revision, re-seeing, can make
for and can take up liberties.

The first of Lowell's sightings of Brunetto is from *Life Studies*
(1959), "For George Santayana":

> Lying outside the consecrated ground
> forever now, you smile
> like Ser Brunetto running for the green
> cloth at Verona—not like one
> who loses, but like one who'd won . . .[63]

In *The Hard Hours,* Hecht had dissimilarly brought Dante to bear
upon Santayana (the Dante of *The Waste Land* I, not of *Little Gid-
ding* II):

> And so it was. The river, as foretold,
> Ran darkly by; under his tongue he found
> Coin for the passage; the ferry tossed and rolled;
> The sages stood on their appointed ground,
> Sighing, all as foretold. The mind was tasked;
> He had not dreamed that so many had died.
>
> ("Upon the Death of George Santayana")

Strange how unlike Eliot's Dantesque rendering in *The Waste Land*
("I had not thought death had undone so many") Hecht succeeds
in being; it must be all those concluding *d*s.

The wry comedy of Lowell's lapidary poem can be felt in
the burial placing of Santayana: "Lying outside the consecrated
ground / forever." For when this proceeds at once to Ser Brunetto,

there is the conviction of Brunetto's lying forever, there in the land of the damned, outside the consecrated ground. Inside the desecrated grounds.

The second of Lowell's meetings with this meeting is from *Near the Ocean* (1967), in the translation "Brunetto Latini":

> Then he turned back, and he seemed one of those
> who run for the green cloth through the green field
> at Verona . . . and seemed more like the one
> who wins the roll of cloth than those who lose.

And third, from *History* (1973), in the first of five unrhymed sonnets that turn upon Dante:

> A man running for his life will never tire:
> his Ser Brunetto ran through hell like one
> who ran for the green cloth through the green fields
> at Verona, looking more like one
> who won the roll of cloth, than those who lost. . . .

In *Notebook,* this sonnet had the title "Winter," and those lines ran:

> *the man running for his life never tires:*
> Ser Brunetto, running like one of those
> who ran for the green cloth through the green fields
> at Verona, looks like the one who won
> the roll of cloth, not like those who lose. . . .

This urged the homophone toward the caricatural: in immediate sequence, "the one who won."

Each of Lowell's engagements has its own grim felicities. Two of the three make play with the homophone "one"/"won." The poem to Santayana positions the two words as end rhymes and then throws in an internal rhyme as well, to make assurance double sure, while having twice the word "one":

> not like one
> who loses, but like one who'd won . . .

The sonnet to Dante rolls the word from the one line to the next—

> looking more like one
> who won the roll of cloth, than those who lost. . . .

—while smiling darkly at its own expanse, for Lowell's line "his Ser Brunetto ran through hell like one" is an inspired dislocation, there in hell, of "ran like hell through."

It is the other version of the three, the straight translation from Dante (insofar as Lowell ever translates anything straight), that waives the homophone instead of waving it:

> and seemed more like the one
> who wins the roll of cloth than those who lose.

Decorum, declining the homophonic gambit, here presents its respects to the master whom Lowell loves and respects. The masters, rather, Eliot as well as Dante.

"The emotion of the passage," Eliot had insisted, "resides in Brunetto's excellence in damnation—so admirable a soul, and so perverse."[64] Brunetto, so fallen. Lowell, so often so perverse. Even Santayana, since the line about him that immediately precedes Lowell's "Lying outside the consecrated ground" is the quoted saying "There is no God and Mary is His Mother." (Lowell writes most touchingly about Santayana in "New England and Further": "Roman Catholic by birth (inheritance) and even taste, though in belief a pious agnostic"; "Of the Catholic Church: 'It's a pity it has no bottom . . . it's too good to be believed.'" Lowell's ellipsis.)[65] But the excellent in damnation, the admirable, the perverse: when these three meet again, it is in Ezra Pound.

Lowell reviewed *Four Quartets* in 1943, saying that if he "were to pick purple passages," the list would begin with part I of *The Dry Salvages* and "the unrhymed terza rima section in *Little Gidding*."[66] The phrase "purple passage" ("a brilliant or ornate passage in a literary composition") is too highly colored for the Dantesque or Dantescan section of *Little Gidding,* but a sibling phrase was to be more appropriately deployed (because meant to be glaringly so) in a translation-imitation found, like "Brunetto Latini," in *Near the Ocean.* This, his version of Juvenal, Lowell was so bold as to call "The Vanity of Human Wishes":

> March, madman, cross
> the Alps, the Tiber—be a purple patch
> for schoolboys, and a theme for declamation!

Imperial, this purple.

Arnold's touchstones were not limited to purple patches or purple passages. When Eliot turned to the Brunetto Latini episode for the first time within his *Dante* (1929), it was by way of returning to Arnold:

> There is a well-known comparison or simile in the great XVth canto of the *Inferno,* which Matthew Arnold singled out, rightly, for high praise; which is characteristic of the way in which Dante employs these figures. He is speaking of the crowd in Hell who peered at him and his guide under a dim light:

e sì ver noi aguzzevan le ciglia,
come vecchio sartor fa nella cruna.

and sharpened their vision (knitted their brows) at us, like an old tailor
peering at the eye of his needle.

The purpose of this type of simile is solely to make us *see*
more definitely the scene which Dante has put before us in the
preceding lines.[67]

There is delicacy of purpose in the movement of Eliot's observation
as to this moment of observation, such as is characteristic of his
criticism at his best: "who peered . . . *sharpened their vision* . . . *peer-*
ing at the eye of his needle . . . to make us *see more definitely* the scene"
(to see the seen). The concentration of (and upon) the eyes returns
within Eliot's rendering of his Brunetto:

> And as I fixed upon the down-turned face
> That pointed scrutiny with which we challenge
> The first-met stranger in the waning dusk

Pointed, as is a needle. Soon, "The eyes of a familiar compound
ghost."

This Dantesque passage, which forms the second part of *Little
Gidding* II (the first part being the lyric on the four elements, "Ash
on an old man's sleeve"), immediately establishes the authority of
its verse movement, unmistakable yet uncoercive.[68]

> In the uncertain hour before the morning
> Near the ending of interminable night
> At the recurrent end of the unending
> After the dark dove with the flickering tongue
> Had passed below the horizon of his homing

ROBERT LOWELL

•

193

While the dead leaves still rattled on like tin
Over the asphalt where no other sound was
  Between three districts whence the smoke arose
  I met one walking, loitering and hurried
As if blown towards me like the metal leaves
  Before the urban dawn wind unresisting.

My first problem was to find an approximation to the *terza rima* without rhyming. English is less copiously provided with rhyming words than Italian; and those rhymes we have are in a way more emphatic. The rhyming words call too much attention to themselves: Italian is the one language known to me in which exact rhyme can always achieve its effect—and what the effect of rhyme is, is for the neurologist rather than the poet to investigate—without the risk of obtruding itself. I therefore adopted, for my purpose, a simple alternation of unrhymed masculine and feminine terminations, as the nearest way of giving the light effect of the rhyme in Italian.[69]

Not altogether so, for the alternation is, rather, that of feminine and masculine terminations. The unstressed final syllables ("morning," "unending," "homing") are the odd numbers, as against the even-numbered terminations ("night," "tongue").

Eliot's metrical decision was masterful and his carrying it out masterly. Perhaps he was influenced by Robert Bridges, who exercised this alternation (feminine endings and then masculine ones) but in combination, further, with full rhyme. This in a poem of 1880 which, like Eliot's passage, is a cityscape of night into morning, of a London night into a London morning.

London Snow

When men were all asleep the snow came flying,
In large white flakes settling on the city brown,
Stealthily and perpetually settling and loosely lying,
   Hushing the latest traffic of the drowsy town;
Deadening, muffling, stifling its murmurs failing;
Lazily and incessantly floating down and down:
   Silently sifting and veiling road, roof and railing;
Hiding difference, making unevenness even,
Into angles and crevices softly drifting and sailing.
   All night it fell, and when full inches seven
It lay in the depth of its uncompacted lightness,
The clouds blew off from a high and frosty heaven;
   And all woke earlier for the unaccustomed brightness
Of the winter dawning, the strange unheavenly glare:
The eye marvelled — marvelled at the dazzling whiteness;
   The ear hearkened to the stillness of the solemn air;
No sound of wheel rumbling nor of foot falling,
And the busy morning cries came thin and spare.
   Then boys I heard, as they went to school, calling,
They gathered up the crystal manna to freeze
Their tongues with tasting, their hands with snowballing;
   Or rioted in a drift, plunging up to the knees;
Or peering up from under the white-mossed wonder,
"O look at the trees!" they cried, "O look at the trees!"
   With lessened load a few carts creak and blunder,
Following along the white deserted way,
A country company long dispersed asunder:
   When now already the sun, in pale display

ROBERT LOWELL

·

Standing by Paul's high dome, spread forth below
His sparkling beams, and awoke the stir of the day.
　For now doors open, and war is waged with the snow;
And trains of sombre men, past tale of number,
Tread long brown paths, as toward their toil they go:
　But even for them awhile no cares encumber
Their minds diverted; the daily word is unspoken,
The daily thoughts of labour and sorrow slumber
At the sight of the beauty that greets them, for the charm
　they have broken.

Bridges's conduct of his cadences is exemplary, and Eliot may have found the example something to hearken to. Eliot's first five lines end with "morning," "night," "unending," "tongue," homing"; Bridges's with "flying," "brown," "lying," "town," "failing." True, what came flying in *Little Gidding* was not the snow but enemy aircraft.

Little Gidding: "First Complete Draft 7 July 1941."[70] This was the year in which Eliot became Bridges's publisher, when Faber and Faber issued *Selected Poems by Robert Bridges,* within their series Sesame Books. "London Snow" is there.[71]

There is further evidence of Eliot's being interested in Bridges, or certainly not uninterested in him. Upon Bridges's death, in the wake of speculation as to who should be the next poet laureate, Eliot was altogether dignified: "One feeling which we are sure all other practitioners of verse had for Bridges is the feeling of respect; and when so unanimous, that is a very fine feeling to inspire." Circumspect, such respect, but still. "It is certain that his experimentation has served a valuable purpose. It has helped to accustom readers of verse to a more liberal conception of verse technique, and to the notion that the development of technique is a serious and unceasing subject of study among verse writers; it has helped to protect other versifiers of less prestige, against the charge of being just 'rebels' or 'freaks'; or as a writer in *The Morning Post* some years ago nicely named them, 'literary Bolsheviks.'" In conclusion: "And even those poets who feel that they owe nothing to him directly, and who cannot join the chorus of praise over *The Testament of Beauty,* have reason to bless his memory."[72] To dispraise of *The Testament of Beauty,* I shall be returning, holding open the possibility that Eliot was, on one occasion, among the poets who owed something to Bridges directly.

Assuredly Eliot was among the poets who owed something to Pound both directly and indirectly. I suggest that Pound is one of the many figures who come to make up the ghost in *Little Gidding* II, given that Pound goes to the making of *Little Gidding* elsewhere.

Pound: "See, they return." Eliot: "See, they return," returning moreover not only to "See, they depart" but to "See, now they vanish," all three within *Little Gidding.* This poem of Pound's, "The Return," is (I believe) to be heard not only in *Little Gidding* III and V but in section II, with its memory of Dante.

> See, they return; ah, see the tentative
>   Movements, and the slow feet,
>   The trouble in the pace and the uncertain
>   Wavering!
>
> See, they return, one, and by one,
>   With fear, as half-awakened;

As if the snow should hesitate
And murmur in the wind,
    and half turn back;

I believe that Pound's turn,

    The trouble in the pace and the uncertain
    Wavering!

assisted two creations in Eliot. First the movement of a moment in
Ash-Wednesday VI:

    Although I do not hope to turn

    Wavering between the profit and the loss

where Eliot profits from Pound without loss to Pound. Second,
the "uncertain" into "-ing" that opens *Little Gidding* II: "In the un-
certain hour before the morning." But I think that there is more
than this to Pound's ghostly presence in the Dantesque passage. I
sense some recollection of what Eliot wrote in his introduction to
Pound's *Selected Poems* in 1928: "Out of discussion of such matters
with Pound rose the spectre of an introduction by myself."[73] "Rose
the spectre of an introduction":

        an incantation
    To summon the spectre of a Rose.
    (*Little Gidding* III)

Dante is there in Eliot's pages on Pound, naturally enough, and so
is Arnaut Daniel, the two poets especially linked for Eliot not only
within *Little Gidding* II but within Eliot's introduction to Pound,
which mentions "the fact that I am totally ignorant of Provençal,
except for a dozen lines of Dante."

Since our concern was speech, and speech impelled us
To purify the dialect of the tribe

— "Technically, these influences were all good; for they combine to insist upon the importance of *verse as speech.*" "Throughout the work of Pound there is what we might call a steady effort towards the synthetic construction of a style of speech."[74]

"Knowing myself, yet being someone other": "the translator is giving the original through himself, and finding himself through the original" (p. xiv).

Eliot came to create something "which did not develop simply out of what precedes, but which was probably in suspension in the poet's mind until the proper combination arrived for it to add itself to." First, there may be a small local likelihood:

Pound:

one, and by one
With fear, as half-awakened;

Eliot:

half recalled,
Both one and many;

— with, seven lines earlier in Eliot, "I met one." In manuscript, "half recalled" had been "and recalled," which is less close to Pound. There may perhaps be a coinciding, and not just a coincidence, in other small overlappings of "The Return" and *Little Gidding* II. Pound, "the wind"; Eliot, "the urban dawn wind," "the common wind." Pound, "the trace of air"; Eliot, "the death of air." Pound, "souls of blood"; Eliot, "body and soul."

But much more crucial, if I am right in thinking that in creating the Brunetto vision Eliot's mind—and more than mind—went back to Pound, is the half-line in "The Return":

And murmur in the wind,
and half turn back;

Brunetto's speaking was over. *"Poi si rivolse . . . Then he turned back . . ."*
It may be worth remembering that the extended passage that Eliot
did not publish (beginning, "Remember rather the essential mo-
ments") had drawn to an end with a direct reference to *"Poi si ri-
volse"*: "He turned away."[75]

At which point, I turn back to Bridges for a moment. For I
think that his "London Snow" mingled, in Eliot's suspensions, with
Pound's unexpected movement in "The Return" into the phrase "As
if the snow." (Tempted to mention the unexpected arrival of snow
in the opening of *Little Gidding*, I fall.) Perhaps Pound's phrase "the
trace of air" mingled likewise with Bridges's "the solemn air" to be-
come Eliot's "This is the death of air." Is there any reason to believe
that a Bridges-Pound-Eliot triangle (as against a Dante-Pound-
Eliot one) ever existed? Some such triangle had been proposed by
the editor of *The Criterion,* to whom Pound had written in mock
dismay that promptly became the real thing. Pound thanked Eliot,
in a way, for the invitation to write about Bridges (25 April 1936).
But: "If the luminous reason of one's criticism iz that one shd. focus
attention on what deserves it, a note by E.P. on Bridges wd. be a
falsification of values."[76]

I believe that in the Eliot phrase that had earlier been "a vague
familiar ghost" but that became "a familiar compound ghost," Eliot
intimates that Pound joins the other shades.[77] It might reasonably
be objected that Pound was not dead in 1942. But, as Helen Gardner
notes, "In this scene of 'meeting nowhere, no before and after' the
distinction between the dead and the living is blurred." Pound, I
suggest, was among the "masters to whom he owed reverence and

gratitude but from whom he felt himself severed."[78] "*I severed men,*
my head and heart / Ye see here severed, my life's counterpart": Eliot in 1918
had praised this figure of Pound's from Dante.

Not that *Little Gidding* II explicitly heralds Pound. The contrast
would be with the roll of drums with which Austin Clarke beats
out the name of Ezra Pound. Part I of Clarke's "Ezra Pound" has its
off-rhyme, listening to what Pound came to:

> Behind barbed wire and in asylum,
> Still he wrote on, louder in silence.[79]

Part II is constituted of on-rhymes, playing—on and on—on the
man's name:

> Rhyme, echo the name of Ezra Pound
> Whom the war capitalists impounded.
> For miserable years he pounded
> The wall of modern verse, expounded
> The madness of dollar, franc and pound.
> Forget the theories he propounded,
> But praise the language he compounded.
> The centuries are in that pound.

This ("But praise the language he compounded") spares more
than a thought for the familiar compound ghost, in converse with
whom,

> I was still the same,
> Knowing myself yet being someone other—
> And he a face still forming;

"I am almost a different person when I come to take up the ar-
gument for Eliot's poems." This single sentence, within a vista of

retrospect, constitutes the laconic paragraph that concludes Pound's "A Retrospect" (1918).[80]

Pound, then, was not only a different person from Eliot, he became (to his mind) almost a different person from himself when he came to take up the argument for Eliot's poems. Something similar, mutatis mutandis, might be said of the Hell that is the Inferno as against the pangs of Purgatory. Hell is not only a different situation ("The dismal Situation waste and wilde," *Paradise Lost,* 1.60) from Purgatory, Hell becomes almost a different situation from itself, when—when what? When Eliot's poem comes to take up the argument for Brunetto Latini (and in a further round, for Pound).

The Dantesque section of *Little Gidding* contemplates both the Inferno and Purgatory, and their denizens. Brunetto is met in—has met—his Inferno. Arnaut Daniel, il miglior fabbro, his Purgatory. The lines of Eliot carry us from the one to the other. But not unthinkingly.

We are to contemplate closely Eliot's contemplating of Dante's contemplating Brunetto—and then with a further twist to the vistas the way in which the contemplating of Brunetto asks that we look at a figure of speech within which this is again happening: *"and sharpened their vision (knitted their brows) at us, like an old tailor peering at the eye of his needle."* Not an eye for an eye, but eyes bent upon eyes bent upon an eye.

When, exactly, within Eliot's sequence does Brunetto modulate into Arnaut? The question might seem idle, in that the ghost is explicitly a compound ghost. But presumably there must be no paltering when it comes to the afterlife, any more than there should be as to whence comes the ghost of Hamlet's father. (From the Inferno? No, from Purgatory.) Whither this ghost goes within— and then from—*Little Gidding* II is clear enough: "And faded on the blowing of the horn." We hear the crowing of the cock. Eliot was determined, whatever revisions he made, to adopt no wording "which would mean my losing the allusion to Hamlet's ghost."[81] "Hamlet's ghost" is good, since father and son bear the same name, compound it.

"What! are *you* here?" "*You,*" here, italicized and all, is Brunetto, who had been named by Eliot at one manuscript stage ("Are you here, Ser Brunetto?"). Even when no longer directly named, his name had been conjured with, four lines earlier, when we glimpsed his "brown baked features." Eric Griffiths and Matthew Reynolds, scrupulously attentive to this sequence, which is more than a sequence of thought alone, identify what is for them the pivotal moment, which occurs sixteen or seventeen lines after "What! are *you* here?":

> These things have served their purpose: let them be.
> So with your own, and pray they be forgiven
>> By others, as I pray you to forgive
>> Both bad and good.

[Note by Griffiths and Reynolds] Prayer for forgiveness is unknown in *Inferno* (Brunetto Latini is keen his works should be remembered). These lines mark a pivotal moment in the passage as Eliot moves from the damned Brunetto Latini to the purged Arnaut Daniel.[82]

But this, which is tellingly adduced, is not entirely consonant with the parallel passage they give for the Eliot lines that come earlier (three or four lines after "What! are *you* here?" and so a dozen lines before those on forgiveness).

And he a face still forming; yet the words sufficed
To compel the recognition they preceded.

Standing firm as to "preceded," Eliot said finely to Hayward: "I mean, to be aware that it is someone you know (and to be surprised by his being there) before you have identified him."[83]

"The recognition they preceded": the words recognized by Griffiths and Reynolds are themselves compelling: "compare Purgatorio 23.43–5." In the translation by Laurence Binyon that Pound loved and improved:

> Him from his aspect had I never guessed,
>> But in his voice was given to me the clue
>> Of what was in his countenance suppressed.[84]

If these lines are to call up a figure from Purgatory and are applied to Brunetto, is it not intimated by Eliot (even if only faintly) that Brunetto — *pace* Dante — may perhaps not be damned through all eternity but may yet be purged?

So is there "a pivotal moment in the passage as Eliot moves from the damned Brunetto Latini to the purged Arnaut Daniel"? Does the passage register any such unwobbling pivot, or clear moment anywhere?

In wondering what moment might be settled upon, we might consider that "Ash on an old man's sleeve," the lyric immediately preceding the Dantesque vision, had in manuscript ended with three lines that are not of the Inferno but of Purgatory (for the textual details, see note 85):[85]

> Fire without and fire within
> Shall purge the unidentified sin.
> This is the place where we begin.

It is true that against the likelihood of any such relenting (from the Inferno to Purgatory), there must be acknowledged much in Eliot's criticism where the greatness of what Dante could do for him (and of what he could do for Dante) depended upon Eliot's marked unsentimentality. I am thinking, for instance, of the Dante essay in *The Sacred Wood,* and of exactly whither it is that Eliot turns, a dozen lines after his speaking of "Brunetto's excellence in damnation—so admirable a soul, and so perverse." This is a humane concession, including the mixed feelings within the phrase "excellence in damnation," with its versatile preposition "in," but it is perilous, and for Eliot it had immediately to precipitate a prophylaxis: "The emotion of the person, or the emotion with which our attitude appropriately invests the person, is never lost or diminished, is always reserved entire, but is modified by the position assigned to the person in the eternal scheme, is coloured by the atmosphere of that person's residence in one of the three worlds. About none of Dante's characters is there that ambiguity which affects Milton's Lucifer. The damned preserve any degree of beauty or grandeur that ever rightly pertained to them, and this intensifies and also justifies their damnation."[86] "Milton's Lucifer": yet Eliot's finely judged and finely judging turn, "Brunetto's excellence in damnation," has something of the high ambiguity or paradox of Milton's Lucifer, Milton's Satan: "Satan exalted sat, by merit rais'd / To that bad eminence" (*Paradise Lost,* 2.5–6).

Within Dante, there can be no doubt that Brunetto, whose name is colored brown and whose figure of speech is colored green (*"one of those who run for the green cloth"*), is eternally among the damned. Within Eliot's lines, I am not sure that this is so, and I am not sure that it was altogether so for Eliot the man. The temporal tension, even if the position is finally unwavering, can be felt strongly enough in "so admirable a soul, and so perverse," even as it can be felt in "the damned master whom he loves and respects."

Eliot could not but return to these matters of justice all his life: "Dante is able to depict pride and exhibit its worldly grandeur simultaneously with its simple sinfulness. The damnation of the damned in Dante's Hell consists chiefly in this, that they remain fixed to eternity in the passions which have damned them; not a character in Dante's Hell that is not damned by its own will, there is not one that is not shown as reprehensible" (*Times Literary Supplement*, 6 January 1928).

Of Milton, the greatest of the English poets sustainedly to contemplate eternal torment, it was said by William Empson: "That his feelings were crying out against his appalling theology in favour of freedom, happiness and the pursuit of truth was I think not obvious to him."[87] I should not want to say of Eliot that his feelings were crying out against his appalling theology, but I believe that when he came to create his compound ghost, something moved him to leave open at least something of a hope that Brunetto might yet be moved from the Inferno to Purgatory. Eliot, who would seldom have concurred with the historian Henry Thomas Buckle about anything, would have been especially disposed to contest Buckle's belief that "The greatest observer and the most profound thinker is invariably the most lenient judge."[88] Yet mercy, which is not leniency, cannot but make its appeal. The Dantesque section, because it compounded its ghosts, did not have to compound Brunetto's reprehensibility but could suggest at least a wish, and perhaps a hope, that his eternity might take a different turn.

The emotion in Dante, in contemplation of a soul in the afterlife, is colored, Eliot said, by "the atmosphere of that person's residence in one of the three worlds." It may be that Eliot found himself moved (very moving this might be in its turn) by a glimpse of the thought that Brunetto might unthinkably have residence in two of the three worlds. Not, in Arnold's vision,

> Wandering between two worlds, one dead,
> The other powerless to be born
>
> ("Stanzas from the Grande Chartreuse"),

but enabled to be present, even if only for an imagined moment within a sequence, in two worlds. Thanks to time, which is (as Blake knew) the mercy of eternity.

> Time is the mercy of Eternity; without Times swiftness
> Which is the swiftest of all things: all were eternal
> torment.[89]

Brunetto, or the ghost within which he is compounded, is met at a particular point and moment, "at this intersection time": "Between three districts whence the smoke arose." (In manuscript, "three angles" and "three corners.")[90]

Why might Eliot wish some such thing for Brunetto? Partly because he is loved and respected. Partly because eternal torment, however indispensable to the religion and however carefully or humanely it is conceived of, is a conviction from which anyone might, at least on occasion, wish release, relief. Partly because, however much Eliot revered Dante, he knew that he was not Dante nor was meant to be. Partly because he wished for some mercy for himself, when he acknowledged, within this very passage,

> The shame
> Of motives late revealed, and the awareness
> Of things ill done and done to others' harm
> Which once you took for exercise of virtue.

"'Oh mercy!' to myself I cried." *Oh mercy to myself! I cried.*

All this, perhaps, and furthermore, perhaps, because Eliot wished that mercy be shown to Ezra Pound.

Pound's being so involved in or with Hell is everywhere in Eliot's sense of him. Back in 1918, there had been "Near Perigord," near Arnaut Daniel and near the damned figure with his own head swinging in his hand. In 1934, Eliot published Pound's review of Binyon's translation, headed "HELL."[91] In this same year, Eliot published *After Strange Gods,* whose pages 41–43 are on Pound's Hell, culminating in some of the most trenchant asseverations that Eliot ever issued:

> It is in fact in moments of moral and spiritual struggle depending upon spiritual sanctions, rather than in those "bewildering minutes" in which we are all very much alike, that men and women come nearest to being real. If you do away with this struggle, and maintain that by tolerance, benevolence, inoffensiveness and a re-distribution or increase of purchasing power, combined with a devotion, on the part of an élite, to Art, the world will be as good as anyone could require, then you must expect human beings to become more and more vaporous. This is exactly what we find of the society which Mr. Pound puts in Hell, in his *Draft of XXX Cantos.* It consists (I may have overlooked one or two species) of politicians, profiteers, financiers, newspaper proprietors and their hired men, *agents provocateurs,* Calvin, St. Clement of Alexandria, the English, vice-crusaders, liars, the stupid, pedants, preachers, those who do not believe in Social Credit, bishops, lady golfers, Fabians, conservatives and imperialists; and all "those who have set money-lust

before the pleasures of the senses." It is, in its way, an admirable Hell, "without dignity, without tragedy."[92] At first sight the variety of types—for these are types, and not individuals—may be a little confusing; but I think it becomes a little more intelligible if we see at work three principles, (1) the aesthetic, (2) the humanitarian, (3) the Protestant. And I find one considerable objection to a Hell of this sort: that a Hell altogether without dignity implies a Heaven without dignity also. If you do not distinguish between individual responsibility and circumstances in Hell, between essential Evil and social accidents, then the Heaven (if any) implied will be equally trivial and accidental. Mr. Pound's Hell, for all its horrors, is a perfectly comfortable one for the modern mind to contemplate, and disturbing to no one's complacency: it is a Hell for the *other people,*[93] the people we read about in the newspapers, not for oneself and one's friends.*

*Consult *Time and Western Man* by Wyndham Lewis.

Eliot's footnote turned from one friend of his, Pound, to another, Wyndham Lewis. Not that Dante was afraid to put his friends as well as his enemies in Hell.

Prior to *Little Gidding,* there is Eliot on Pound in 1918 and (doubly) in 1934. Subsequent to *Little Gidding,* there is Eliot in 1950 on "What Dante Means to Me." I have to admit at once that there is no explicit mention of Pound in this talk of Eliot's. But I think that by such a date it might have been difficult for Eliot, however fully attentive to Dante he was being, not to have the necessarily repeated word "canto" colored by *The Cantos.* I even admit that I like to imagine a typo, *tezra rima.* But genuinely germane, I believe, to the matter of any pivotal moment in distinguishing the

Inferno from Purgatory is Eliot's valuably unsettling and unsettled movement hereabouts. "Twenty years after writing *The Waste Land*, I wrote, in *Little Gidding*, a passage which is intended to be the nearest equivalent to a canto of the Inferno or the Purgatorio, in style as well as content, that I could achieve. The intention, of course, was the same as with my allusions to Dante in *The Waste Land*: to present to the mind of the reader a parallel, by means of contrast, between the Inferno and the Purgatorio, which Dante visited and a hallucinated scene after an air-raid." "The nearest equivalent to a canto of the Inferno or the Purgatorio": and yet "or" might perhaps have been *and*, since even if the exact pivotal moment may be "Both intimate and unidentifiable," Eliot's canto announces its residing in two of the three worlds. Arnaut is known by Dante to be in Purgatory, not in the Inferno. Is Brunetto (within this equivalent to a canto) known by Eliot to be assuredly in the Inferno, not in Purgatory?

Eliot's intention ("of course," with masterly reassurance from him) was "to present to the mind of the reader a parallel, by means of contrast, between the Inferno and the Purgatorio, which Dante visited and a hallucinated scene after an air-raid." The syntax of this may have its brief velleity, for Eliot's phrasing "a parallel, by means of contrast, between the Inferno and the Purgatorio" must make it seem for a moment as though the parallel/contrast is between the Inferno and the Purgatorio; yet once the sentence fully unrolls, the parallel/contrast is seen to be between (a) the Inferno-and-the-Purgatorio and (b) the hallucinated scene after an air-raid. This is compounded by Eliot's not having a comma after "Dante visited," and (to the same effect) his having one after "Purgatorio," so that the antithesis is not altogether clarified, intriguingly.[94]

So that when these various elements, infernal and purgatorial, are put together, a coloring may attend upon a remarkable comment of Eliot's. We learn from Helen Gardner that John Hayward had queried the disappearance (by name, that is) of Ser Brunetto. "Eliot replied that this was necessary because of the change he had made in the speech of the 'dead master.'" He gave two reasons: "The first is that the visionary figure has now become somewhat more definite and will no doubt be identified by some readers with Yeats though I do not mean anything so precise as that. However, I do not wish to take the responsibility of putting Yeats or anybody else into Hell and I do not want to impute to him the particular vice which took Brunetto there. Secondly, although the reference to that Canto is intended to be explicit, I wished the effect of the whole to be Purgatorial which is much more appropriate."[95] ("The particular vice which took Brunetto there": sodomy. Eric Griffiths and Matthew Reynolds supply the crucial information that "Only Dante supplies the information that he was a homosexual.")[96]

Exactly what weight should we give to "or anybody else" within Eliot's saying that "I do not wish to take the responsibility of putting Yeats or anybody else into Hell"? Does "anybody else" include Brunetto? Dante may indeed have taken the responsibility of putting Brunetto in Hell. Eliot may have wished, even if he did not judge, otherwise. For the immediate sequence of his thinking is clear: "Secondly, although the reference to that Canto is intended to be explicit, I wished the effect of the whole to be Purgatorial which is much more appropriate." If the reference to Canto XV of the Inferno is intended to be explicit (and yes, it is), can the effect *of the whole* be Purgatorial? Well, it can, because "of the whole" is a designedly loose phrase, and may mean "taken as a whole, irrespective of the effect of any particular parts within it." Nevertheless, some small escape route is left open by such phrasing, and if the effect of the whole, in the stronger sense (as who should say "the effect of *the whole*"), is Purgatorial, then the lines about Brunetto will be affected and their judgment to some degree alleviated.

"Between two worlds become much like each other": these are the worlds of the living and the dead, yes, but the thought may be colored by the ways in which the worlds of the afterworld may become much like each other. In manuscript this had been "become so like each other." Gardner speaks of "the insignificant change of 'so like' to 'much like.'"[97] But "so like" is not so like "much like" as to be an insignificant change. Another variant, "Between two states so much alike each other," has an odd redundancy but might serve to remind us that although it is true that the state of being dead differs from that of being alive, the word *state* is one that Eliot had italicized and then twice repeated: "It reminds us that Hell is not a place but a *state:* that man is damned or blessed in the creatures of his imagination as well as in men who have actually lived; and that Hell, though a state, is a state which can only be thought of, and perhaps only experienced, by the projection of sensory images."[98]

> From this distance the many barbed divisions
> between Purgatory and Hell appear blurred.
>
> (Geoffrey Hill, *The Orchards of Syon* LVII)

That the divisions between Purgatory and Hell may even have appeared blurred, on occasion, to Eliot is perhaps suggested not only by the shifting sequence but also by his contemplating (in manuscript) the word "dismissal" at the end of the Dantesque section, when—within the lines as he finally gave them—Brunetto has been succeeded by Arnaut Daniel. "He turned away, and in the autumn weather": this had been "He turned away with his motion of dismissal," and then "with his movement of dismissal." "This *surprise,* at its highest, could by nothing be better illustrated than by the final lines with which Dante dismisses the damned master whom he loves and respects."[99]

It is possible that Eliot's feelings in *Little Gidding* II came to him as something of a surprise. "Although the reference to that Canto [XV, Brunetto] is intended to be explicit, I wish the effect of the whole to be Purgatorial which is much more appropriate": might this be more appropriate, too, for Brunetto, "so admirable a soul," "a loved master"? I hear at least an aching in the thought of "the damned master whom he loves and respects." Eliot always took to heart his own words as well as those of others. With a chastening sense of our responsibility for what we conceive, he had said in 1929 that Dante reminds us "that man is damned or blessed in the creatures of his imagination as well as in men who have actually lived."[100]

The question has even been raised as to whether Dante is damned or blessed in his assigning of the creatures of his imagination. There is a most challenging letter by Anthony Hecht to R. W. B. Lewis (26 August 2001), thanking him for his "brilliant and lively life of Dante":

> I was brought up in the old school of hermeneutics, the four-fold reading of Dante as of scripture, and yours is a refreshing liberation from the undeviating solemnity of that school. But your biographical approach, enchanting as it is, raises its own problems. I was struck by this especially in your account of Brunetto Latini (your pages 38–9). If Brunetto was really not homosexual; if he is placed by Dante in Hell with the sodomites simply because Dante feels a sense of rivalry and competitiveness with him, Dante, then,

by your own thesis that the Comedy is an exercise in self-knowledge and self-confrontation, must have realized that he was himself profoundly guilty of one of the seven deadly sins. Moreover, Dante's placement of Brunetto cannot be likened to Ezra Pound's assignment of all those he despises (with a good number of Jews among them) to some inferno of his own making, since Pound clearly does not believe in his own Hell, and is merely being venomous, whereas Dante has the whole orthodoxy of the Church, the Summa Theologica, canon law, the "works" behind his condemnation. To put someone in Hell who does not belong there must surely be a sinful act. Even to put someone in the wrong circle of Hell is wicked, if you believe, and want your readers to believe, that the whole order of the Cosmos justifies eternal punishments as meted out by this design.

In a further letter to Lewis (4 March 2002), Hecht returned to this, in discussing the "familiar compound ghost" in *Little Gidding* II: "As you can see, Eliot seems to have been far more scrupulous about consigning people to Hell than Dante was in regard to Brunetto, if your surmise is right."

Back to Pound, then, and to the triangle that is Pound and Eliot and Dante's Hell. Since it would be of particular service to me if a Pound instance to which I shall now turn were to have its link with Dante's Brunetto, I must be wary of imagining things. But I believe that it is Pound who is doing the imagining when various elements come together in 1936 to form the opening lines of his Canto XLVI:

> And if you will say that this tale teaches . . .
> a lesson, or that the Reverend Eliot

has found a more natural language . . . you who think you
will

get through hell in a hurry . . .[101]

(Pound's ellipses have a calculatedly perverse effect upon the thought of "in a hurry," since an ellipsis has a way of musing; there is a bizarre play of dot dot dot against those extended spacings in the last line.)

For a start, near the beginning, Eliot is there by name, emphasized by his being put in orders, collared. Then there is the mischievous solecism that dubs him "the Reverend Eliot." One can imagine Eliot wincing—if he *must* be bantered as the Reverend, do at least follow not the American but the English practice, for it was the Church of England that Eliot had entered: the Reverend Thomas Eliot, or the Reverend Mr. Eliot, but never, never "the Reverend Eliot." Mr. Eliot's Sunday Morning Service would not, in England, be conducted by someone called the Reverend Eliot. In "Mr Eliot's Solid Merit" (1934), Pound had been moderately sly: "During the past 20 years the chief or average complaint against the almost reverend Eliot has been that he exaggerated his moderations."[102]

One piece of evidence for the appreciative belief that "the Reverend Eliot / has found a more natural language," or rather that he did so a few years after Pound expressed his skepticism, would be Eliot's Dantesque lines, lines which speak (in a verse draft) of "the life for language" and (in a prose draft) of "the battle of language" and finally (as published) of "last year's language."[103]

And Dante? He it was who had imagined in Brunetto a man whose "tale teaches" still (even there, in the Inferno), a teacher associated—in his way—with the thought that one might get through hell in a hurry. Or, in Pound's spacing and pacing,

> you who think you will
>
> get through hell in a hurry . . .

"Then he turned back, and seemed like one of those who run for the green cloth at Verona through the open field; and of them he seemed like him who wins, and not like him who loses." Pound in 1936 well knew Eliot's book on Dante (1929), which was reprinted in full within *Selected Essays* (1932). Pound's lines are earlier than the Dantesque section of *Little Gidding,* and Eliot's lines in 1942 may include some memory of Pound's having brought together in Canto XLVI a brightly lit reference to him (Eliot), alongside what looks like a darkly hatched allusion to Brunetto and to running through hell: "get through hell in a hurry." (Carroll F. Terrell glosses this: "Because Pound sees hell as the locus of greed, Geryon, and usury as the dominating thrust of Western civilization, he does not believe anyone will traverse it quickly"; this general reflection would not conflict with a thought of Brunetto, given the Reverend Mr. Eliot's thoughts of Brunetto.)[104]

> Between three districts whence the smoke arose
> I met one walking, loitering and hurried.

If, paradoxically, not only hurried but loitering ("hurried and yet unhurried" in manuscript),[105] then unlikely to be able to "get through hell in a hurry."

Getting through hell in a hurry would be one thing; getting out of hell, if only into Purgatory, would be something else, something not to be achieved in a hurry. Lowell on Dante:

> his Ser Brunetto ran through hell like one
> who ran for the green cloth through the green fields

Lowell, like Eliot, pondered Dante's assignings or consignings in the afterlife, and created an inspired, startling, and inaccurate mercy in the *Commedia:* "Pope Boniface VIII is its devil, though paradoxically consigned to Purgatory, not Hell."[106]

Pound came to ask mercy. Cryptically and self-protectively enough, but still.

> Many errors,
>
> > a little rightness,
>
> to excuse his hell
>
> > and my paradiso.
>
> (Canto CXVI, 1962)

His hell, my paradiso. But then whose purgatory?

"Charity I have had sometimes" (Canto CXVI, again). "I have had" as bestowed by Pound or upon him?

Two years later, Pound bestowed a gift upon Lowell, upon Dante, upon us all, and upon himself, by recording Lowell's translation of the Brunetto Latini episode.[107] The date was 27 September 1964, a few months before Eliot died (4 January 1965). Lowell's lines were to appear in *Near the Ocean* (1967).

It should be hard for anyone, and has proved impossible for me, to hear Pound's recorded uttering of the great lines that are greatly translated anew by Lowell and refuse all mercy to Pound. There is in Pound's voice such agèd pain, such patience, and such self-suppression as to bring to us some such complication of due feelings as are evoked by Dante in contemplating Brunetto, so admirable a soul, and so perverse, the damned master (whether damned or not in the eternal end) whom Lowell loves and respects. Pound's self-condemnation to silence or all-but-silence had yet left him free to utter this tribute, at once his to Dante and Lowell, and Lowell's to

Dante, and Dante's to Brunetto. At two moments in the reading, this old man—he was about to turn seventy-nine—slips into a word that has its erroneous aptness: into *learning,* for Lowell's "lamenting," and into *steps* for "star." There is immense fatigue, and there is indomitability. Brunetto is here, and his creator Dante, and Dante's re-creator Lowell, and now Pound, the re-creator of Lowell. All forming and re-forming a familiar compound ghost that had been (as both Lowell and Pound knew) the especial re-creation of—of and by—Eliot. "Are you here Ser Brunetto?" "What! are *you* here?"

> So I assumed a double part, and cried
> And heard another's voice cry: "What! are *you* here?"

So Eliot had assumed a double part, and then not only his and the ghost's, but his and Dante's, a triple part or more. So Pound assumed a double part, not only his and Brunetto's, but his and Dante's, and certainly his and Lowell's, a triple part and more, for does not Eliot take part, too?

> And last, the rending pain of re-enactment
> Of all that you have done, and been;

—of which Eliot wrote to John Hayward: "I want to preserve the association of 'enact'—to take the part of oneself on a stage for oneself as the audience."[108]

Dante's lines are full of piety, of many kinds. The lineage that is fatherly and filial is itself then something that is to be heard again when Lowell's lines are uttered by Pound, a ghostly father of his. Griffiths and Reynolds have pointed out that "only Virgil and Brunetto Latini address Dante as 'son' in hell (the endearment is repeated in the Italian where Lowell repeats it at line 36)," and

they have brought home Lowell's bringing of this home: the third
occurrence ("'O Son'") in Lowell is not in Dante at this point. These
are the particular lines from Lowell's "Brunetto Latini" that Pound
voiced:

"are you here Ser Brunetto?"
He answered, "Do not be displeased, my Son,
if Brunetto Latini turn and walk a little
downward with you, and lets this herd pass on."
Then I, "I'll go with you, or we can sit
here talking as we used to in the past,
if you desire it, and my guide permit."
"O Son," he answered, "anyone who stands
still a moment will lie here a hundred years,
helpless to brush the sparks off with his hands.
Move on, I'll follow. Soon enough I must
rejoin my little group of friends who walk
with me lamenting their eternal lust."
Then since I dared not leave my bank and move
over the flames of his low path, I bent
my head to walk with reverence and love.
Then he, "What brings you here before your day?
Is it by accident, or Providence?
Who is this man who guides you on your way?"
I answered, "In the world that lies serene
and shining over us, I lost my path,
even before the first young leaves turned green.
Yesterday morning when my steps had come
full circle, this man appeared. He turned me round,
and now he guides me on my journey home."

ROBERT LOWELL

•

"O Son," said he, "if you pursue your star,
you cannot fail to reach the glorious harbor.
And if the beautiful world, less sinister,
had let me live a little longer, I too
might have sustained your work and brought you comfort,
seeing how heaven has befriended you.["]

Pound (who himself had been forced reluctantly to acknowledge, "I lost my path") had yet been Lowell's guide, had sustained his work, and had befriended him—more, was doing so in the very instance of uttering and recording Lowell's lines.

Lowell wrote gratefully to Pound:

March 8, 1966

Dear Ezra:

Olga was kind enough to send me a tape of your reading of my "Brunetto." I must say your voice stays in my head constantly and that the lines really sound like Dante, like you and Dante, so much that I now think of them as yours. I've been doing a little piece on Ford's last poems, and you have been much in mind—I think of you both as comrades and travellers on the long shining road from Provence to pre-War London.

I follow the news of you and read your rare public statements. I think you rather stand alone in facing those purgatorial moments we all face and don't, the good and ill of our lives—you do it with glorious humor and sorrow. Hope to get to Italy sometime and renew the years with you.

Affectionately,

Cal

P.S. The Dante took me about a month of hard work. Some-

time in some pause in my life and time, I'd like to do ten or
so more. May the gods go with you and all your family![109]

Dante's voice had become Lowell's, and then had become Pound's.
Pound is understood by Lowell to have been in Purgatory; Bru-
netto is understood to have been in the Inferno, but Lowell—like
Eliot?—renders the lines as though he wished "the effect of the
whole to be Purgatorial which is much more appropriate." And
when Lowell thinks of Pound and Ford Madox Ford "as comrades
and travellers on the long shining road from Provence to pre-War
London," I recall Eliot's letter to John Hayward with its two con-
secutive sentences about *Little Gidding* II: "I want something hold-
ing good for the past also—something as universal as Dante's old
tailor threading his needle. On the other hand, any references to
the reverberes [French streetlamps] will take the reader directly to
pre-war London."[110] For Provence too is heard in *Little Gidding* II, the
voice of Arnaut Daniel as well as of Brunetto.

But more directly pertinent to Lowell's letter is one of Pound's
"rare public statements," of which Lowell was certainly aware, the
tribute to Eliot upon his death in 1965, the year that intervened be-
tween the recording and the letter from Lowell. It was within this
public statement of homage and grief (public and private both) that
Pound recalled the time when he "went from Excideuil to meet a
rucksacked Eliot. Days of walking—conversation? literary?"

Am I to write "about" the poet Thomas Stearns Eliot? or my
friend "the Possum"? Let him rest in peace. I can only repeat,
but with the urgency of 50 years ago: READ HIM.

E.P.

["]Give
me no pity. Read my *Tesoro*. In

my book, my treasure, I am still alive."

Then he turned back, and he seemed one of those
who run for the green cloth through the green field
at Verona . . . and seemed more like the one
who wins the roll of cloth than those who lose.

Brunetto's closing utterance, dismissing us, and then his self-
dismissal, and then his dismissal by Dante.

"READ HIM." In 1923, the woman whom Eliot loved then, and
whom in the end he came to dismiss (when at last the death of
Vivien Eliot released him into the possibility of marrying her), had
been given by him a copy of *Ara Vos Prec,* inscribed:

For Emily Hale
   with the author's
      humble compliments.
        T.S. Eliot
5. ix. 23.
    SIETI RACOMMENDATO
        IL MIO TESORO
     NELLO QUAL VIVO ANCOR
      E NON PIÙ CHIEGGIO.
    POI SI REVOLSE.[111]

Then (decades later) he turned back, and turned away. More like
the one who wins than those who lose? It is bitter to have loved and
lost. For all concerned.

But read their treasures. Read Eliot and Pound. Read Geoffrey
Hill, Anthony Hecht, and Robert Lowell, whether or not under the
sign of Eliot and Pound.

Notes

CHAPTER 1. GEOFFREY HILL

1. Blake's Marginalia in a copy of Joshua Reynolds's *Works* (1798); see G. E. Bentley, Jr., *The Stranger from Paradise* (2001), pp. 52–53.
2. Note by an editor: Geoffrey Keynes, *The Complete Writings of William Blake* (1957), p. 157; note by a later editor: *The Early Illuminated Books,* ed. Morris Eaves, Robert N. Essick, and Joseph Viscomi (1993), p. 219.
3. *The Guardian,* 26 February 2005.
4. *Scenes from Comus* is divided into three sections: (1) "The Argument of the Masque," which consists of poems numbered 1 to 20; (2) "Courtly Masquing Dances," with poems numbered 1 to 80; and (3) "A Description of the Antimasque," with poems numbered 1 to 20. Further textual citations will either be to the named section and poem number or to the section and poem number.
5. "Geoffrey Hill: At-one-ment" (1984), in Christopher Ricks, *The Force of Poetry* (1984), pp. 319–55.

6. *Flaubert, Joyce and Beckett: The Stoic Comedians* (1964), p. 39.
7. "Geoffrey Hill: 'The Tongue's Atrocities'" (1978), in Ricks, *Force of Poetry*, pp. 285–318.
8. "Eros in F. H. Bradley and T. S. Eliot," in Geoffrey Hill, *Collected Critical Writings*, ed. Kenneth Haynes (2008), p. 550.
9. "The Style of the Master" (1948), in *Argufying* (1987), ed. John Haffenden, p. 361.
10. *Canaan* (1996), Hill's ellipsis.
11. "Tradition and the Individual Talent" (1919), in T. S. Eliot, *Selected Essays* (1932; 1951 ed.), p. 16. Hill quotes this in "Word Value in F. H. Bradley and T. S. Eliot," in Hill, *Collected Critical Writings*, p. 541.
12. See Helen Gardner, *The Composition of "Four Quartets"* (1978), p. 174.
13. "An Interview with Frederick Seidel" (1961), in Robert Lowell, *Collected Prose* (1987), p. 265.
14. *After Strange Gods* (1934), p. 43.
15. "Eros in Bradley and Eliot," p. 553.
16. "Word Value in Bradley and Eliot," p. 535.
17. *Encounter* (July–August 1984).
18. "Poetry as 'Menace' and 'Atonement'" (1977), in Geoffrey Hill, *The Lords of Limit* (1984), p. 3, and Hill, *Collected Critical Writings*, p. 4.
19. *The Threepenny Review* (Spring 2004).
20. *The Nation* (15 January 1944).
21. *Stand* 13, no. 1 (n.d. [1971?]).
22. *All What Jazz* (1970; 1985 ed.), p. 27.
23. This appeared only on the American edition (Counterpoint, 2000); the English jacket copy (Penguin, 2001) makes different points.
24. Preface to Harry Crosby, *Transit of Venus* (1931).
25. Eliot on Pound (1946, with a 1950 postscript), in *An Examination of Ezra Pound*, ed. Peter Russell (1950), p. 25, reprinted in an issue of *Agenda* (Autumn–Winter, 1985–86), where the names that move down the cover are Geoffrey Hill, Ezra Pound, and T. S. Eliot.
26. *The Criterion* 16 (1937): 667.
27. A lecture in Dublin (1936), published in *Southern Review* (Autumn

1985) and then in *T. S. Eliot: Essays from the "Southern Review,"* ed.
James Olney (1988), as "Tradition and the Practice of Poetry," p. 13.
28. *Centuries of Meditation*. It owes its currency to C. S. Lewis, who used it
as the epigraph to chapter 9 of *A Preface to "Paradise Lost"* (1942).
29. "Yeats" (1940), in T. S. Eliot, *On Poetry and Poets* (1957), p. 252.
30. Acceptance speech for the T. S. Eliot Prize, *Image: A Journal of the Arts
and Religion* 28 (Fall 2000): 72–77.
31. I wrote on how much the young Hill astonishingly learnt from Eliot
in *The Force of Poetry*, pp. 304–11, 330–31, 342–46.
32. *The Athenaeum* (11 April 1919).
33. *The Egoist* 4 (1917): 151.
34. *The Criterion* 1 (1923): 421.
35. "Christopher Marlowe" (1919), in Eliot, *Selected Essays*, p. 123.
36. Bruce Bairnsfather (1888–1959), a soldier and an artist, was the creator
of the "Old Bill" cartoons of the Great War. For Hill's respect for
Bairnsfather's art (and his dissent from a remark by Wilfred Owen
that "the men are just as Bairnsfather has them—expressionless
lumps"), see "Tacit Pledges," in Hill, *Collected Critical Writings*, pp.
711–12, a note to p. 420.
37. Similarly, "this was not farce" (poem 34), and "what was I think-
ing— / Bergmanesque tragic farce?" (poem 69).
38. Eliot wrote on Isaac Rosenberg, briefly and without carrying convic-
tion, in "A Commentary," *The Criterion* 14 (July 1935): 611.
39. Hill on *Speech! Speech!* in *Poetry Book Society Bulletin* (Winter 2001).
40. See Ronald Schuchard, *Eliot's Dark Angel* (1999), chaps. 4 and 5; David
Chinitz, *T. S. Eliot and the Cultural Divide* (2003); John M. Lyon,
"'What Are You Incinerating?': Geoffrey Hill and Popular Culture,"
English 54, no. 209 (Summer 2005): 85–98.
41. I have written about this in my *T. S. Eliot and Prejudice* (1988), pp.
204–7.
42. "Geoffrey Hill: At-one-ment," p. 320.
43. "Word Value in Bradley and Eliot," p. 535.
44. Ibid., p. 545.

45. Ibid., p. 544.
46. *English Literature in Our Time and the University* (1969), p. 102.
47. "Eros in Bradley and Eliot," p. 560.
48. *English Literature in Our Time,* p. 122.
49. "Word Value in Bradley and Eliot," pp. 535, 538; "Eros in Bradley and Eliot," p. 556.
50. "Poetry as 'Menace and 'Atonement,'" in Hill, *Collected Critical Writings,* pp. 10–11.
51. "Word Value in Bradley and Eliot," p. 534.
52. *Humanism and Poetry in the Early Tudor Period* (1959), pp. 203–21, 246–48.
53. "Word Value in Bradley and Eliot," p. 543.
54. "Il Cortegiano: F. T. Prince's Poems (1938)," *PN Review* (September–October 2002).
55. "Word Value in Bradley and Eliot," p. 544.
56. *The Threepenny Review* (Spring 2004).
57. *Cambridge Quarterly* 26, no. 3 (1997): 263–69.
58. *The All-Sustaining Air* (2007), p. 172, O'Neill's ellipsis.
59. I have a chapter on tone in *T. S. Eliot and Prejudice.*
60. Hill's review of Eliot's Clark Lectures (1926; published as *The Varieties of Metaphysical Poetry,* ed. Ronald Schuchard, 1993) was published in *Agenda* (Summer 1996) and subsequently formed part of *Style and Faith* (2003; p. 156, where it reads, "which assuaged"); it is also re-printed in Hill, *Collected Critical Writings,* p. 377.
61. *Style and Faith,* pp. 156–57, and *Collected Critical Writings,* pp. 377–78.
62. "Word Value in Bradley and Eliot," pp. 540–41.
63. Eric Griffiths drew my attention to this felicity of give and take.
64. "Eros in Bradley and Eliot," pp. 558, 555.
65. *Little Review* 5 (1918): 46, originally published in *The Egoist* (January 1918).
66. *After Strange Gods,* p. 60.
67. "Philip Massinger" (1920), in Eliot, *Selected Essays,* p. 208.
68. "Eros in Bradley and Eliot," p. 562.
69. *New Statesman and Nation* (9 December 1939); *The Times,* 17 May 1945;

The Listener, 19 December 1946; the *Standard Edition* of Charles Williams (1947), my ellipsis.

70. "Eros in Bradley and Eliot," p. 562.

71. Ibid., pp. 554, 552.

72. Gardner, *Composition of "Four Quartets,"* p. 191.

73. Here I draw on my *T. S. Eliot and Prejudice,* p. 213.

74. "A Postscript on Modern Poetics," in Hill, *Collected Critical Writings,* p. 573.

75. *Times Literary Supplement,* 5 April 1928 and 22 July 1929, discussed in T. S. Eliot, *Inventions of the March Hare,* ed. Christopher Ricks (1996), p. xxviii.

76. "What Devil Has Got into John Ransom?" in Hill, *Collected Critical Writings,* pp. 132, 141, 145.

77. The title poem of the volume *A Treatise of Civil Power* (2005) was dropped from the 2007 edition, and some sections of it were then re-formed as new short poems.

78. "Translating Value," in Hill, *Style and Faith,* pp. 158–59, reprinted in Hill, *Collected Critical Writings,* p. 379, omitting "which Eliot had acutely diagnosed in 1920."

79. "Dividing Legacies," in Hill, *Style and Faith,* pp. 203–4, reprinted in Hill, *Collected Critical Writings,* pp. 700–701. In *Collected Critical Writings,* the effect is markedly different; in *Style and Faith,* the book proper comes to an end but is immediately followed by the notes that conclude with the foot-long footnote, whereas in *Collected Critical Writings,* after the last page of *Style and Faith* (now p. 379) there is a leap of more than three hundred pages (to p. 700) to reach the final note of triumph.

80. My appreciation of Larkin abuts the two of Hill in *The Force of Poetry.* I have a further praise of Larkin's poetry in *Dylan's Visions of Sin* (2003), pp. 13–15, and of his prose in *Reviewery* (2001), pp. 201–9.

81. With no more than a cumulative plausibility (if that): Larkin, a field-glass; Hill, a field. Larkin, At Grass; Hill, at times.

82. *Image* (Fall 2000): 73.

83. "London Letter," *The Dial,* 72 (1922): 512.

84. *Image* (Fall 2000): 75.

85. Pound's letter is probably of 24 January 1922 (not 24 December 1921) and was published in *The Letters of Ezra Pound, 1907-1941*, ed. D. D. Paige (1950), p. 169; it was reprinted in *The Letters of T. S. Eliot, Volume 1, 1898-1922*, ed. Valerie Eliot (1988), pp. 497–98. A revised edition of the first volume of Eliot's letters was published by Faber and Faber in 2009. I have removed the needless editorial addition of "[a]" ("without [a] break") since Pound's "without break" is swift and clear; I have also corrected, from the typescript letter, "English" to "Englisch" (with thanks to Jim McCue). The first ellipsis ("from April . . . to") is Pound's, the second is mine.

86. Eliot's letter is probably of 26, not 24, January 1922, published in *Letters of Eliot, Volume 1*, p. 504.

87. *Examination of Pound*, p. 29.

88. "Ulysses" (1922), in *The Literary Essays of Ezra Pound*, ed. T. S. Eliot (1954), p. 406.

89. "Our Word Is Our Bond" (1983), in Hill, *Collected Critical Writings*, pp. 146–47.

90. Pound set his poem in italics.

91. *The Enemy's Country: Words, Contexture, and Other Circumstances of Language* (1991), p. 83, reprinted in Hill, *Collected Critical Writings*, p. 243.

92. *Enemy's Country*, 87–88, reprinted in Hill, *Collected Critical Writings*, p. 247.

93. *Enemy's Country*, 97–98, reprinted in Hill, *Collected Critical Writings*, p. 255, my ellipsis.

94. The title poem of *A Treatise of Civil Power* (2005), dropped in 2007, was in a sense replaced by "A Précis or Memorandum of Civil Power," a very different undertaking.

95. The first line was famously created from a textual error not of Eliot's making, the reading of a line in *The Changeling* as "I am that of your blood . . ." instead of the correct "I that am of your blood . . ." The mistaken text is quoted by Eliot in his persuasively amazing essay on Middleton.

96. "Poetry as 'Menace' and 'Atonement,'" in Hill, *Collected Critical Writ-*

ings, p. 17, quoting from "Thomas Middleton" (1927), in Eliot, *Selected Essays,* p. 163.

97. "The Three Voices of Poetry" (1953), in Eliot, *On Poetry and Poets,* p. 93.

98. "*Clarissa*] A new Character introduced in the subsequent Editions, to open more clearly the MORAL of the Poem, in a parody of the speech of Sarpedon to Glaucus in Homer" (Pope).

99. "Eros in Bradley and Eliot," p. 563.

100. Interview with Hill, *Paris Review* (Spring 2000): 284–85, on "the harshest critics of *The Triumph of Love.*" On resentment and on what should be said against and for it, see the deeply patient and illuminating book by Charles Griswold, *Forgiveness: A Philosophical Exploration* (2007).

101. "T. S. Eliot," in E. M. Forster, *Abinger Harvest* (1936), p. 90.

CHAPTER 2. ANTHONY HECHT

1. "Dante" (1929), in T. S. Eliot, *Selected Essays* (1932; 1951 ed.), p. 248.

2. Introduction to *Ezra Pound: Selected Poems* (1928), p. xv.

3. Interview with Hecht, *Paris Review* 108 (Fall 1988): 197.

4. See Hecht's letter to Ronald B. Schwartz (9 July 1997), sent as a contribution to Schwartz's *For the Love of Books* (1999).

5. *Anthony Hecht in Conversation with Philip Hoy* (1999), p. 42. The interview is collected in *Seven American Poets in Conversation* (2008).

6. *The Venetian Vespers* (1979).

7. *Hecht in Conversation with Philip Hoy,* p. 65, my ellipsis.

8. See the informative responsive essay on the poem by John Frederick Nims, "'The Venetian Vespers': Drenched in Fine Particulars," in *The Burdens of Formality: Essays on the Poetry of Anthony Hecht,* ed. Sydney Lea (1989), pp. 120–41.

9. The likeness is noted by Nims, ibid., p. 127.

10. Here are some alignments of Hecht with Eliot that are further to those commented on in the body of this book. From *A Summoning of Stones* (1954): Hecht, "The Song of the Beasts," and Eliot, "Marina"; "Christmas Is Coming" and "The Hollow Men"; "A Roman Holiday"

and *The Waste Land* V; "A Lesson from the Master" and "Preludes." From *The Hard Hours* (1967): "The Vow" and "Sweeney Among the Nightingales" as well as *The Waste Land* IV. From *Millions of Strange Shadows* (1977): "Green: An Epistle" and *Little Gidding* II; "Exile" and "Journey of the Magi"; "The Odds" and *East Coker* IV. From *The Venetian Vespers* (1979): "The Short End" and "Burbank with a Baedeker: Bleistein with a Cigar"; "The Venetian Vespers" and *Little Gidding* IV. From *The Transparent Man* (1990): "Antapodosis" and "The Boston Evening Transcript"; "Envoi" and "Gerontion" as well as "Sweeney Among the Nightingales"; "Poem Without Anybody" and "Gerontion." From *Flight Among the Tombs* (1996): "Death the Film Director" and "Sweeney Erect." From *The Darkness and the Light* (2001): "Late Afternoon: The Onslaught of Love" and "Marina"; "Poppy" and "Marina"; "The Road to Damascus" and "Journey of the Magi" as well as "A Song for Simeon."

11. "'Thought' and Emotional Quality," *Scrutiny* 13 (1945): 59, collected in F. R. Leavis, *The Living Principle* (1975).

12. In Hecht, *The Transparent Man.*

13. *Hecht in Conversation with Philip Hoy*, p. 42, my ellipsis.

14. William Matthews, "Horatian Hecht," in Lea, *Burdens of Formality,* p. 148.

15. Ashley Brown, "The Poetry of Anthony Hecht," ibid., p. 24.

16. Allusion as often delighting in such enactments of its own nature is the subject of much of my book *Allusion to the Poets* (2002); I draw here on my review of Erving Goffman (collected in *Reviewery,* 2002).

17. *Hecht in Conversation with Philip Hoy*, p. 61, my ellipsis.

18. In Hecht, *The Transparent Man.*

19. Reported by Richard Woodhouse and reproduced in *The Keats Circle,* ed. Hyder Edward Rollins (2nd ed., 1965), vol. 1, p. 129; here I have expanded the contractions and elided the cancelled readings.

20. Keats to B. R. Haydon, 11 May 1817, in *The Letters of John Keats, 1814–1821,* ed. Hyder Edward Rollins (1958), vol. 1, p. 142.

21. On *between,* see my *T. S. Eliot and Prejudice* (1988), pp. 212–14.

22. *7 Greeks* (1980; 1995 ed.), p. 79. Davenport uses brackets to indicate the fragmentary nature of Sappho's lines.

23. In Hecht, *A Summoning of Stones.*

24. In Hecht, *The Darkness and the Light.*

25. *The Waste Land* II.

26. *Seven Types of Ambiguity,* pp. 77–78; the first ellipsis ("air . . .") is Empson's, the second is mine. On Eliot and the reading *carven,* see *The T. S. Eliot Collection of the University of Texas at Austin,* compiled by Alexander Sackton (1975), p. 117, which reproduces Eliot's autograph correction in the first English edition of *The Waste Land* (1923): "coloured" (wrongly repeated from the preceding line) being corrected not to "carvèd" but to "carven." See also James Smith, "A Note on the Text of *The Waste Land*" (*Transactions of the Cambridge Bibliographical Society* 6 [1973]: 131–33). Perhaps Eliot's decision to stay, after all, with "carved" (the reading in the typescript drafts), subsequently "carvèd," was influenced by his repeated marshaling of *-ed.*

27. The text of the poem in a letter of 27 February 1998 to William Maxwell had "Swirled," not "Swiveled," the latter being one of several telling improvements made upon publication. "This poem, as of now untitled, came out of a story of Chekhov's called, in the rather elderly edition that I own, 'The Boys.'" The title "A Certain Slant" was then in the offing only.

28. In Hecht, *The Transparent Man.*

29. *Hecht in Conversation with Philip Hoy,* pp. 91–92.

30. *Yorkshire Post,* reprinted in *The Bed Post: A Miscellany of the "Yorkshire Post"* (1962), ed. Kenneth Young, pp. 43–44.

31. *Hecht in Conversation with Philip Hoy,* p. 72.

32. "Apprehensions," in Hecht, *Millions of Strange Shadows.*

33. *Ash-Wednesday* V: "Against the Word the unstilled world still whirled." *East Coker* II: "Whirled in a vortex that shall bring / The world to that destructive fire." *Burnt Norton* III: "Whirled by the cold wind," "This twittering world," followed by five further uses of *world.*

34. In Hecht, *Millions of Strange Shadows.*

35. In Hecht, *The Hard Hours.*

36. *Four Quartets Read by the Author* (1947), with a thirteen-line sleeve note by Eliot; a reprint of the note was issued with the original H.M.V. recording (Donald Gallup, *T. S. Eliot: A Bibliography,* 1969, p. 361).

37. Letter to Ronald B. Schwartz (9 July 1997).

38. For a meticulous and moving account of Hecht's military service, see Geoffrey Lindsay, "Anthony Hecht, Private First Class," *Yale Review* 96 (July 2008): 1–26.

39. Letter to John Hollander (23 August 1984). Hecht wrote deeply considered letters about Eliot and anti-Semitism to Norman Williams (11 March 2003) and to Ronald Schuchard (27 April 2003).

40. "*The Merchant of Venice:* A Venture in Hermeneutics," a ninety-page essay or monograph within *Obbligati: Essays in Criticism* (1986), p. 168. Relatedly, see Anthony Hecht, *On the Laws of the Poetic Art* (1995), the Andrew W. Mellon Lectures in the Fine Arts, pp. 164–68.

41. I learn from Kenneth Haynes that the manuscript and the typescript of Canto XLV, as reproduced in Eva Hesse's *Ezra Pound: Usura-Cantos XLV und LI* (1985), have "CONTRA NATURA," which is incorrect, though it does bring about a rhyme with "usura." Some printings of the Cantos have the correction to "NATURAM," as in Hecht's quotation and as adopted here.

42. *Obbligati,* pp. 223–24.

43. *Merchant of Venice,* I.iii, II.iv, II.vi.

44. Canto 94, in Ezra Pound, *Section: Rock-Drill* (1955).

45. I am grateful, too (I cannot conceal), for his words about my *T. S. Eliot and Prejudice* in his conversation with Philip Hoy (p. 95).

46. *Parade of Ghosts:* had this not been the title of a book of poems (1976) by Hecht's brother Roger Hecht, it would have served Anthony Hecht well. "I've watched the welding of these ghosts which led, / Still lead me, God knows where," from Hecht's "Sonnet" in the *Bardian* (8 September 1942, when he was nineteen). Here follow some ghosts further to those adduced in this chapter. From *A Summoning of Stones:* "Signed with the famous scrawl of our most traveled ghost" ("La Condition Botanique"); "the cause / That ghosts return upon us to be fed" ("Hallowe'en"). From *The Hard Hours:* "ghostly creatures" ("Ostia

Antica"); "The pale ghost of a leaf / Haunts those uncanny softnesses" ("The Origin of Centaurs"); "If that ghost was a girl's, I swear to it" ("The Vow"). From *Millions of Strange Shadows:* "a ghost / Of foison" ("An Autumnal"); "like a little hovering ghost" ("A Birthday Poem"); "these dim, weathery ghosts" ("After the Rain"); "his ghostly role" ("'Gladness of the Best'"). From *The Venetian Vespers:* "their ghostly wreckage" ("The Short End"). From *The Transparent Man:* "Ghostly crepuscules" ("Antapodosis"); "poor generous ghost" ("In Memory of David Kalstone"). One consequence of Hecht's repudiation of fifteen poems from his first volume, *A Summoning of Stones,* is that these then appear as ghost poems within our evocations of his life and art. Earlier there is the *Kenyon Review* (Spring 1952) "Elegy": "Loom as a ghost unclearly, / all alien and apart". Ghosts in the French language are alien and apart from those in English. Hecht's translation from Baudelaire, "The Swan" (1961) — "I see what seem the ghosts of these royal barracks" — takes a sardonic liberty with "Je ne vois qu'en esprit tout ce camp de baraques." Hecht summons a ghost from "en esprit," and (perhaps) from *spectre/scepter* an intimation of what was originally unremarked, the royal.

47. In Hecht, *The Darkness and the Light.*

48. "For James Merrill: An Adieu," in Hecht, *Flight Among the Tombs.*

49. In Hecht, *The Darkness and the Light.*

50. See in particular Hecht, *On the Laws of the Poetic Art.*

51. In Hecht, *The Venetian Vespers.*

52. Hecht's poem "The Dover Bitch" has been both reveled in and reviled. Hecht wrote to Sandra McPherson (4 October 1992), "I have always admired the Arnold poem on which it is based, and yet I also felt a marked impatience with Arnold's way of making love into a form of redemption and substitution for any other form of transcendent experience. Putting that much weight on human fidelity in a love relationship is to burden it beyond the limits of any lightness or carefree spontaneity. It was to make love into something grimly solemn, like Victorian organ music, for which the word 'lugubrious' could have been coined. The title of my poem was suggested to me

by my friend, who at the time was also my colleague, Daniel Aaron. On the basis both of the poem and its title I have been accused of sexism, though when I wrote the poem I intended only to bring a spirit of levity and informality to the relations between men and women in the persons of Arnold's poem."

53. Often attributed to Herman Goering, these words were said by a storm trooper in a 1934 play by the Nazi writer Hanns Johst.

54. Hecht, letter to David Lehman, 15 December 1980.

55. In "Songs for the Air, or Several Attitudes About Breathing," a cloud had been "Bellowed into conspicuous ectoplasm. / It is a lake's ghost that goes voyaging" (*A Summoning of Stones*). The poem, which moves to "The jovial ghost to mimic and to ape," was not reprinted by Hecht, a ghost poem. "The Ghost in the Martini" has the young reprover remind the old pretender: "You only got where you are / By standing upon my ectoplasmic shoulders" (*Millions of Strange Shadows*).

56. In T. S. Eliot, *Inventions of the March Hare,* ed. Christopher Ricks (1996), pp. 52 (poem), 199–200 (notes).

57. Originally published in *A Summoning of Stones,* this unreprinted poem thereafter became a ghost poem.

58. *Hecht in Conversation with Philip Hoy,* p. 42. ("The lines . . . is . . . it": read, say, "The passage . . . is.")

59. Hecht in an interview, *Harvard Advocate* 107 (Fall 1973): 11.

60. "Poetry and Drama" (1951), in T. S. Eliot, *On Poetry and Poets* (1957), pp. 84–85; "Reflections on 'Vers Libre'" (1917), in T. S. Eliot, *To Criticize the Critic* (1965), p. 187.

61. In Hecht, *The Transparent Man;* Eliot, "Humouresque. (After J. Laforgue)," in *Harvard Advocate* (12 January 1910) reprinted in T. S. Eliot, *Poems Written in Early Youth* (1967).

62. "What Dante Means to Me," in Eliot, *To Criticize the Critic,* pp. 126–27.

63. In Hecht, *Flight Among the Tombs.*

64. In Hecht, *Millions of Strange Shadows.*

65. This appears forty pages earlier in Hecht, *Millions of Strange Shadows.*

66. "*Millions of Strange Shadows:* Anthony Hecht as Gentile and Jew," in Lea, *Burdens of Formality*, pp. 101–2.

67. "Mr. Browning," *Literary Essays* (1871): 242.

68. "Song of Myself," 6. I owe this recognition to William H. Pritchard.

69. "Almost every line of Eliot's poetry seems forged of the most durable steel, and while poems like 'Prufrock' or *The Waste Land* were mocked at or puzzled over at their first appearances, they are now, pretty much line for line, a part of our mental life, and are fixed in the memory of many of us. The careful skill of these poems, and of virtually all of Eliot's poems, is undeniable. And so, one is obliged to add with regret, is the malice of the earlier poems, up to perhaps 'Ash-Wednesday'" (*Hecht in Conversation with Philip Hoy*, p. 97).

70. Letter to David Havird, 21 January 1998.

71. In Hecht, *The Hard Hours*.

72. "Our Common Lot" (1979), in Lea, *Burdens of Formality*, p. 46.

73. Letter of 14 November 1979.

74. Letter to David Havird (30 December 1997).

75. *Kenyon Review* 9, no. 2 (Spring 1947): 223–24.

76. In Eliot, *Collected Poems, 1909–1935* (1936); *Burnt Norton* was issued separately in 1941.

77. *Times Literary Supplement* (23 May 2008).

78. *Nation and Athenaeum* (21 February 1931). These sentences are not included in *Argufying* (1987), ed. John Haffenden, where only the part of Empson's review on Eliot's "Marina" is reprinted (p. 356).

CHAPTER 3. ROBERT LOWELL

1. "Telling the Time," *Salmagundi* 1 (1966–67): 22.

2. From the dust jacket of each volume.

3. "A Commentary," on *I'll Take My Stand: The South and the Agrarian Tradition* in *The Criterion* 10 (April 1931): 483–85.

4. Letter to Herbert Read, quoted in *T. S. Eliot: The Man and His Work*, ed. Allen Tate (1966), p. 20.

5. First published in *Impact* (1960), reprinted in Ezra Pound, *Selected Prose, 1909-1965*, ed. William Cookson (1973), p. 133.

6. Letter to Charles Eliot Norton (28 August 1891), reprinted in Henry James, *Letters*, ed. Leon Edel, vol. 3 (1980), p. 353.

7. John McCormick, "Falling Asleep over Grillparzer: An Interview with Robert Lowell," *Poetry* 81, no. 4 (January 1953): 277, ellipses in the original.

8. "John Maynard Keynes," *New English Weekly* (16 May 1946).

9. "Credo," *Front* 1 (December 1930), reprinted in Pound, *Selected Prose*, p. 53 (but there with "English").

10. "T. S. Eliot: Two Controversial Questions," in Robert Lowell, *Collected Prose* (1987), p. 51.

11. Letter to the editor, *New English Weekly* (14 June 1934).

12. "Isolated Superiority," *Dial* 84 (January 1928): 5.

13. "Dr Williams' Position" (1928), in *Literary Essays of Ezra Pound* (1954), ed. T. S. Eliot.

14. Ezra Pound, *Poems and Translations*, ed. Richard Sieburth (2003), p. 1283.

15. Item 76 in Donald Gallup's *Ezra Pound (1885-1972): The Catalogue of an Exhibition in the Beinecke Library, 30 October-31 December 1975, Commemorating His Ninetieth Birthday* (*Yale University Library Gazette*, January 1976). The phrase of praise had been used by Pound as the title of the second chapter of *The Spirit of Romance* (1910).

16. "The Method of Mr. Pound," *The Athenaeum* (24 October 1919).

17. "Eliot: Two Controversial Questions," p. 51.

18. For word of these, I am grateful to Charles Tomlinson.

19. Beddoes, *Death's Jest-Book*, III.iii, "The old crow of Cairo"; "Luz is an excellent joke," Beddoes, quoted by H. W. Donner in his edition (1950), p. xxxviii (*luz*, the bone which "withstands dissolution after death, out of which the body will be developed at the resurrection").

20. "The Three Voices of Poetry" (1953), reprinted in Eliot, *On Poetry and Poets* (1957), p. 94. The Beddoes quotation is from *Death's Jest-Book*, III.iii.

21. On Eliot and Beddoes, see my "Thomas Lovell Beddoes: 'A Dying Start,'" in *The Force of Poetry* (1984), pp. 140–43.

22. I draw on my *T. S. Eliot and Prejudice* (1988), pp. 259–60.

23. *Notebook, 1967-68* (1969), *Notebook* (1970), *History* (1973).

24. T. S. Eliot, *The Use of Poetry and the Use of Criticism* (1933; 1964 ed.), p. 106.

25. Letter to H. F. Cary (7 November 1817) in *Collected Letters of Samuel Taylor Coleridge*, ed. Earl Leslie Griggs, vol. 4 (1959): 782.

26. In *Brief Lives*, ed. John Buchanan-Brown (2000), p. 203.

27. "Johnson as Critic and Poet" (1944), reprinted in Eliot, *On Poetry and Poets*, p. 175; "Milton II" (1947), in Eliot, *On Poetry and Poets*, p. 158.

28. "Eliot: Two Controversial Questions," p. 51.

29. *Harvard Advocate* 125, no. 3 (December 1938), 20, 41; this is not included in Lowell's *Collected Prose*. Lowell's unlovely word "unautochthonous" anticipates Eliot's justified unloveliness: "Driven by dæmonic, chthonic / Powers" (*The Dry Salvages* V). In what follows, I draw on my memorial pages "For Robert Lowell," on his death in 1977, published in *Harvard Advocate*, 113, nos. 1–2 (November 1979).

30. Frederick May Eliot is the "Master Frederick" who is repeatedly bantered, or mocked, in letters from Eliot to Eleanor Hinkley; see, e.g., letters of 3 January, 27 January, and 21 March 1915, and 5 September 1916 ("Tell me what Frederick is preaching about"), in *The Letters of T. S. Eliot, Volume 1, 1898-1922*, ed. Valerie Eliot (1988), pp. 77, 82–83, 90, 148. The epigraph to "Mr. Eliot's Sunday Morning Service" is "Look, look, master, here comes two religious caterpillars" (*The Jew of Malta*). Lyndall Gordon says of Eliot: "In particular, he resented Sunday morning services conducted by his cousin Frederick May Eliot, who graduated from Harvard a year behind him, in 1911, went on to Harvard Divinity School, and was ordained as a Unitarian minister" (*T. S. Eliot: An Imperfect Life* [1998], p. 110).

31. *The Lowells and Their Seven Worlds* (1947), p. 361.

32. Lowell's *Collected Prose*, p. 210, has someone's misleading typo: "Of Pound: Eliot remembered Pound would walk for two hours and then say, '*You* speak.' But by then one had absolutely nothing to say."

(From the three pages on Eliot in Lowell's twenty-five-page essay "New England and Further" [1960s–1977], posthumously published; this essay's attentions can easily be overlooked, since they are not itemized in the table of contents and the book has no index.)

33. *The Letters of Robert Lowell,* ed. Saskia Hamilton (2005), pp. 3–4.

34. Ibid., p. 227.

35. Letter of 10 November 1969, ibid., p. 525.

36. Letter of 8 November 1969.

37. Humphrey Carpenter, *A Serious Character: The Life of Ezra Pound* (1988), pp. 872, 874, 876, 877, 882, 891, 869, 883–84.

38. "A Conversation with Ian Hamilton" (1971), in Lowell, *Collected Prose,* p. 279.

39. "To Ezra Pound?" no date, September 1947? in *Letters of Lowell,* pp. 71, 690: "This letter, which survives only as a fragment, may have been addressed to both Ezra and Dorothy Pound; it may otherwise have been a letter of application to Pound's doctor for visiting privileges."

40. Letter, no date, fall 1948, ibid., p. 114.

41. Ibid., p. 227.

42. For Pound's intense quizzing of the text of "Gerontion," see T. S. Eliot, *Inventions of the March Hare,* ed. Christopher Ricks (1996), pp. 349–52. Eliot's receiving but not heeding Pound's advice contrasts intriguingly with the revision of *The Waste Land.*

43. Letter to William Carlos Williams, with "carbon outline," 18 March 1922, in *The Selected Letters of Ezra Pound, 1907–1941,* ed. D. D. Paige (1950), pp. 172–73, my ellipsis.

44. "Ezra Pound," in *An Examination of Ezra Pound,* ed. Peter Russell (1950), pp. 26–27.

45. Mary de Rachewiltz, *Discretions* (1971), pp. 255–56. For Lowell's knowing her, see *Letters of Lowell,* pp. 417, 419 (February 1963).

46. Cryptic or reticent, this doesn't *say* that Eliot was the visitor, though one can see why Frank Bidart and David Gewanter have a note: "I.e., Eliot was '. . . here with a black suit and black briefcase'" (Robert Lowell, *Collected Poems,* ed. Bidart and Gewanter [2003], p. 1111).

47. "Notes on Elizabethan Classicists" (1917), in *Literary Essays of Ezra Pound,* p. 238.

48. Eliot, introduction to *Literary Essays of Pound,* pp. xi–xii.

49. Quoted in Donald Davie, *Pound* (1975), pp. 48–49. Pound's five letters to Hardy (written between 1920 and 1925) appeared the year before Lowell published his Pound sonnet; see Patricia Hutchins, "Ezra Pound and Thomas Hardy," *Southern Review* 4, no. 5 (January 1968): 97–103.

50. Griffiths and Reynolds supply invaluable annotations to *Little Gidding* II, an imaginative multiplicity of references to Dante.

51. Quoted in Carpenter, *Serious Character,* p. 864.

52. Noel Stock, ibid., p. 871.

53. "T. S. Eliot (1888–1965)," *Sewanee Review* 74, no. 1 (Winter, 1966): 109, reprinted as *T. S. Eliot: The Man and His Work,* ed. Allen Tate (1966), p. 89. (The volume did not include Eliot's essay "American Literature and the American Language," which had appeared in the posthumous collection *To Criticize the Critic* [1965].)

54. "'T. has 7 blisters,' Pound recorded by post-card to Dorothy; and so . . . 'le papier Fayard was then the burning topic' of their conversation. 'Will probably proceed by train tomorrow,' he told Dorothy, but 'le papier Fayard' must have eased the blisters since it seems they walked on to Bourdeilles" (A. David Moody, *Ezra Pound: Poet,* vol. 1: *The Young Genius* [2007], p. 360).

55. Pound italicized these lines.

56. *Discretions,* p. 306.

57. "A Visiting Card," written in Italian and first published in Rome in 1942. The translation, by John Drummond, was first published by Peter Russell in 1952, reprinted in Pound, *Selected Prose,* p. 290.

58. "Immediate Need of Confucius," *Aryan Path* 8 (August 1937), in Pound, *Selected Prose,* p. 91.

59. Quoted in Carpenter, *Serious Character,* p. 879 (ellipsis in the original).

60. "Dante" (1929), in Eliot, *Selected Essays,* p. 247.

61. Geoffrey Hill deals boldly with Dryden's poem in *The Enemy's Coun-*

try: Words, Contexture, and Other Circumstances of Language (1991), pp. 73–80.

62. In Eliot, *Selected Essays,* pp. 18–19.

63. Lowell's ellipsis, as also in the next three quotations.

64. From yet another place where Eliot turns to Brunetto, the review of Henry Dwight Sidgwick (previously "Dante as a 'Spiritual Leader'"), reprinted as "Dante" (1920), in T. S. Eliot, *The Sacred Wood* (1920), p. 166.

65. In Lowell, *Collected Prose,* pp. 205–6.

66. "T. S. Eliot: Four Quartets," ibid., p. 48.

67. In Eliot, *Selected Essays,* pp. 243–44.

68. This section of seventy-two lines occupies twenty-six pages of Helen Gardner's superb book *The Composition of "Four Quartets"* (1978). For Eliot's revisions of the opening lines, see my *Eliot and Prejudice,* pp. 263–65.

69. "What Dante Means to Me," in Eliot, *To Criticize the Critic,* p. 128.

70. Gardner, *Composition of "Four Quartets,"* p. 153.

71. In the same series was *A Selection of Poems by Ezra Pound,* and the Bridges was advertised on the back of *The Waste Land and Other Poems.* I owe this to Jim McCue.

72. "A Commentary," *The Criterion* 9 (July 1930): 587–88.

73. In Ezra Pound, *Selected Poems* (1928), p. vii.

74. Ibid., pp. xii, ix (emphasis Eliot's), xiv.

75. Gardner, *Composition of "Four Quartets,"* pp. 174, 184.

76. In Pound, *Selected Letters,* p. 280.

77. In the manuscript there is no "compound": "The remoteness of a vague familiar ghost" (Gardner, *Composition of "Four Quartets,"* p. 174).

78. Ibid., p. 185.

79. *Old-Fashioned Pilgrimage and Other Poems* (1967).

80. Included by Eliot in *Literary Essays of Ezra Pound,* p. 14.

81. Eliot to Hayward, quoted in Gardner, *Composition of "Four Quartets,"* p. 196.

82. *Dante in English* (2005), p. 320.

83. Quoted in Gardner, *Composition of "Four Quartets,"* p. 180.

84. *The Divine Comedy*, Agenda Editions, in enlarged format (2003). "This edition includes extensive revisions to the translation of the *Inferno* Laurence Binyon made before his death probably partly as a result both of his long correspondence with Pound concerning his version of the *Purgatorio* . . . and the detailed criticism Pound had made of his *Inferno* in *The Criterion*" (publisher's note).

85. Gardner, *Composition of "Four Quartets,"* p. 168. Helen Gardner says: "The coda was rightly cancelled as inconsistent with the lyric as written." The lines would have further complicated, at least, the sequence from the Inferno to Purgatory. Jim McCue points out to me that the lines never actually appear on the same leaf as the lyric. In manuscript, they are on their own leaf, and in typescript they are at the top of a new leaf, perhaps stationed between the lyric and the narrative.

86. In Eliot, *The Sacred Wood* (1920), p. 151. The error "character" (for "characters") creeps into later editions; for instance, the seventh edition (1950), p. 167, as well as the edition that was published by Faber (1997), p. 14.

87. *The Structure of Complex Words* (1951), p. 104.

88. *History of Civilization* (1857), cited in *OED*, s.v. "lenient."

89. *Milton*, pl. 23, ll. 72–73, reprinted in *William Blake's Writings*, ed. G. E. Bentley, Jr. (1978), vol. 1, p. 369.

90. Gardner, *Composition of "Four Quartets,"* pp. 172–73.

91. Included by Eliot in *Literary Essays of Ezra Pound.*

92. Pound, Canto XIV.

93. For "the *other people,*" see my *Eliot and Prejudice*, pp. 7–8.

94. In Eliot, *To Criticize the Critic*, p. 128.

95. Gardner, *Composition of "Four Quartets,"* p. 176.

96. *Dante in English*, p. 374, among the notes to Lowell's translation of Canto XV.

97. Gardner, *Composition of "Four Quartets,"* pp. 188, 190.

98. "Dante," p. 250.

99. Gardner, *Composition of "Four Quartets,"* p. 184; "Dante," p. 247.

100. "Dante," p. 250.
101. Published 1936, collected in Ezra Pound, *The Fifth Decad of Cantos* (1937).
102. In Ezra Pound, *Polite Essays* (1937), p. 98.
103. Gardner, *Composition of "Four Quartets,"* pp. 186, 190.
104. *A Companion to the Cantos of Ezra Pound* (1980), p. 180.
105. Gardner, *Composition of "Four Quartets,"* p. 172.
106. "Epics" (posth., 1980), in Lowell, *Collected Prose*, p. 217. This is inaccurate (Rosanna Warren points out to me) because in *Inferno* XIX Pope Nicholas III mistakes Dante for Boniface and foresees that he will be damned (*will*, because he yet lives).
107. There is a copy of the recording at the Woodberry Poetry Room, Houghton Library, Harvard University; my thanks to Don Share.
108. Quoted in Gardner, *Composition of "Four Quartets,"* p. 194.
109. In *Letters of Lowell*, p. 469.
110. Quoted in Gardner, *Composition of "Four Quartets,"* p. 178.
111. Private communication from R. A. Gekoski, Rare Books and Manuscripts (London), September 2008.

Credits

Publishing Company. Excerpts from "Animula," *Ash-Wednesday,* "Coriolan (I. Triumphal March—1931)," "Landscapes (I. New Hampshire)," "The Hollow Men," and "To Walter de la Mare" in *Collected Poems, 1909- 1962,* by T. S. Eliot, copyright © 1936 by Houghton Mifflin Harcourt Publishing Company and renewed 1964 by T. S. Eliot, reprinted by permission of the publisher. Excerpt from "La Figlia Che Piange" in *Collected Poems, 1909-1962,* by T. S. Eliot, reprinted by permission of Faber and Faber Ltd.

ANTHONY HECHT: "A Voice at a Séance," "'More Light! More Light!,'" "Pig," "Still Life," "The Ghost in the Martini," "The Venetian Vespers," "Persistences," "A Deep Breath at Dawn," from *Collected Earlier Poems,* by Anthony Hecht, copyright © 1990 by Anthony E. Hecht, used by permission of Alfred A. Knopf, a division of Random House, Inc. "A Certain Slant," "Curriculum Vitae," "Humoresque," "Death the Hypocrite," "Despair," "Devotions of a Painter," "Envoi," "Meditation," "Memory," "The Witch of Endor," from *Collected Later Poems,* by Anthony Hecht, copyright © 2003 by Anthony Hecht, used by permission of Alfred A. Knopf, a division of Random House, Inc. "Seascape with Figures" from *A Summoning of Stones* (Macmillan, 1954), copyright © 1954 by Anthony E. Hecht, reprinted by permission of the estate of Anthony Hecht. "Motes," originally published in the *New Yorker* (November 1, 2004), copyright © 2004 by the estate of Anthony Hecht, reprinted by permission of Helen Hecht. Letters of Anthony Hecht, copyright © 2010 by the estate of Anthony Hecht, printed by permission of Helen Hecht. Excerpts from "Anthony Hecht in Conversation with Philip Hoy," from *Seven American Poets in Conversation* (Between the Lines, 2008), © 1999 by Anthony Hecht, reprinted by permission of Helen Hecht.

GEOFFREY HILL: Excerpt from "On Reading *The Essayes or Counsels, Civill and Morall*" from *A Treatise of Civil Power,* by Geoffrey Hill (Penguin Books, 2007), copyright © 2007 by Geoffrey Hill, reprinted by permission of Penguin Group UK. Excerpt from "Scenes with Harlequins" from *Canaan,* by Geoffrey Hill (Penguin Books, 1996), copyright © 1996 by Geoffrey Hill, reprinted by permission of Penguin Group UK. Ex-

CREDITS

•

244

cerpt from "Song of Armenia" from *King Log,* by Geoffrey Hill (Penguin Books, 1992), copyright © 1968 by Geoffrey Hill, reprinted by permission of Penguin Group UK. Excerpts from Part 1 and Part 3 from *Scenes from Comus,* by Geoffrey Hill (Penguin Books, 2005), copyright © 2005 by Geoffrey Hill, reprinted by permission of Penguin Group UK. Excerpts from "28," "29," "99," and "107" from *Speech! Speech!* by Geoffrey Hill (Viking, 2001), copyright © 2001 by Geoffrey Hill, reprinted by permission of Penguin Group UK. Excerpts from "II" and "LVII" from *The Orchards of Syon,* by Geoffrey Hill (Penguin Books, 2002), copyright 2002 by Geoffrey Hill, reprinted by permission of Penguin Group UK. Excerpts from "XII," "XXIII," "LII," and "CXXI," from *The Triumph of Love,* by Geoffrey Hill (Penguin Books, 1999), copyright © 1998 by Geoffrey Hill, reprinted by permission of Penguin Group UK. Excerpts from "Pindarics" 14, 18, 21 from *Without Title,* by Geoffrey Hill (Penguin Books, 2006), copyright © 2006 by Geoffrey Hill, reprinted by permission of Penguin Group UK. Excerpt from "Scenes with Harlequins" from *Canaan,* by Geoffrey Hill, copyright © 1996 by Geoffrey Hill, reprinted by permission of Houghton Mifflin Harcourt Publishing Company, all rights reserved. Excerpts from *The Triumph of Love,* by Geoffrey Hill, copyright © 1998 by Geoffrey Hill, reprinted by permission of Houghton Mifflin Harcourt Publishing Company, all rights reserved. 780w from *Collected Critical Writings* (2008), by Geoffrey Hill, edited by Kenneth Haynes, reprinted by permission of Oxford University Press. Excerpts from *Speech! Speech!* and *The Orchards of Syon,* by Geoffrey Hill, reprinted by permission of Geoffrey Hill.

PHILIP LARKIN: "At Grass," reprinted from *The Less Deceived,* by Philip Larkin, by permission of the Marvell Press, England and Australia.

ROBERT LOWELL: Excerpts from "For George Santayana," "Ezra Pound," "T. S. Eliot," "Dante 1," "Milton in Separation," and "Brunetto Latini" from *Collected Poems,* by Robert Lowell, copyright © 2003 by Harriet Lowell and Sheridan Lowell, reprinted by permission of Farrar, Straus and Giroux, LLC. Excerpt from "Winter" from *Notebook,* revised and expanded edition, by Robert Lowell, copyright © 1967, 1968, 1969, 1970

Index

Hill, Geoffrey (continued)
  "Style and Faith," 5
  Style and Faith, 5, 18, 32, 35, 49–
    51, 68, 79, 226–27
  "Tacit Pledges," 225
  "Translating Value," 49–50,
    227
  "Weight of the Word, The," 5
  "What Devil Has Got into John
    Ransom?" 49, 227
  "Word Value in F. H. Bradley
    and T. S. Eliot," 16, 28–31,
    62, 224–26
Hinkley, Eleanor, 237
Hoffman, Daniel, 130–31
Hollander, John, 232
Homer, 160–61
Horace, 91
Housman, A. E., 23, 100
Hoy, Philip, 95
Hughes, Ted, 21
Hutchins, Patricia, 239
Hutton, Richard Holt, 128

Isis, The, 22

James, Henry, 36–37, 57, 69, 81,
    88, 146
Jeffers, Robinson, 141
Johnson, Daniel, 22
Johnson, Samuel, 161
Jonson, Ben, 26, 81
Joyce, James, 57

Julian of Norwich, Dame, 15–
    16
Juvenal, 192

Kavanagh, Patrick, 21
Keats, John, 40, 84, 160
Kenner, Hugh, 5
Kermode, Frank, 34
Keynes, John Maynard, 147
King Lear (Shakespeare), 67, 120
Kingsmill, Hugh, 100
Kipling, Rudyard, 18–19
Knight, G. Wilson, 120
Kunitz, Stanley, 144
Kuppner, Frank, 3

Laforgue, Jules, ix, 57, 121
Landor, Walter Savage, 69, 147
Larkin, Philip, 3, 19, 21, 48–55,
    224, 227
Lawes, Henry, 59–60, 67
Lawrence, D. H., 21, 37
Lea, Sydney, 229
Leavis, F. R., 28–29, 78–80
Lehman, David, 234
Lewis, C. S., 38, 225
Lewis, R. W. B., 213–14
Lewis, Wyndham, 153–54, 209
Lindsay, Geoffrey, 232
Listener, The, 164
Lowell, A. Lawrence, 165–66
Lowell, Amy, 166
Lowell, James Russell, 146

Whibley, Charles, 15, 29
Whitman, Walt, 22, 129, 189
Williams, Charles, 37–38, 68
Williams, Norman, 232
Williams, Oscar, 23
Williams, William Carlos, 102,
   151, 172
Wootten, William, 3

Wordsworth, William, ix, 8
Wyatt, Thomas, 31

Yeats, W. B., 21, 28, 53–54, 56,
   104, 120, 153–54, 211

Zinik, Zinovy, 140–41
Zukofsky, Louis, 106